IMAGES
of America

THE UNCOMPAHGRE VALLEY

I0807615

On the Cover: A peach-packing crew poses at the Paonia Excelsior Ranch, about 1912 or 1913. An uncropped version of this image appears on page 79. (Photograph courtesy of the Delta County Historical Society, donated by Mr. and Mrs. Lloyd Miller.)

IMAGES
of America

The Uncompahgre Valley

Theajo "Tj" Davis
and Royal C. "Whitey" Huff Sr.

ARCADIA
PUBLISHING

ISBN 978-0-7385-8071-5

Published by Arcadia Publishing
Charleston SC, Chicago IL, Portsmouth NH, San Francisco CA

Printed in the United States of America

Library of Congress Control Number: 2009941859

For all general information contact Arcadia Publishing at:
Telephone 843-853-2070
Fax 843-853-0044
E-mail sales@arcadiapublishing.com
For customer service and orders:
Toll-Free 1-888-313-2665

Visit us on the Internet at www.arcadiapublishing.com

To Steve Baughn, my life partner and best friend, for being my biggest cheerleader, and to the early settler families of the Uncompahgre Valley for their life stories

Contents

Acknowledgments

Several years ago, I said I was going to write a book about the crazy things I have experienced in my life. Unknown to me, the path of my book would be the history of a community that I had never even been to at the time. I have been a chamber of commerce president by trade, and my career path led me to some interesting places, including, eventually, Delta, Colorado. In Palm Harbor, Florida, I had volunteered to help save the North Pinellas Historical Museum from closing. There I met Charley and Winona Jones. Winona had written *Around and About Palm Harbor* for Arcadia Publishing in 2005. She inspired me to think that one day I, too, could write a book.

Shortly after moving to Delta as the chamber executive director, I met Whitey Huff Sr. I had in the past loved learning about the histories of the places where I lived. I always looked forward to meeting natives of the area who could share their stories with me. As Whitey Huff Sr., my coauthor of this book, visited me every couple of weeks, telling of the history of Delta and the Uncompahgre Valley, he brought wonderful old photographs. I looked forward to Whitey's visits. As time passed, I suggested we write a book using all the wonderful old photographs Whitey and his friends and associates owned from times past. With some encouragement, the 84-year-old Whitey was up to the project.

Thank you to the Delta County Historical Society, Delta Area Chamber of Commerce, and Uncompahgre Valley Water Users Association for information and photographs, and to Shirley Bradbury for scanning some of the photographs, and to my good friend Renee McRay for helping to caption the photographs. My young personal assistant Erica Dixon helped pull it all together. Every effort was made to give credit to the original photographers of the photographs used here. Special thanks are owed to Whitey Huff Sr., who made the contacts and introductions to the Uncompahgre Valley area's pioneering families.

The Uncompahgre Valley and the Gunnison Tunnel: A Description of Scenery by Barton Walter Marsh (published in 1905 by Marsh and Torrence: Montrose, Colorado) was the foundation and information guideline referenced for the introduction and text of this book.

The photographs in this book came from many sources, including the personal collections of Royal C. "Whitey" Huff Sr., other Uncompahgre Valley residents, the Delta County Historical Society, and the Uncompahgre Valley Water Users Association.

—Theajo "Tj" Davis

INTRODUCTION

The Uncompahgre is not a large valley. It contains about 185,000 acres of irrigable land. It is about 35 miles long and has an approximate width of 12 miles. The Uncompahgre River flows through the valley, and from this stream part of the valley's water supply is drawn. The lay of the land in the Uncompahgre Valley is ideal for farming. It is completely surrounded by the everlasting hills, and water runs through it.

In 1881, the Utes were removed to a reservation in Utah and the Uncompahgre Valley was opened for settlement. A great number of new settlers were anxiously waiting on the drawing of borders for the territory, for the arrival of the day when they would be able to stake out their own pieces of land.

A large portion of the valley's arable land was claimed within a short period. During this time, the soil's great potential for fertility was unknown; the land was barren, and no system of irrigation had been developed to supply it with moisture. The valley was only awaiting the assistance of human ingenuity to bring forth a harvest both amazing in its size and variety. The Uncompahgre River provided a sufficient water supply for all of the valley's farmlands. The digging of irrigation ditches began. Farmers rapidly built homes and laid out farms from Delta to Montrose. The countryside began to take on the shape of an industry and a community.

It was soon discovered that all the dirt in the valley possessed remarkable fertility. With water and careful cultivation, the valley yielded enormous crops. Along with this pleasing fact, however, came the sad reality that the river could not supply enough water to irrigate all of the sprawling farms planted by entrepreneurial farm families. As time passed, the new ditches were taken out, and the water supply for all settlers in the valley dwindled. Many early settlers were forced to abandon their promising farms because of the lack of water. These actions caused the valley to begin to relapse into a wilderness.

Only 16 miles away was the Gunnison River, a mighty source of water rushing through the Black Canyon. There was one major problem with tapping into the abundant water source: it was separated from the Uncompahgre Valley by a massive mountain range. In the early years, nobody dared to dream of a diversion project that might bring the much-needed Gunnison river water to the parched rich lands of the valley.

The Uncompahgre Valley soils vary greatly from location to location. The river bottomland was prime for grazing and is home to countless sheep and cattle. The lands of the mesa are red sandy loam, gray, and red adobe. Deposits washed down from the mountains formed black sandy loam. Soil experts pronounced this land to be the most fertile land in the world at the start of the 20th century. All types of fruits and vegetables were grew in abundance. At the Western Slope Fair held at Montrose, in the fall of 1904, a single planter exhibited 117 varieties of vegetables, all grown on his farm.

The valley's bounty included potatoes, onions, sugar beets, corn, pumpkins, wheat, and grains. The principal tree fruits grown in the valley were peaches, apples, pears, cherries, apricots, plums, prunes, quince, and nectarines. The berry culture was an important industry in the valley, producing raspberries, blackberries, and dewberries, among others. Of all the berries grown here, however, the strawberry was grown most. At the time, honey was a very important part of the industry as well; about 5,700 colonies of bees existed in the valley. White honey was produced from the blossom of the alfalfa plant. Crops of hay and honey could be taken from the same field. At the St. Louis World's Fair in 1904, the local honey took the first-place prize, which brought much pride to the valley. The Uncompahgre Valley's sunshine and flowers were—and continue to be—essential to the production of good honey. Many of the other crops are still grown in the valley today, also.

Land crops were not the only commodities produced in the valley. Farmers and ranchers raised cattle, sheep, horses, and poultry. The Uncompahgre Valley was ideal countryside for stock producing; when the stock was properly fed, no severe weather prevented it from fattening up. The winters were never severe enough to demand shelter; the skies never produced cold sleets that covered the animals with ice, therefore causing them to shiver or contract colds. The surrounding mountain ranges also yielded superior grazing for thousands of cattle, horses, and thoroughbred white leghorns (sheep). The high altitude, combined with constant climbing, produced lung expansion that developed the animals into the hardiest livestock of their time. The steers of the Uncompahgre Valley were awarded both first- and second-place prizes at the Chicago and St. Louis World's Fairs. The raising of poultry was another significant industry in the Uncompahgre Valley. Hens and roosters thrived in the valley's soils, and the climate proved ideal for raising poultry.

All of this bountiful harvest came despite a limited water supply for irrigation. At the time, farmers drew 95 percent of the water needed for irrigation from the Uncompahgre River. The river waters are a combination of spring water and run-off from snow in the San Miguel Mountain Range. From springtime until the dog days of summer, the melting snowpack usually provided enough water to irrigate the entire valley. When the snowmelt was gone, however, the water supply produced by the springs was barely enough to irrigate 10,000 acres of land. Insufficient rainfall was always a threat. For 20 years, the valley's farmers struggled with the water shortage, frustrated that their valley, blessed with some of the most fertile soils in the world, was cursed by a limited water supply.

A Frenchman named Lauzon became convinced that it was possible and practical to divert the Gunnison River, one of the largest streams in Colorado, into the Uncompahgre Valley. Throughout the valley, he touted the idea of diverting the Gunnison River to irrigate their farms. Many questioned his logic. By 1904, the valley's citizens were finally convinced to fund a survey. On August 27, 1904, the Ouray, Montrose, and Delta Counties directed civil engineers Walter Fleming and Richard Whinerah to run level lines from the Uncompahgre Valley to the Gunnison River to determine how much of the valley lands could be covered by water from the Gunnison River—assuming that the diversion were possible in the first place. The idea was to cut a ditch out from the canyon and run it over the mountains to the river. The water would flow from the Gunnison through pipes and flumes and then drop into the valley. Fleming and Whinerah soon determined that the ditch idea was impractical—if water were to be drawn from the Gunnison to the valley, they decided one night while sitting around a campfire, they must bore a hole through the mountain. With this in mind, they ran a line from a point 8 miles east of Montrose in a northeastern direction to Black Canyon. It revealed that a tunnel following this path could provide enough water to cover every farm in the valley.

Now that the Gunnison River concept had proven merit, it still needed capital to bring it to fruition. Fortunately, farmers were not the only ones interested in the project. The mining companies in the San Juan district needed electrical power to drive their machinery. The Denver and Rio Grande Railroad needed a way to get their trains into the Uncompahgre Valley without having to climb the mountains. For these reasons, local leaders made appeals to the state and federal governments for funding. Fortunately, the U.S. Bureau of Reclamation, created by a 1902 act of Congress, had been created specifically to provide funding for irrigating arid lands in the

West. The overpopulated eastern states had supported the bill because they needed an outlet for their excess populations. If the dry lands of the West could be made fertile, the immigrants and poor packed into eastern cities could move west to farm them.

The Gunnison Tunnel project began in 1905. On September 23, 1909, the completion of the Gunnison Tunnel in the Uncompahgre Valley marked the dawn of a new era for the valley. Pres. William Howard Taft presided over the opening of the gates at the dedication celebration. At the time of its completion, the 5.8-mile-long Gunnison Tunnel was the longest irrigation tunnel in the world.

A number of other projects would follow over the following years. One of these later projects, the Blue Mesa Dam, created the Blue Mesa Reservoir, Colorado's largest body of water. Colorado congressman Wayne N. Aspinall was instrumental in implementing the Blue Mesa project. Completed in 1965, the lake is 36 miles long and has 96 miles of shoreline. To achieve the reservoir, a vast amount of land was flooded. This submerged land had possessed riches of its own: prior to the construction of the dam, the land was home to the Carpenter family and their well-known hunting lodge, the Sportsman's Hotel in Cabolla. Hunters came from all over the world to stalk game across the valley's beautiful mesas and deep, narrow canyons, and to fish the frith-like lakes teeming with trout.

Over the past 130 years, the Uncompahgre and Gunnison Rivers have unlocked the valley's secret riches. These rivers, and the people who thought to use them, are responsible for the great harvests reaped annually from one of the nation's great breadbaskets.

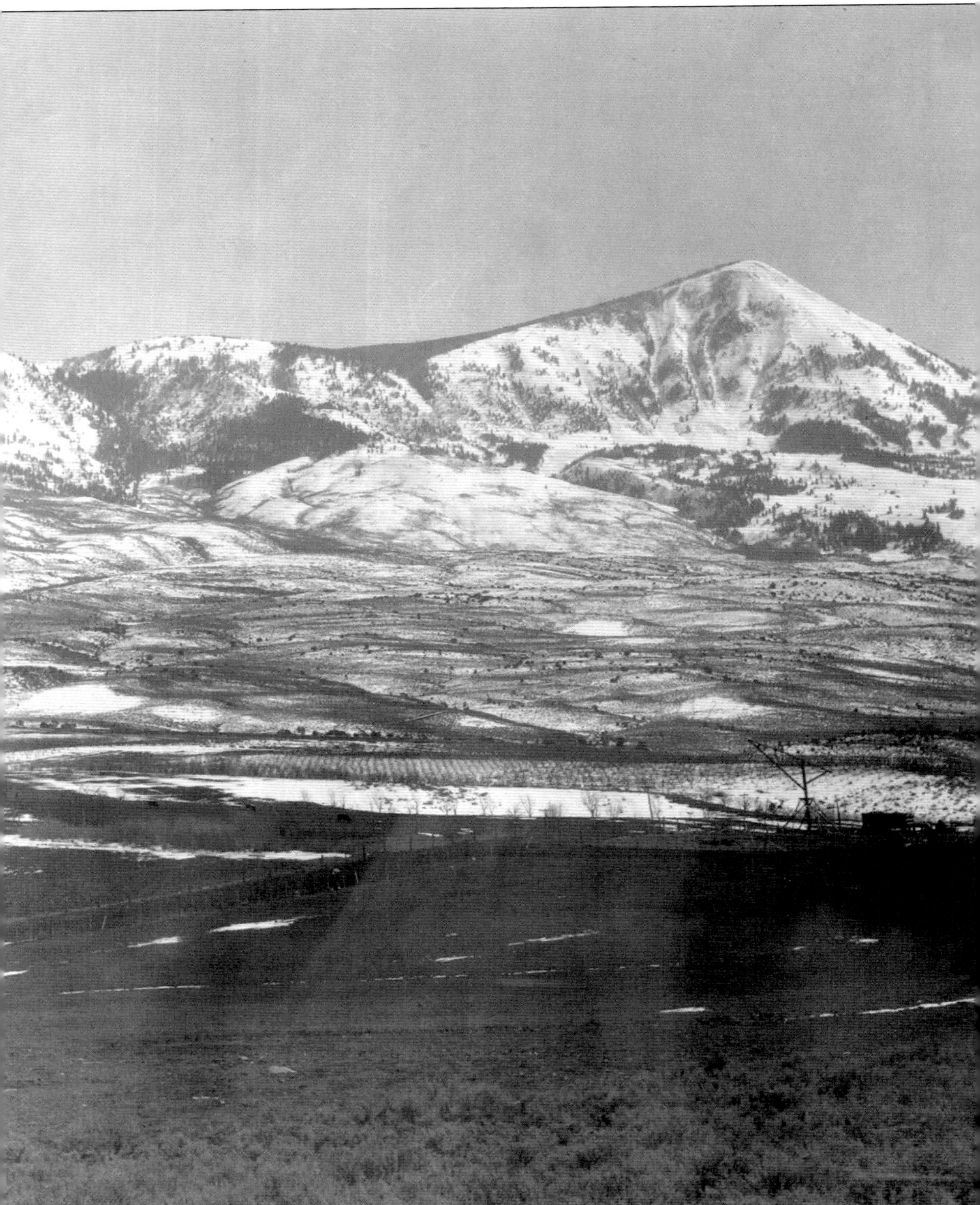

This view of the Uncompahgre Valley was photographed by Ritchie's Studio.

One

Gunnison Tunnel

It took two engineering expeditions, 10 years, several thousand man-hours and dollars, and many interesting events to create the Gunnison Tunnel. The names of such men as Lauzon, Fleming, Whinerah, Hammond, Bell, Pelton, Torrence, Fellows, Tobin, and Dodge will forever be associated with the landmark project. On October 5, 1904, the government opened bids for the construction of the great bore. Almost five years later, on September 23, 1909, Pres. William Howard Taft declared the tunnel opened. It had taken five years to complete the gigantic project.

The tunnel enters the valley 8 miles east of Montrose at an elevation of about 6,000 feet, near the little station of Cedar Creek. The tunnel is reached by a 12-mile roadway built by the government at a cost of several thousand dollars for the purpose of transporting equipment and supplies.

The tunnel is 30,600 feet long and 11-by-13 feet. The South Canal is 12 miles long, 70 feet wide at the surface, and 10 feet deep. It carries waters from the tunnel to the Uncompahgre River. The West Canal irrigates 65,000 acres of land to the west of the Uncompahgre River. The 25-mile-long East Canal irrigates 65,000 acres of erstwhile desert lands east of the river.

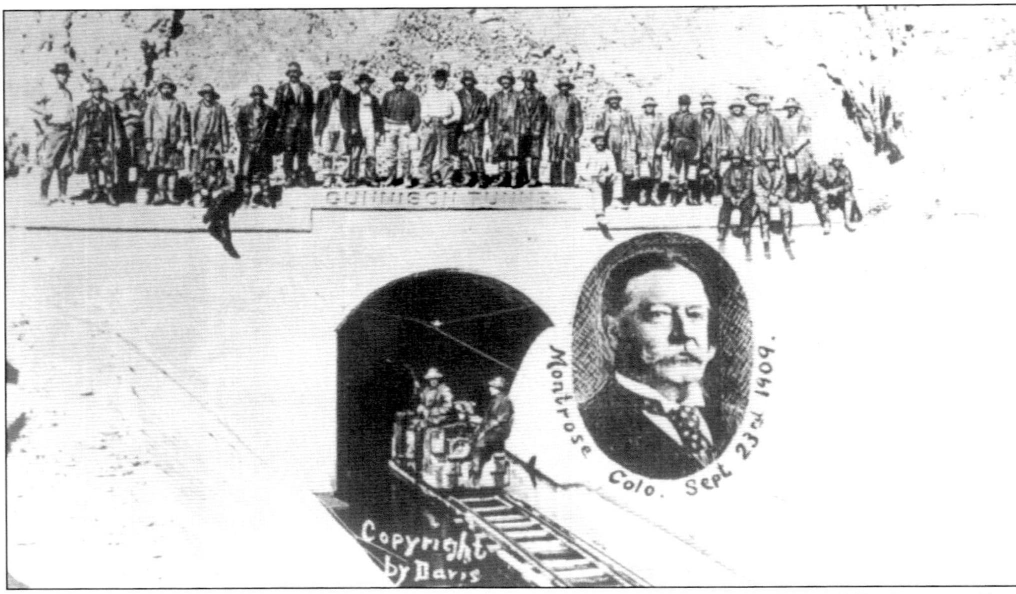

Pres. William Howard Taft served as master of ceremonies on Gunnison Tunnel Dedication Day, September 23, 1909. This photograph shows a number of the workers who were involved in this project on the wall and entrance of the Gunnison Tunnel. Note the group of workmen on the rail carts used to carry them in and out of the tunnel.

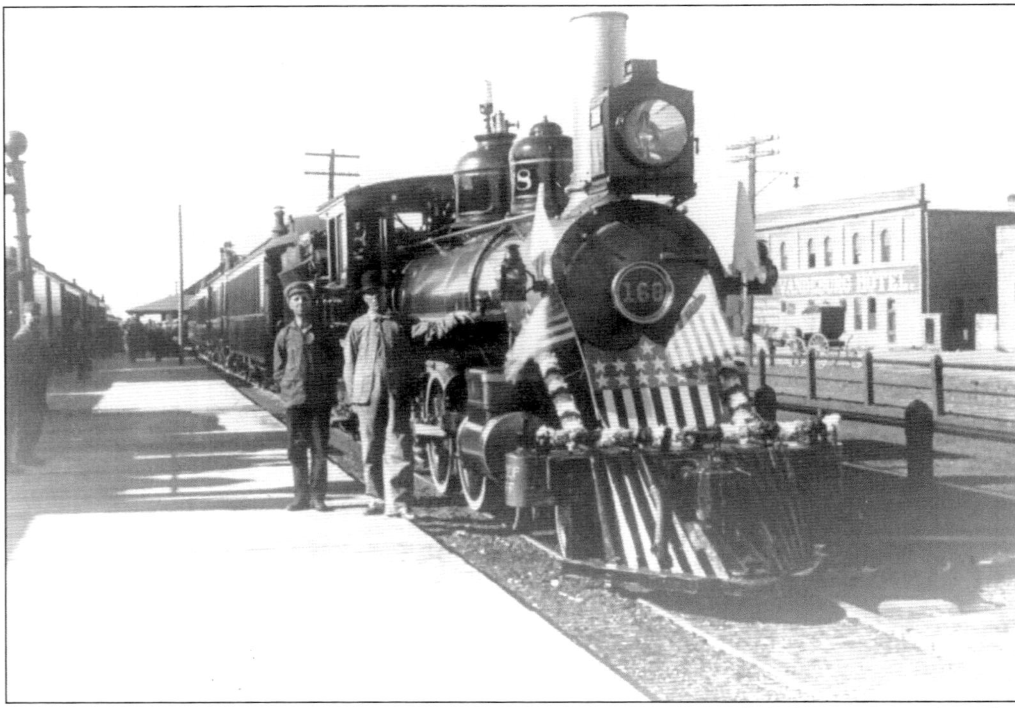

President Taft's train arrived in Montrose for the Gunnison Tunnel dedication on Thursday, September 23, 1909. President Taft made several stops along the way to the tunnel. Several hundreds of people came to attend the tunnel dedication and see the president in person.

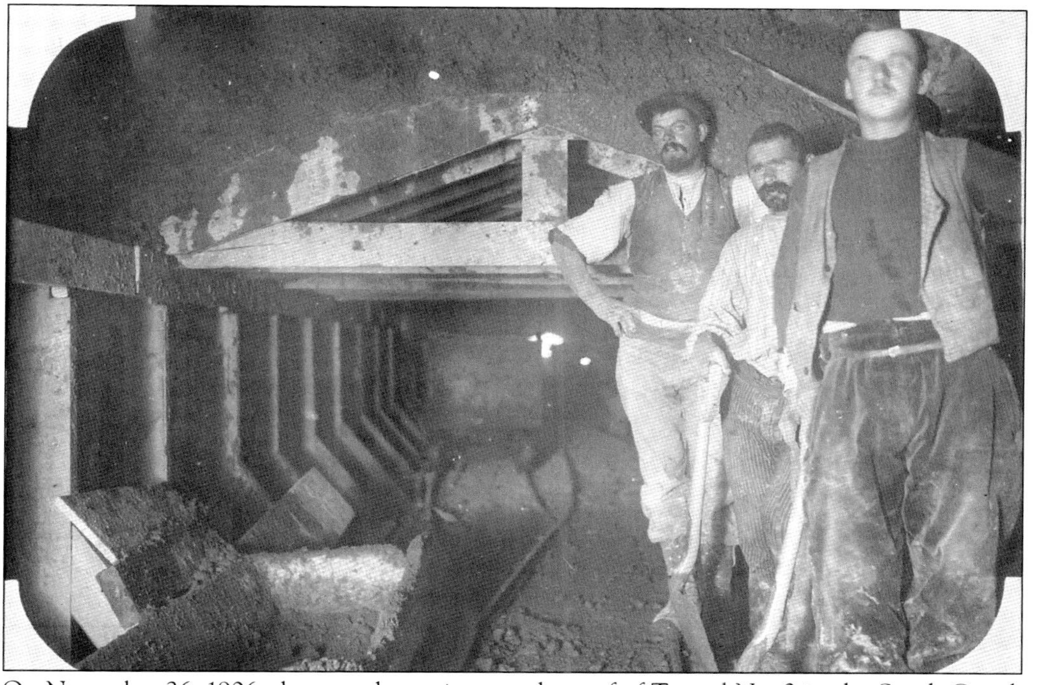

On November 26, 1906, three workmen inspect the roof of Tunnel No. 3 in the South Canal. The two men in the front of the photograph pose with the shovels used in this process.

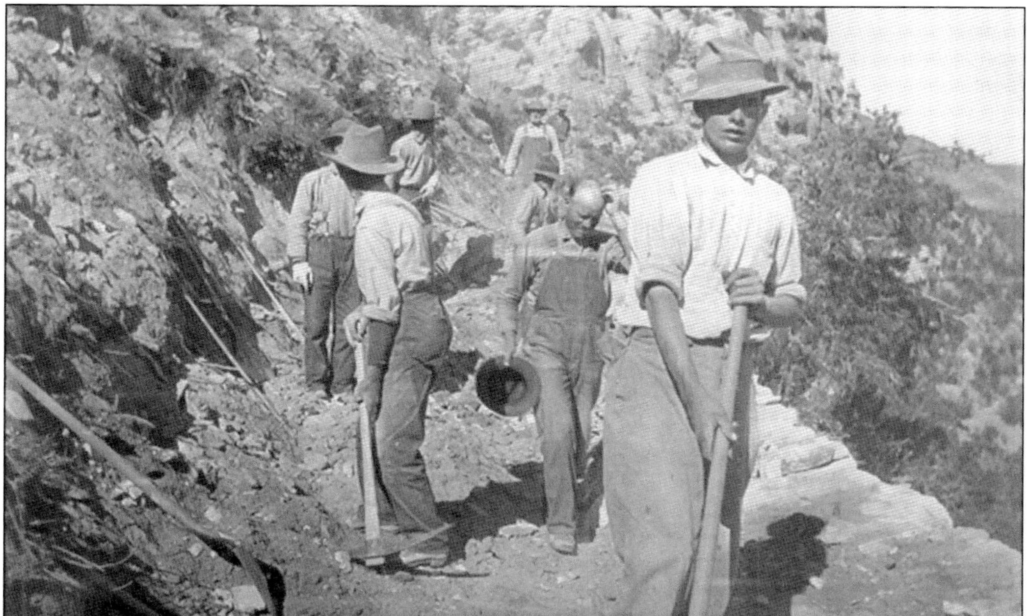

This image captures labor crews at work widening a section of road on the Rainbow Route. Piles of shale are stacked on the outer edge of the road, perhaps to serve as a solid support and prevent erosion. Notice the broad age spectrum of the men working together in the hot sun.

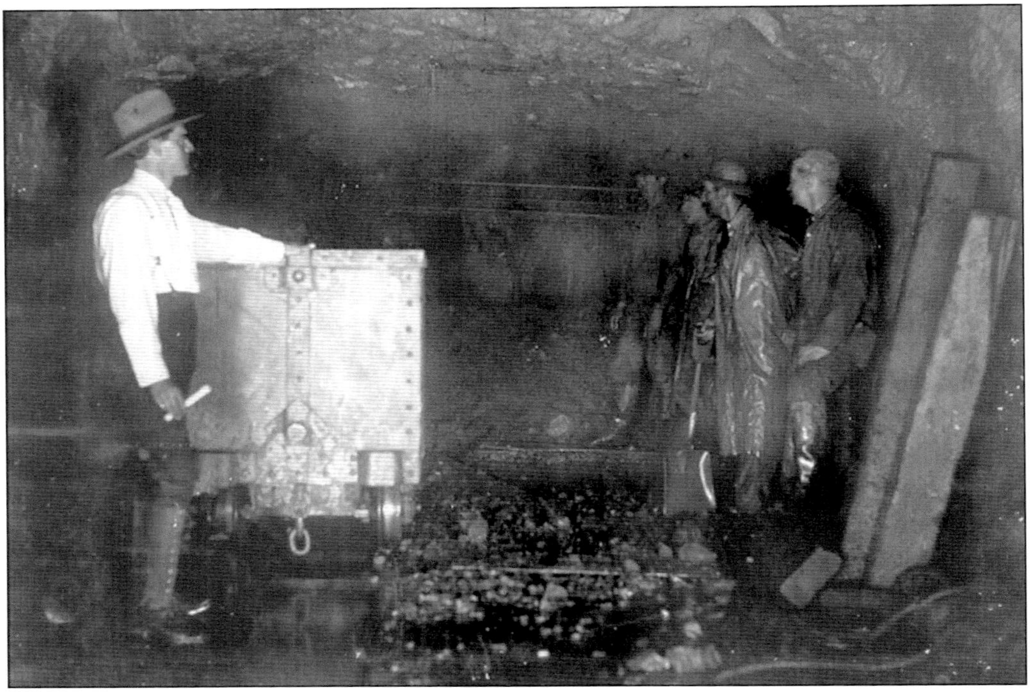

A supervisor is pictured here with his crew working at the head of the tunnel. Rock and debris had to be removed by hand. Then the underground crew loaded it into the rail cart and sent it to the surface for disposal. The large timbers along the wall on the right will be used to shore the tunnel as it progresses.

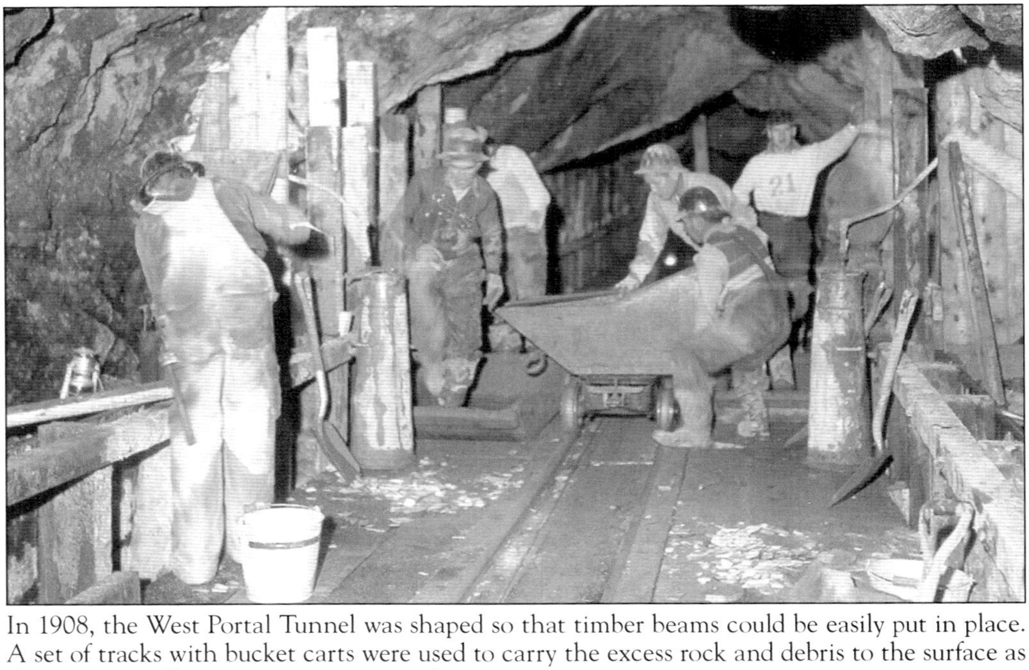

In 1908, the West Portal Tunnel was shaped so that timber beams could be easily put in place. A set of tracks with bucket carts were used to carry the excess rock and debris to the surface as the support wall construction continued.

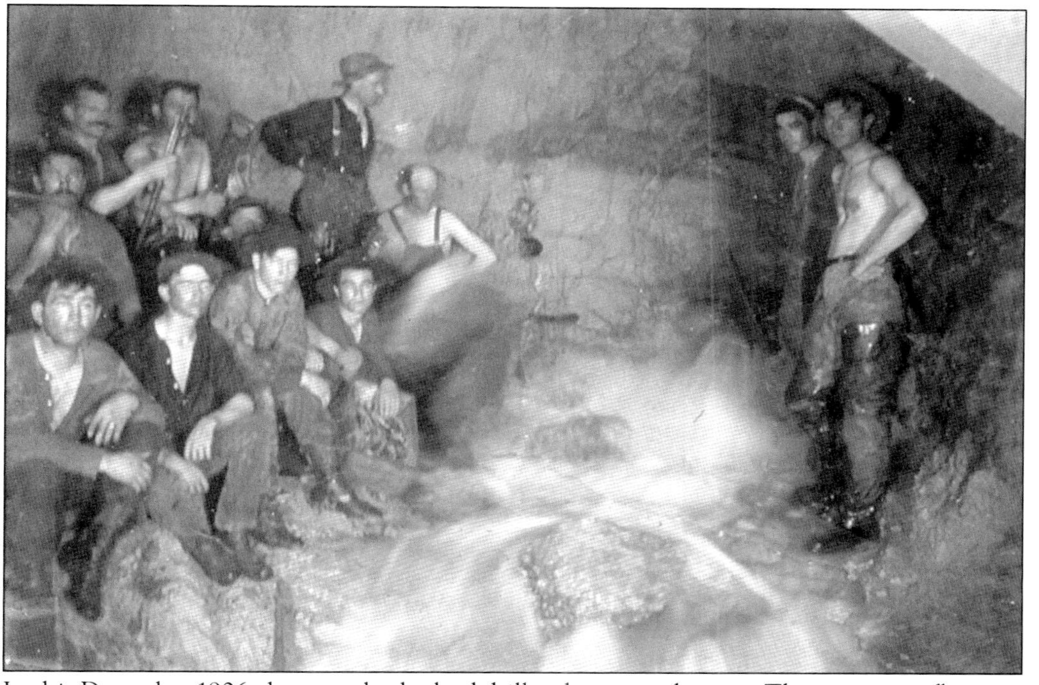

In this December 1906 photograph, the lead drillers have struck water. The maximum flow was about 20 cubic feet per second; the temperature of the water was about 90 degrees. This pocket of water was so large that its jets shot out about 40 feet into the tunnel, knocking the drillers from their machines. The hot, steaming water made the working area unbearably hot and halted work for six months.

Inside the East Portal, notice the lunch buckets on the wall on the left. In the distance, the rail dips down into the shaft. The tunnel, when completed, would be nearly 6 miles long and 10 by 12 feet wide. Workers drilled from both sides of the mountain and met in the middle.

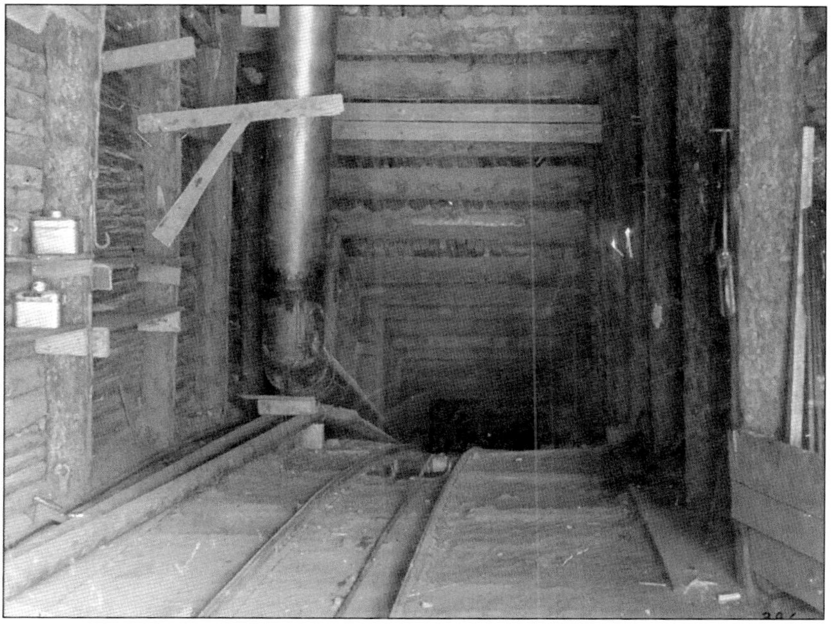

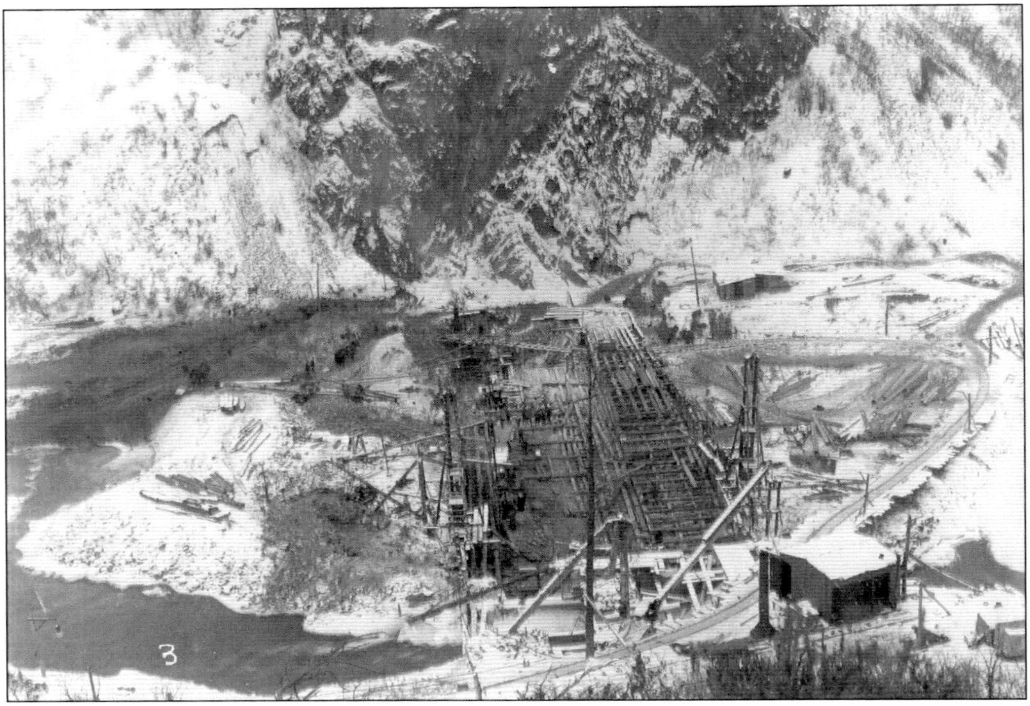

Work on a secondary tunnel to divert some of the surging spring waters of the Gunnison River into the Gunnison Tunnel was started in 1913. The timber seen here was Oregon fir imported from the Northwest. Green timber was used so that it would not swell or float when submerged. The East Portal Dam measures 240 feet across East Portal Weir. It sits 14 feet above the streambed. Workers men dug a channel to ride lower than the riverbed. It took more than three years to build; they could not work in the spring because of high water. The submerged fir timbers have never been replaced.

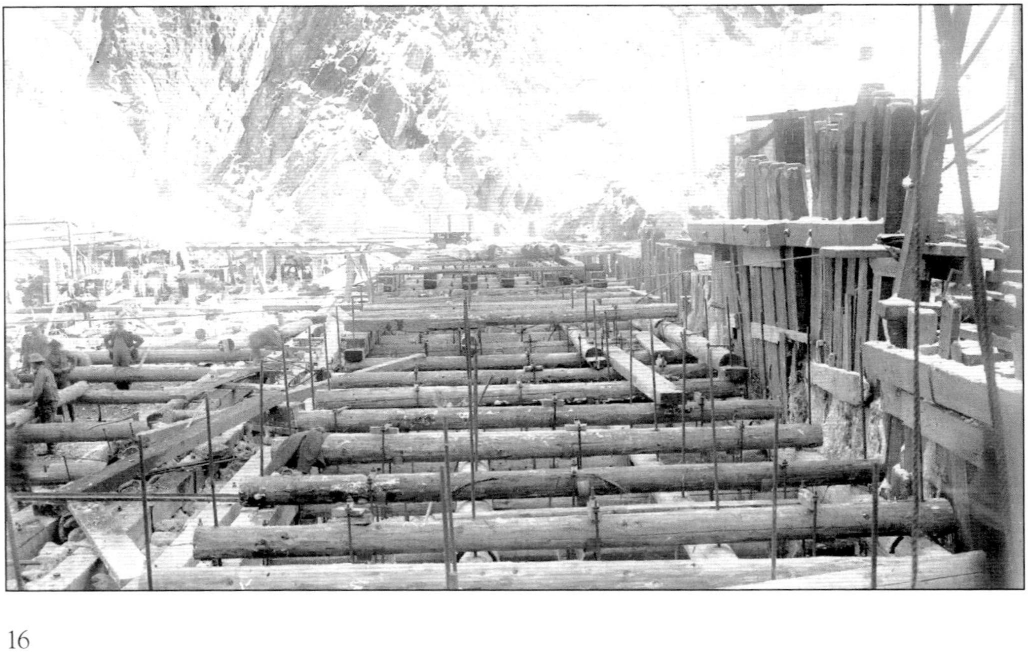

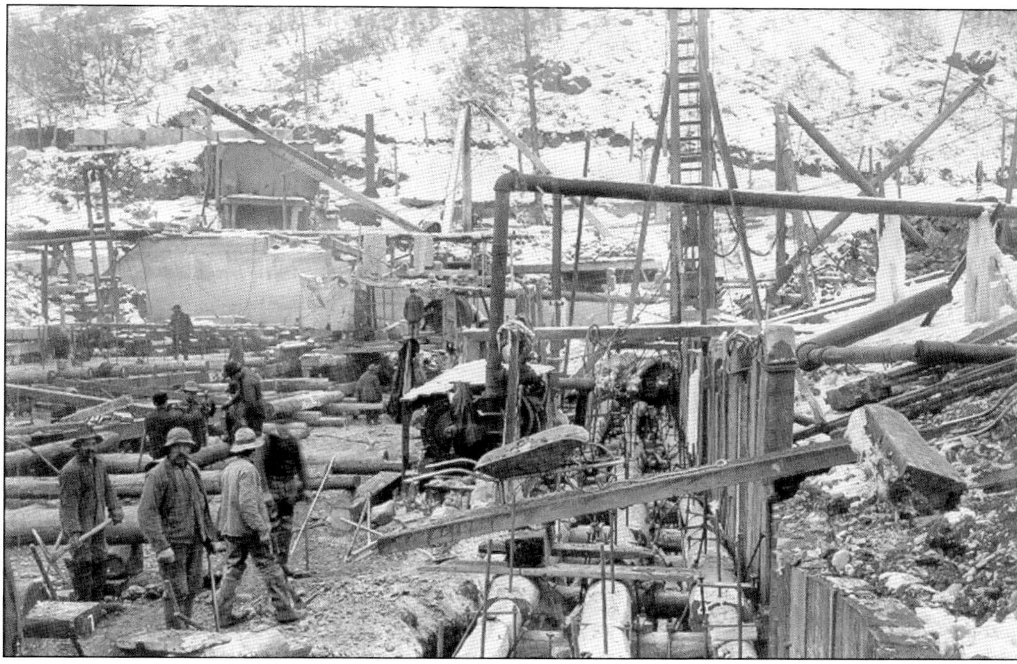

On a frigid day, December 22, 1911, crews of men from Gunnison River Weir Construction brave the elements to work on a lower cut-off wall. Giant logs have been sawn and fitted as crude but effective supports. In the distance, a train (at the top of the photograph) waits to transport workers and supplies.

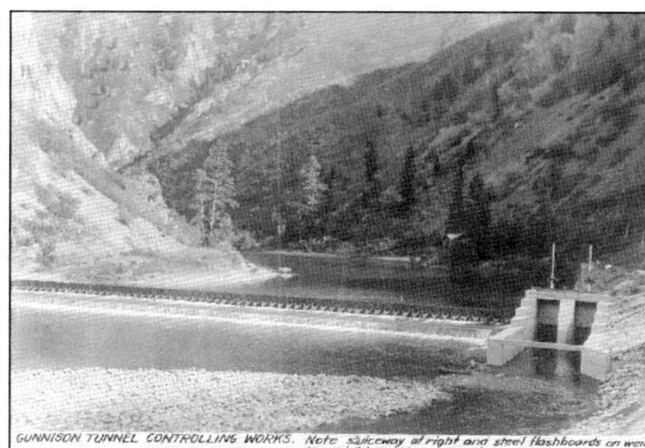

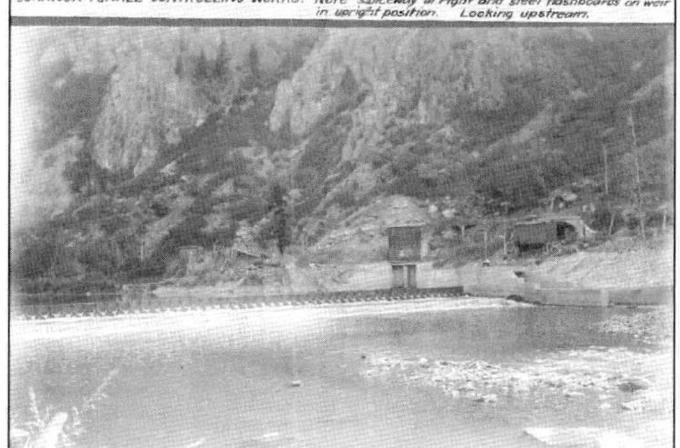

These photographs show the Gunnison Tunnel's controlling works. In the above picture, a close look at the steel flashboards shows that they are in an upright position. The image below shows the view looking upstream from the left bank with the sluiceway at the right and the intake for the tunnel in the center.

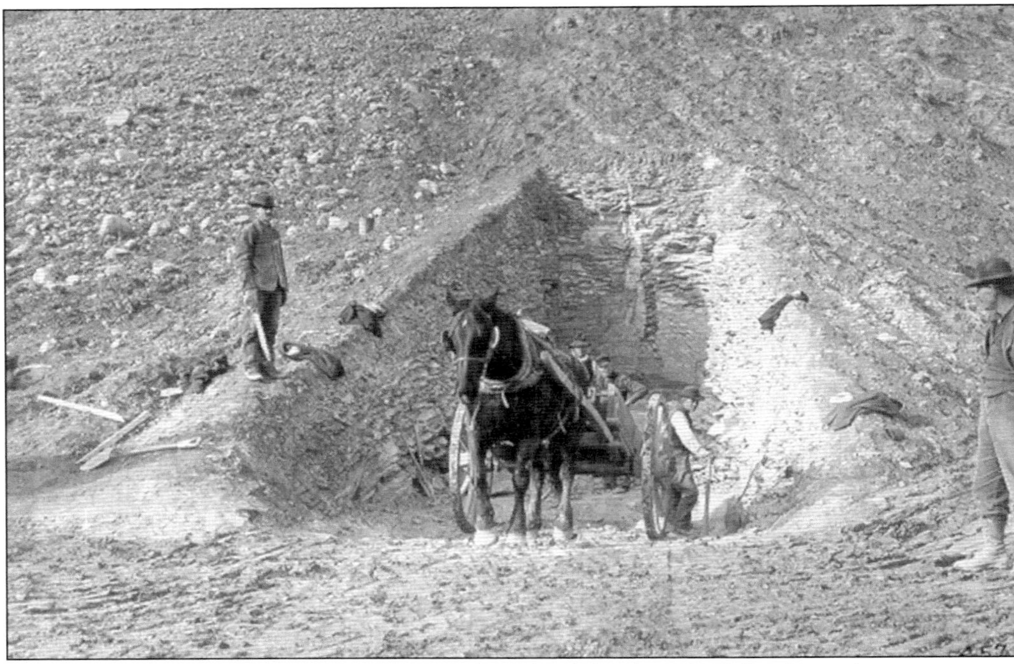

In this 1906 photograph, a man stands on the side of the deep ditch bank watching a crew and horse-drawn wagon below digging trenches to prevent water from flowing through layers of shale. The area around appears desolate, totally lacking in the rich vegetation that irrigation will soon provide.

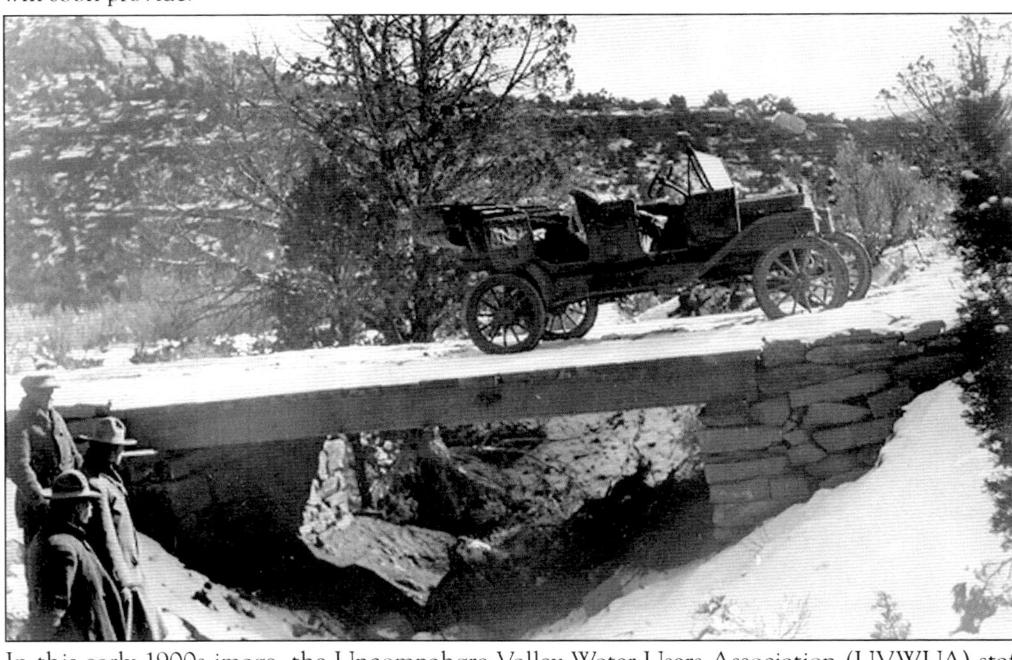

In this early 1900s image, the Uncompahgre Valley Water Users Association (UVWUA) staff and government agents inspect the water flow through ditches across the valley. Keeping the ditches clear of obstructions was critical work. These men were called ditch riders.

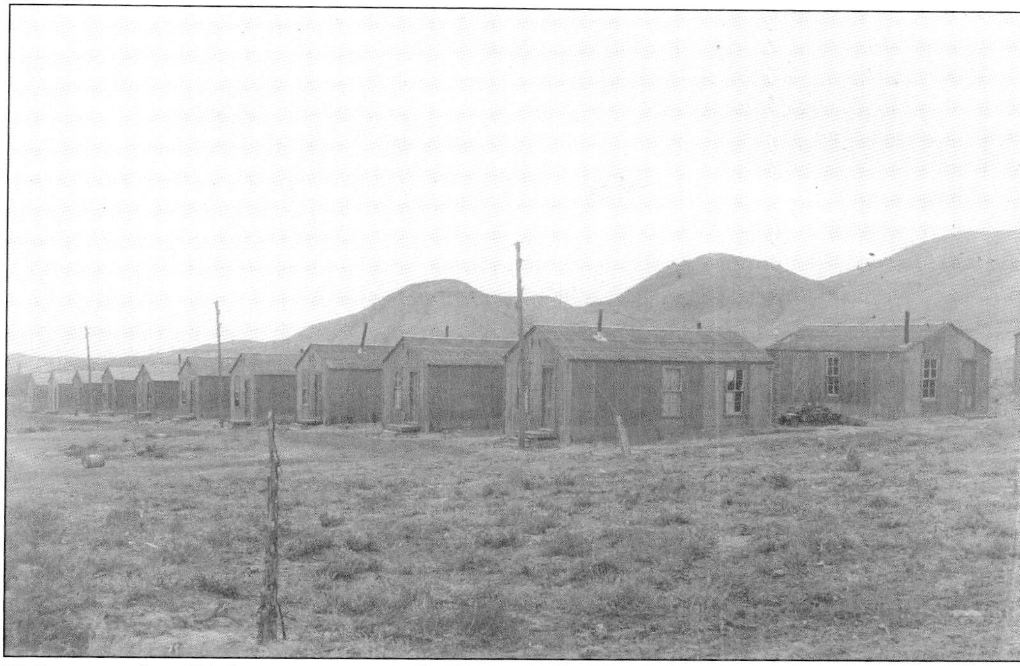

Tight rows of small laborer quarters mark the town of Lajane, which sprang up at the West Portal east of Montrose in 1906. These tiny shanties housed the families of workers who had come to build the Gunnison Tunnel.

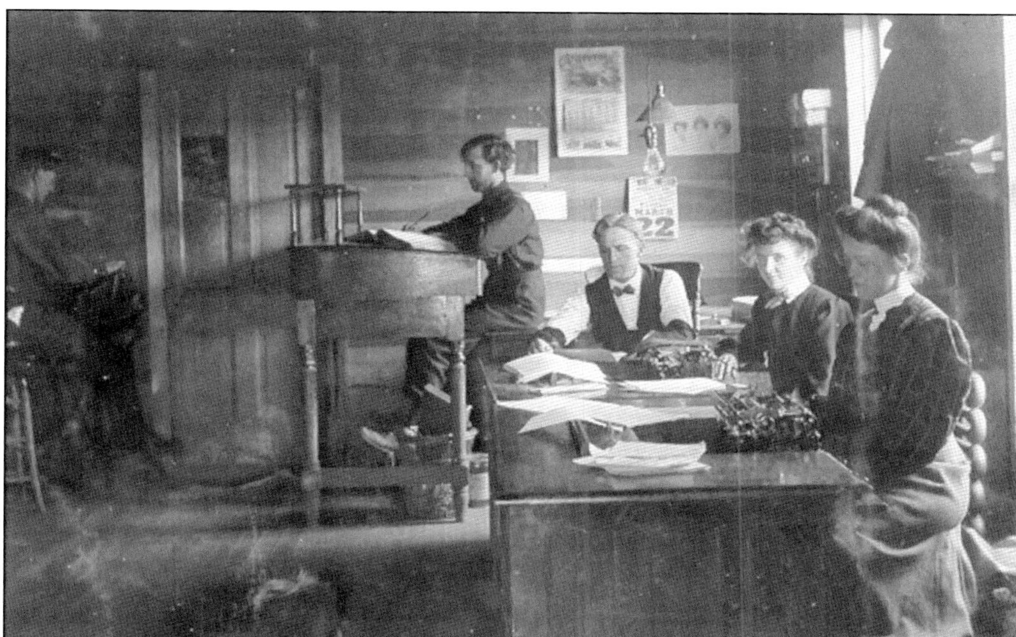

Shown here during the early 1900s, this office staff is busily working at Lajane. These unidentified workers were a small but important part of the tiny town's history.

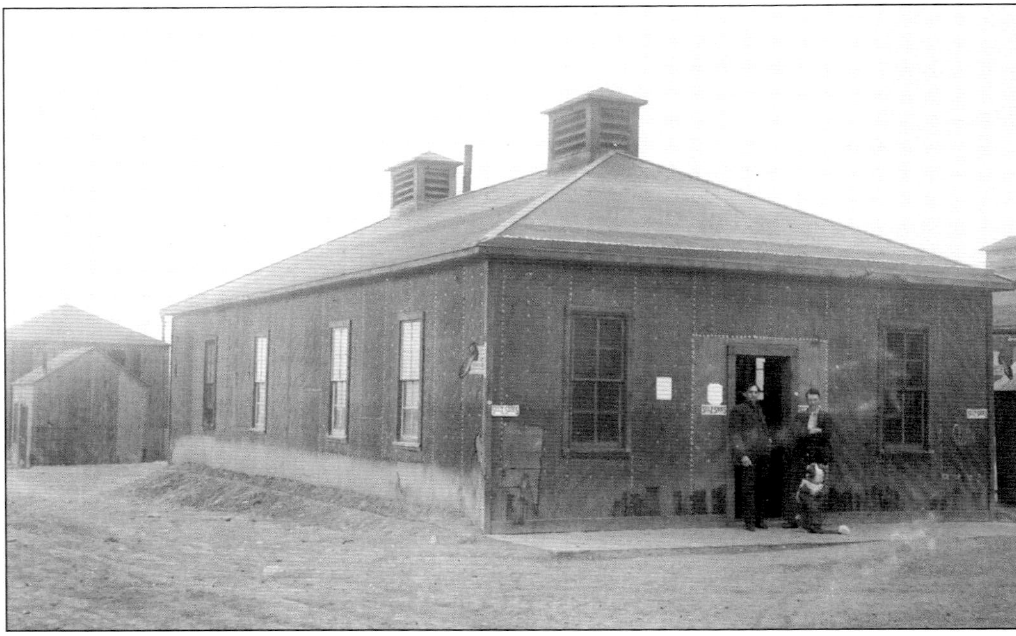

In the first decade of the 1900s, the general store at Lajane stands ready to serve the tunnel workers and their families. This simple rectangular building was large enough to require two chimneystacks. Its proud owners seem to be waiting to greet shoppers. Inside the store, shelves are stacked all the way to the top of the high ceiling. The center of the store is also packed full of items. To further maximize space, even more goods are displayed hanging from the rafters. It appears that every square inch is neatly used in hopes of meeting the needs of this bustling work camp. (Photograph UVWUA.)

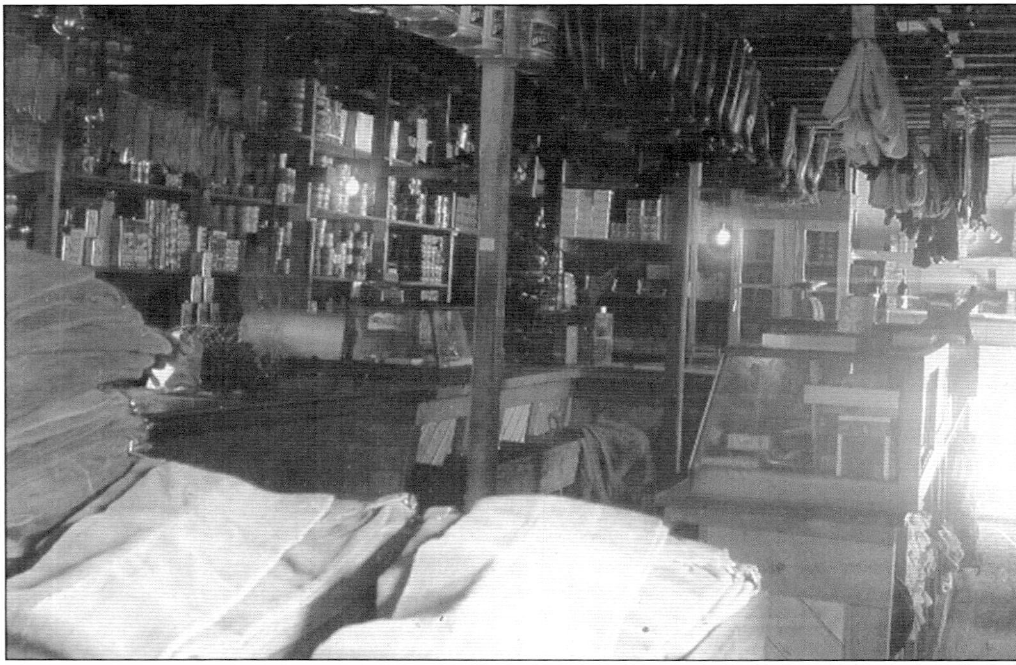

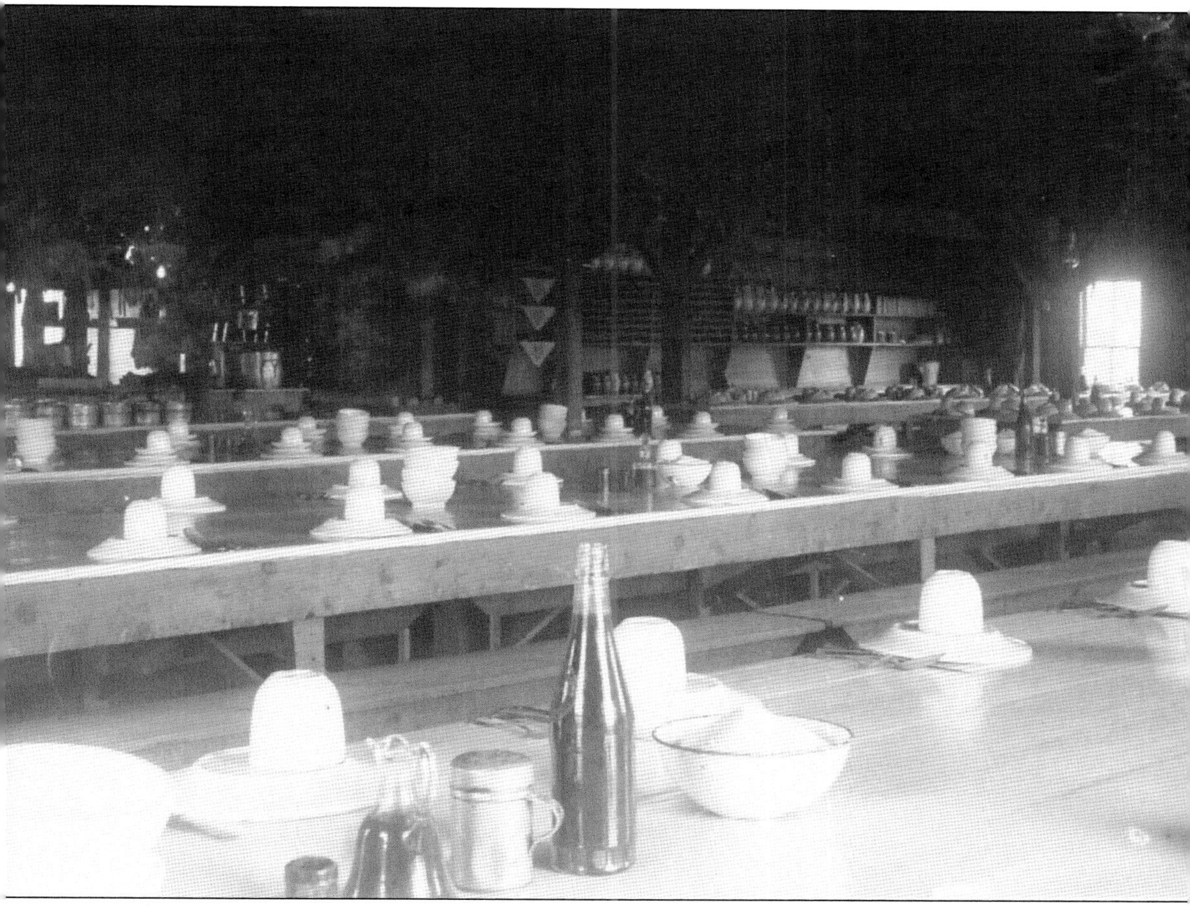

Here is the interior of the Lajane Dining Room. Virginia Smith Wilkins wrote that her grandmother cooked at the bunkhouse along with a married couple. Virginia spent all week with her grandma and said the most amazing thing was seeing the men come and eat in shifts. The long tables were set with tin dishes. Breakfast was bacon, eggs, potatoes, big puffy biscuits, and bacon gravy. The canned milk was tasty on oatmeal (with lots of sugar). The cooks baked pies and bread all day, along with all the beans, potatoes, and meat that the hungry men could eat. The room here was always filled with loud laughter and friendly banter. (Photograph by Clarence Dahl.)

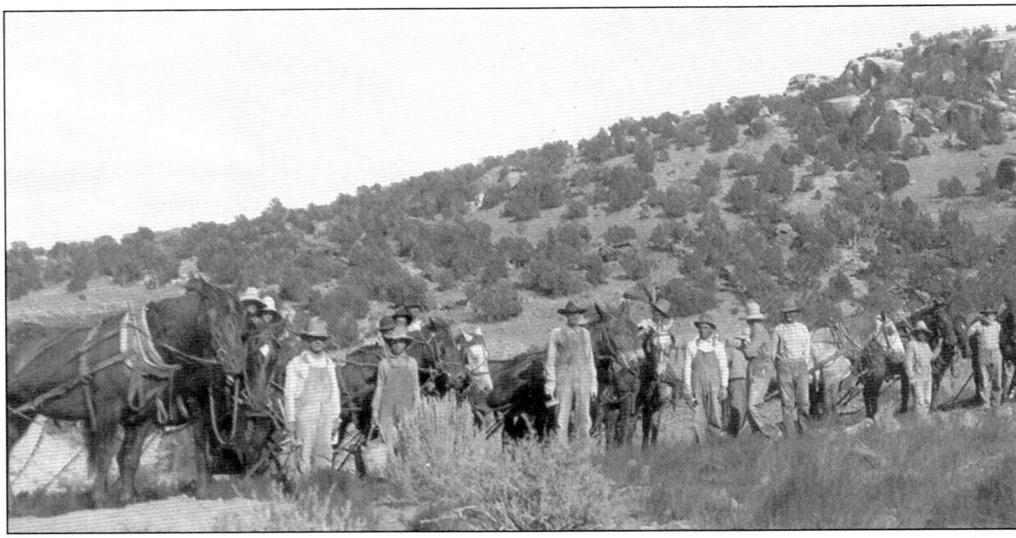

Workers' camps like Lajane required numerous supplies for the construction of the tunnel and canals. The wagon and horse were still the current mode of transportation; these caravans of supply haulers would travel to the nearby towns, pick up construction supplies and goods for the workers and their families, and take them back to the camps for distribution.

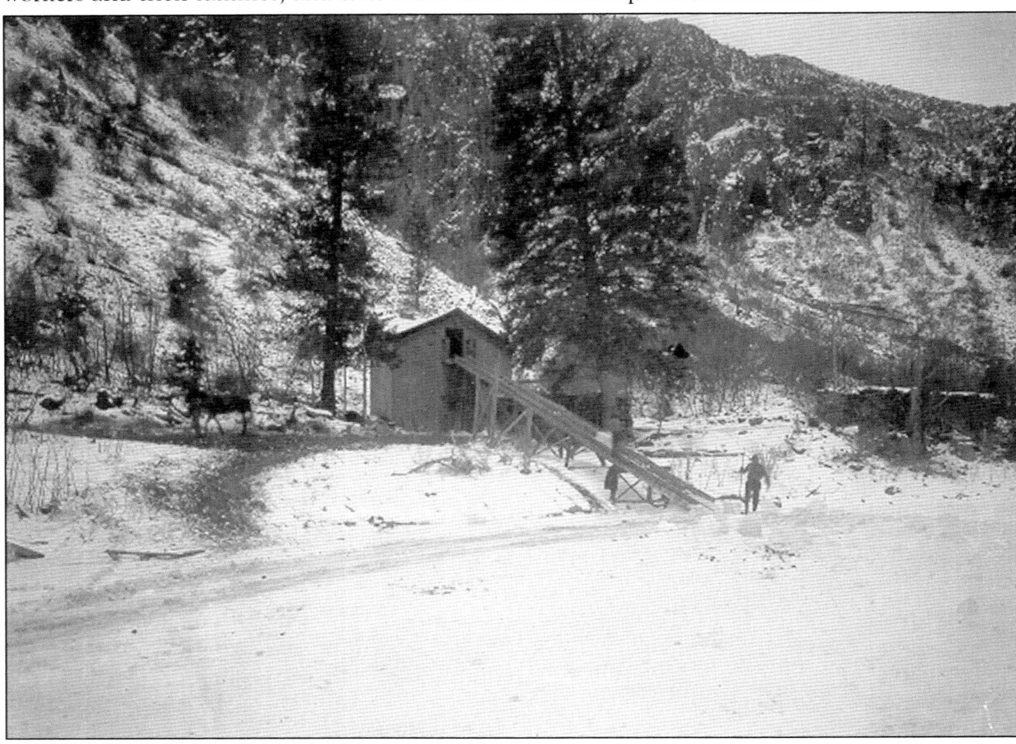

In the early 1900s, it was important to plan ahead. Here in January 1908, a man harvests ice for the River Portal icehouse. Ice harvesting provided a means of early refrigeration, which kept food fresh during the summer months, when hundreds of hungry men would need a hearty meal and an occasional iced drink to sustain them through the long workdays.

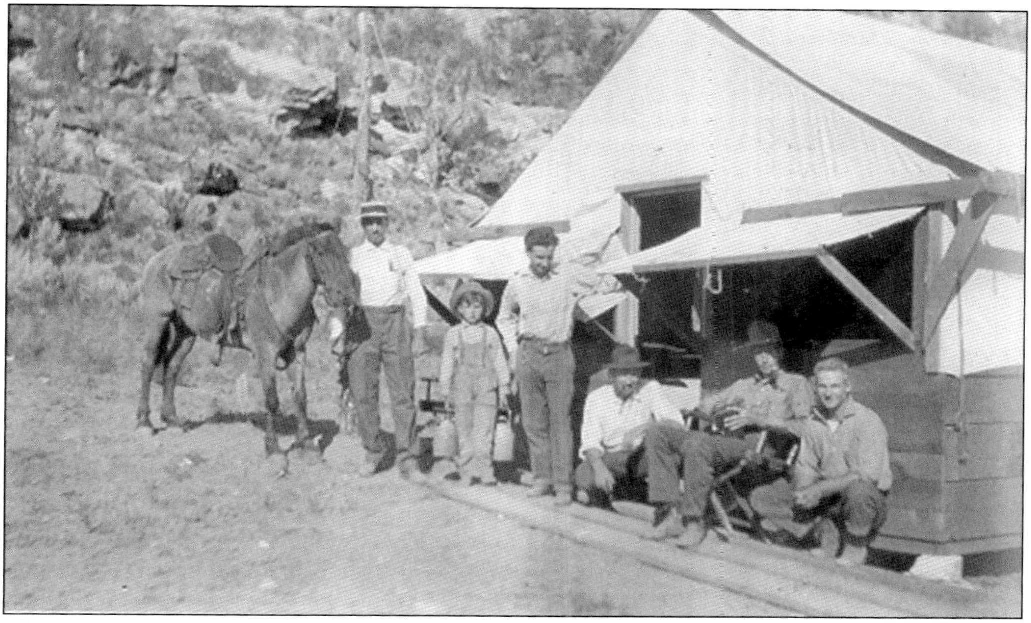

This is typical tent housing for labor crews on the Rainbow Route. The young boy carrying canisters shows that all ages helped out around the camp. The structure here looks sound, but winter snows will be the true test of its stability.

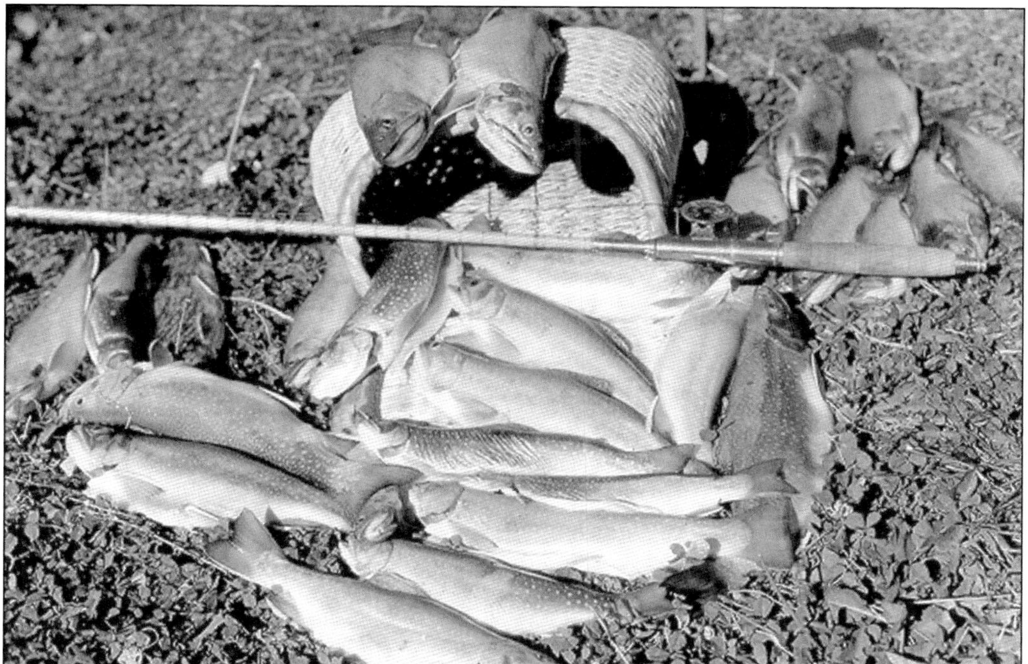

With vast streams brimming with fish near the work camps, workers would often spend their off-hours angling for a fish dinner. Apparently, this was a good day for fishing. Seen here are over 20 nice-sized trout caught with the fly rod and basket pictured.

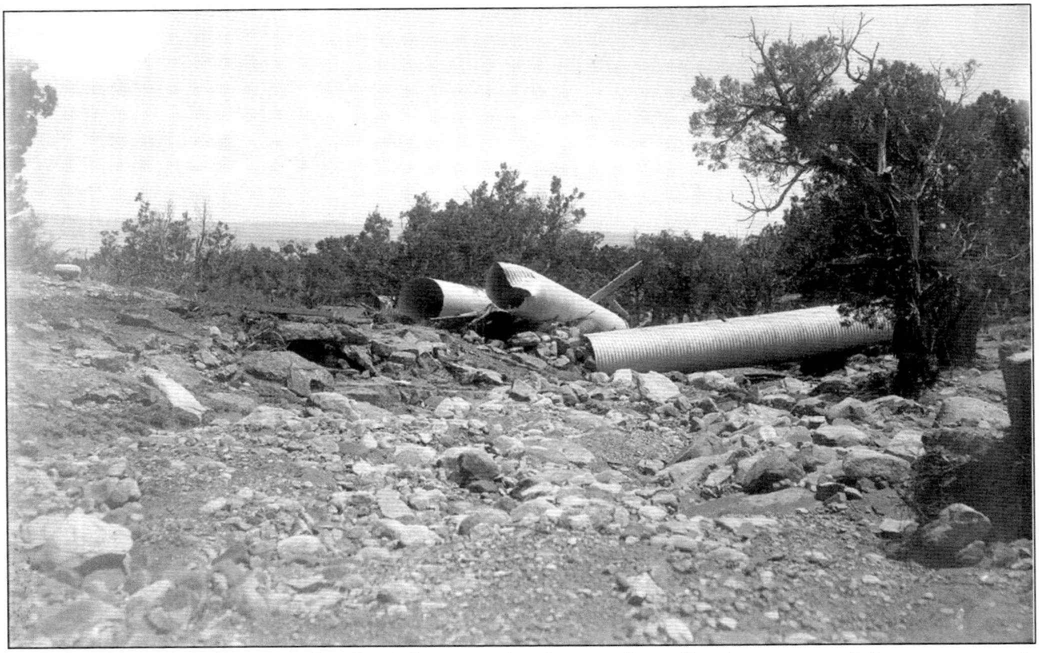

This photograph, taken on July 16, 1912, shows the damage from floodwaters to a 3-foot corrugated iron culvert at Station No. 425 of the West Canal. Notice the line where the flood waters traveled, dragging metal, wood, and boulders along its path. The forces of nature have uprooted the culvert and crumpled its ends like paper. As seen here, in moments, storm floods could cause damage that would take multiple crews of men weeks to repair.

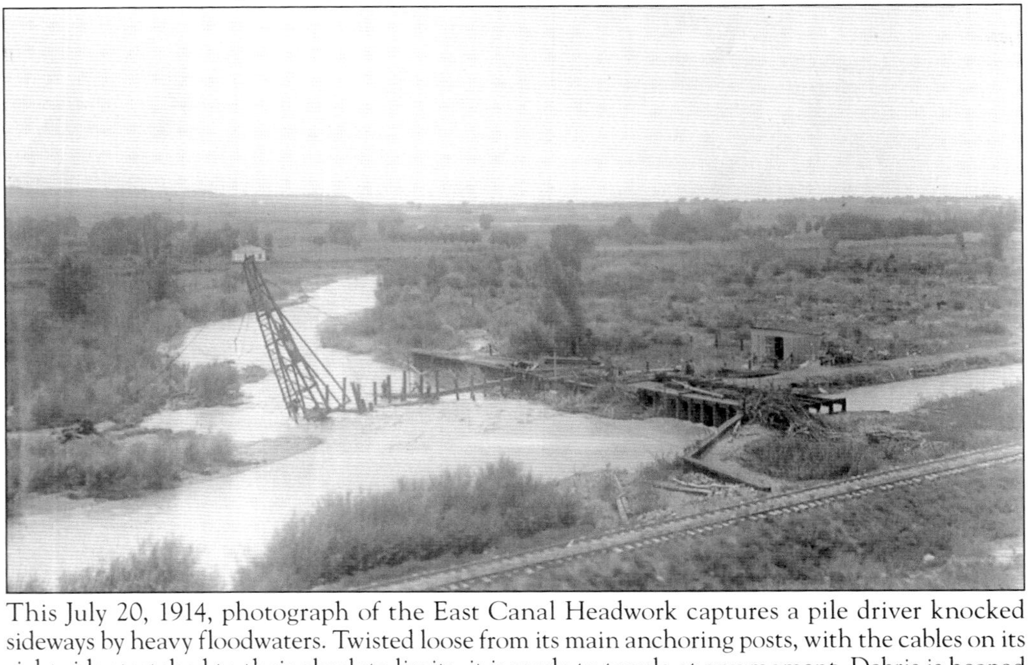

This July 20, 1914, photograph of the East Canal Headwork captures a pile driver knocked sideways by heavy floodwaters. Twisted loose from its main anchoring posts, with the cables on its right side stretched to their absolute limits, it is ready to topple at any moment. Debris is heaped everywhere, blocking roads and choking parts of the canal.

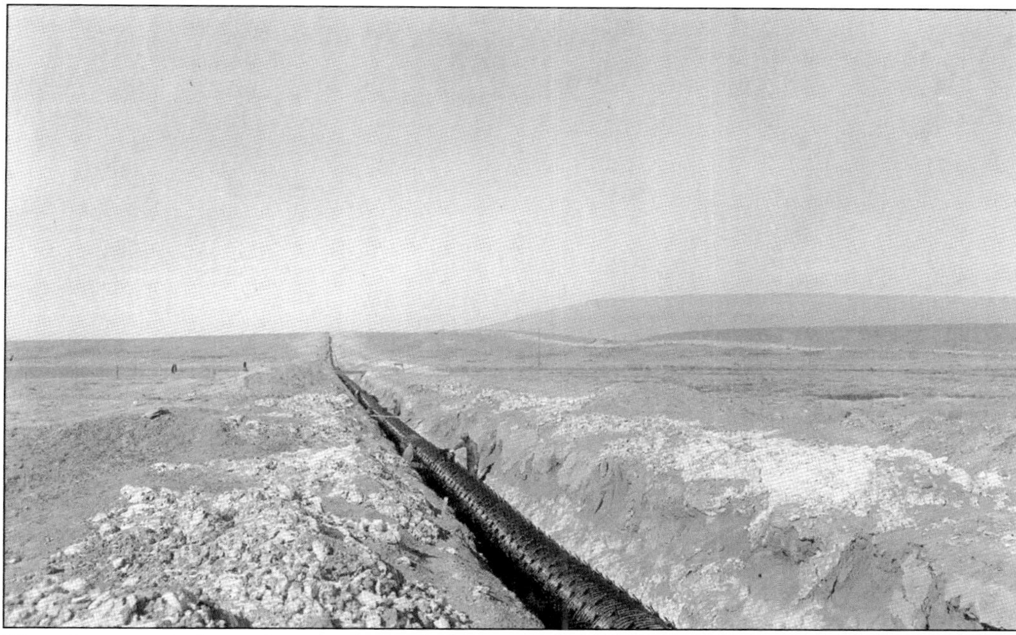

This photograph shows the trench for the Garnet Mesa Siphon in its final stages of completion, stretching for miles across the desolate earth. (The crew seen here is busily applying a second coat of paint.) It is hard to imagine that one day this dry desert scene would be replaced with lush farms and quaint, tree-lined neighborhoods.

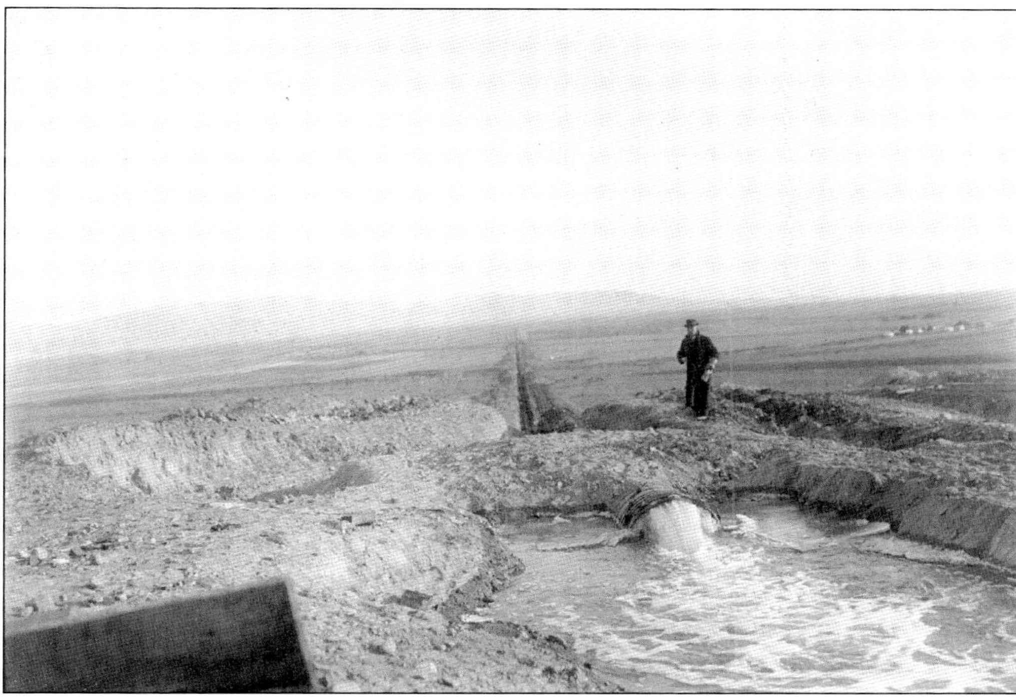

This December 12, 1914, photograph shows an outlet of the Garnet Mesa Siphon near the end of its preliminary testing.

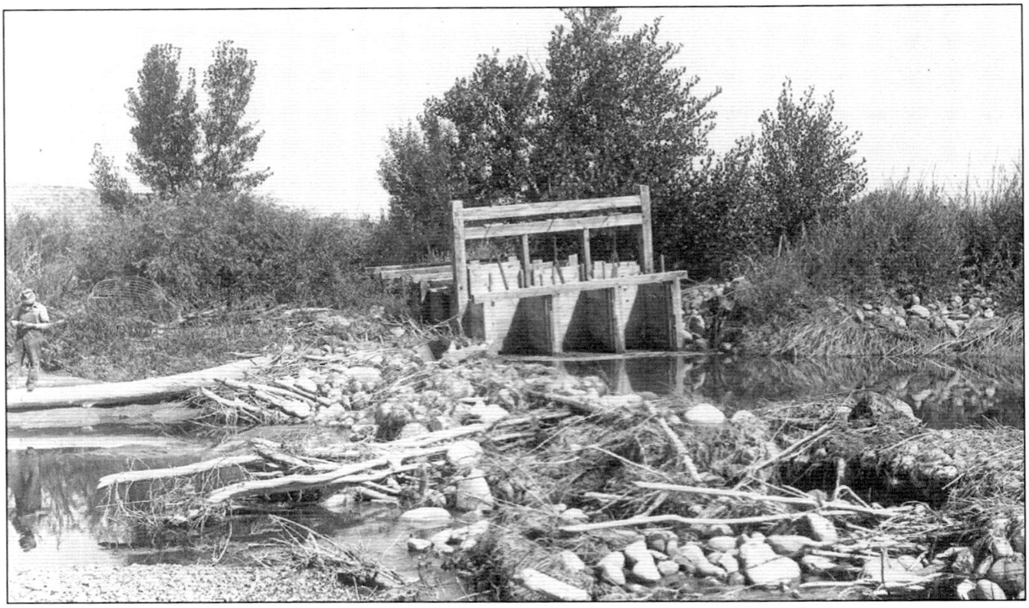

This view of the Garnet Ditch shows the head gate and the makeshift dam spanning the Uncompahgre River. The dam was constructed largely from brush and river debris. (Early settlers' means for controlling the waters were crude but apparently effective.) The picture illustrates the typical condition of the structures found on the private canals acquired by the United States Government during the early days of the U.S. Bureau of Reclamation.

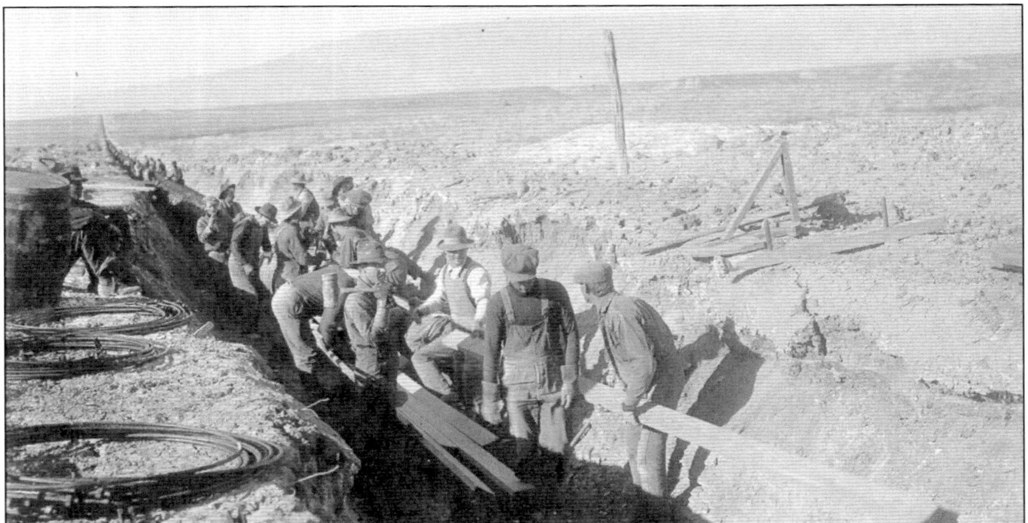

One of the first stages of the Garnet Mesa Siphon's construction consisted of assembling the staves— the strips of wood placed side by side to form a barrel, or, in this case, a long, wooden pipeline. The crew of men in the foreground holds the boards together, and the next crew bands the boards together and completes the first cinching. The crew farther down the pipe are completing the second cinching. The far in the distance is painting the pipeline as quickly as it is completed. The band distributor sitting to the left of the trench is waiting until the men below are ready for more metal bands.

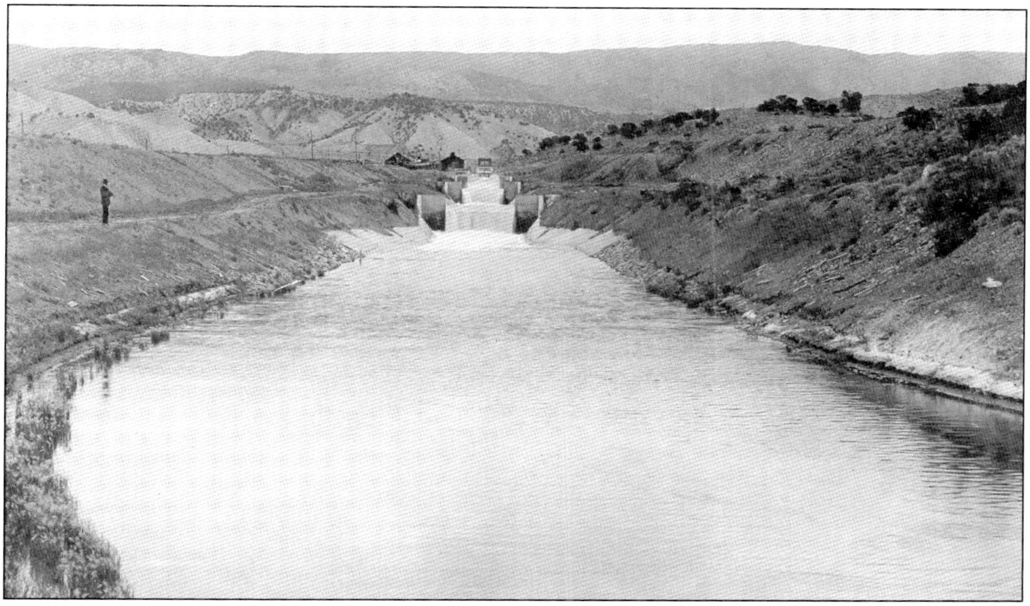

The South Canal's several drops just below the West Portal compensated for the drop in elevation.

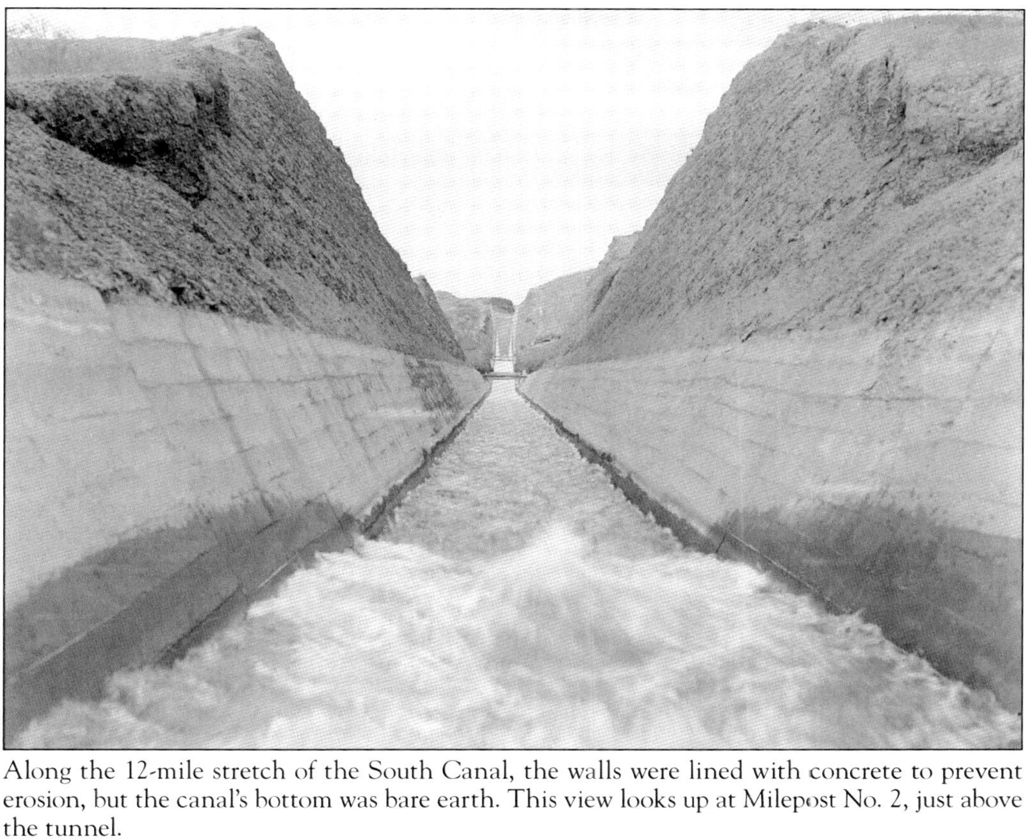

Along the 12-mile stretch of the South Canal, the walls were lined with concrete to prevent erosion, but the canal's bottom was bare earth. This view looks up at Milepost No. 2, just above the tunnel.

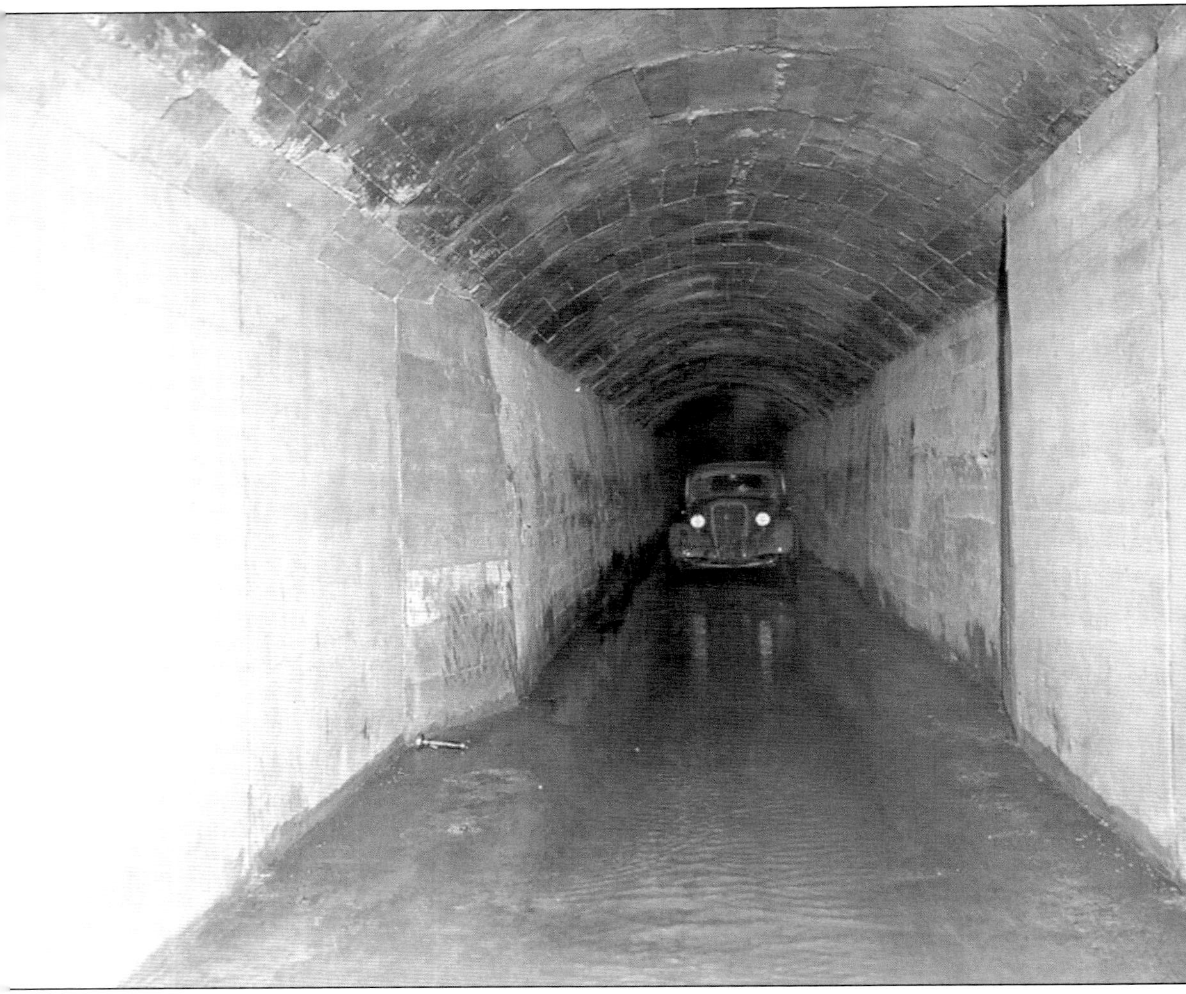

Inspecting the vast Gunnison Tunnel would have taken many hours on foot, so the U.S. Bureau of Reclamation inspectors pictured here in the 1930s have chosen to travel by automobile. Inspectors would inspect the tunnel's walls and roof for damage. After problems were noted, a full inspection team returned to the location to evaluate what equipment and manpower the repairs would require. This inspection process continued through the years. This photograph shows a section of the repaired walls being inspected via automobile.

The man crouched in this photograph is pointing out a crack in the floor of the South Canal above Tunnel No. 1, likely caused by the heaving or swelling of the earth. The winter ground freeze and melting also caused cracks in concrete and was a regular nemesis for the Gunnison Tunnel. Even today, the tunnel requires regular maintenance due to these natural phenomena.

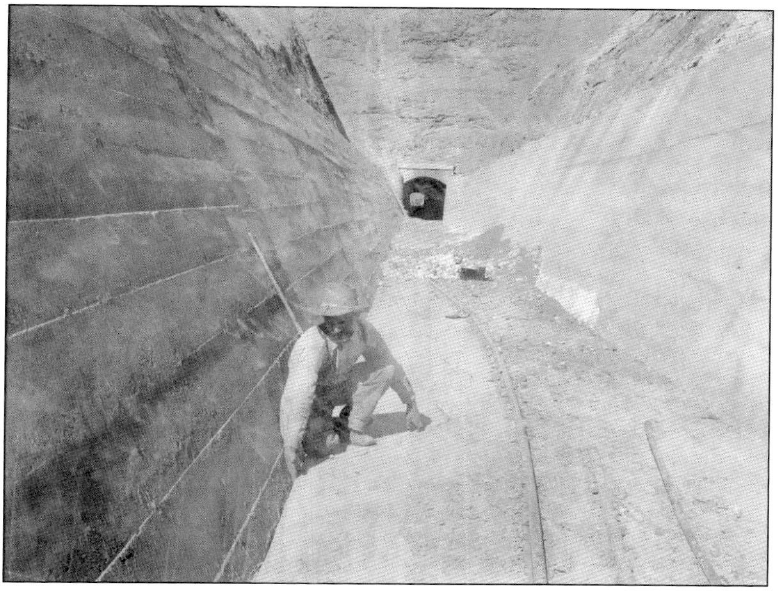

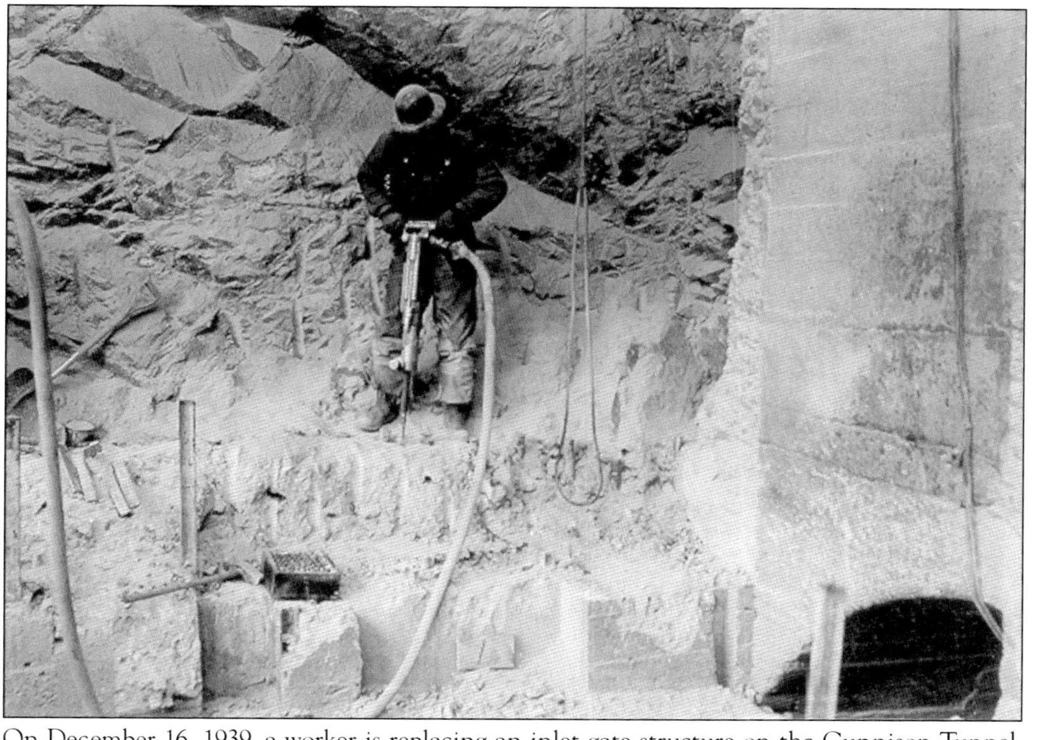

On December 16, 1939, a worker is replacing an inlet gate structure on the Gunnison Tunnel. Nearly all rock and concrete excavation was done by drilling and wedging, rather than blasting. This more time-consuming method was chosen to prevent damage to the operating house above, but it added many hours of backbreaking labor for the tunnel workers.

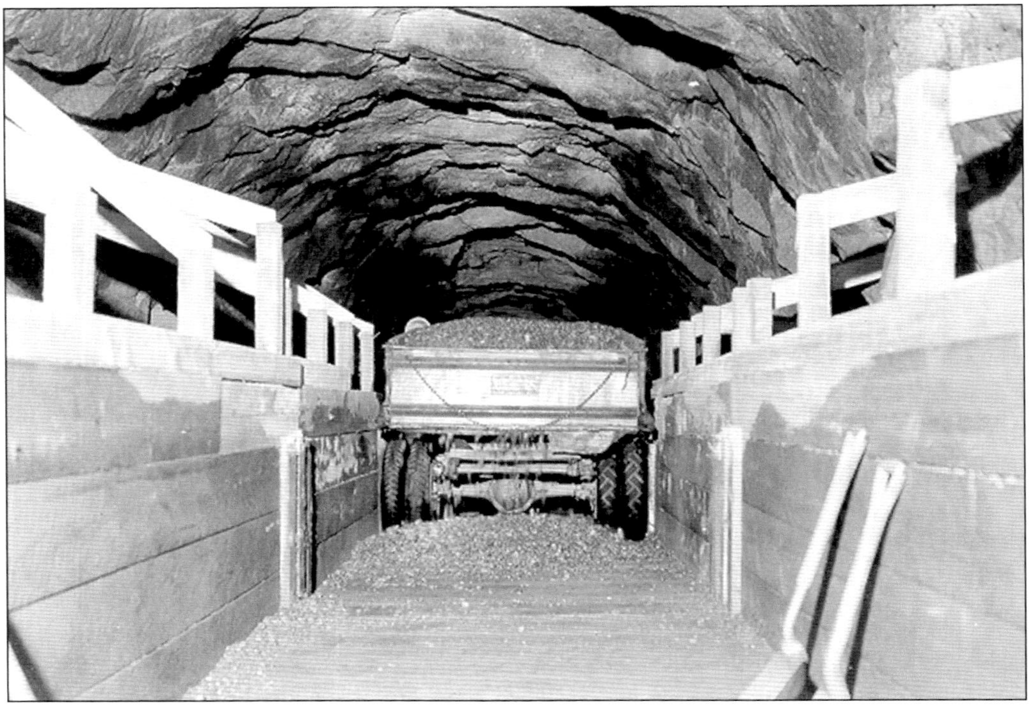

Repair work in the Gunnison Tunnel became much easier with the arrival of motorized vehicles. This 1930s image shows one such vehicle bearing a load of material through the narrow tunnel. The shovels against the wall, however, attest that much of the work was still done by hand during this era.

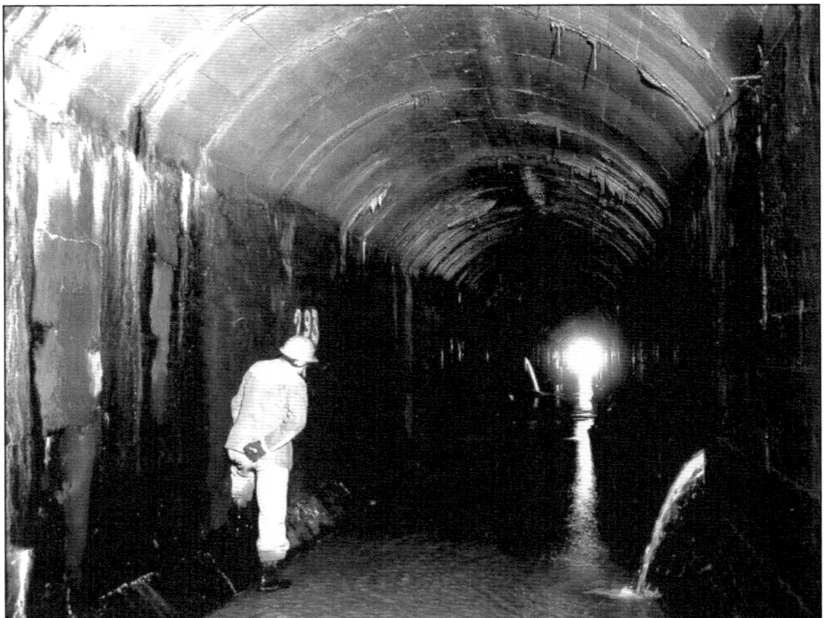

In the inspections of the 1930s, the walls were found to be weeping water. Here, an inspector from the Bureau of Reclamation views a former weep site that has turned into a full flow. Major repairs loom ahead.

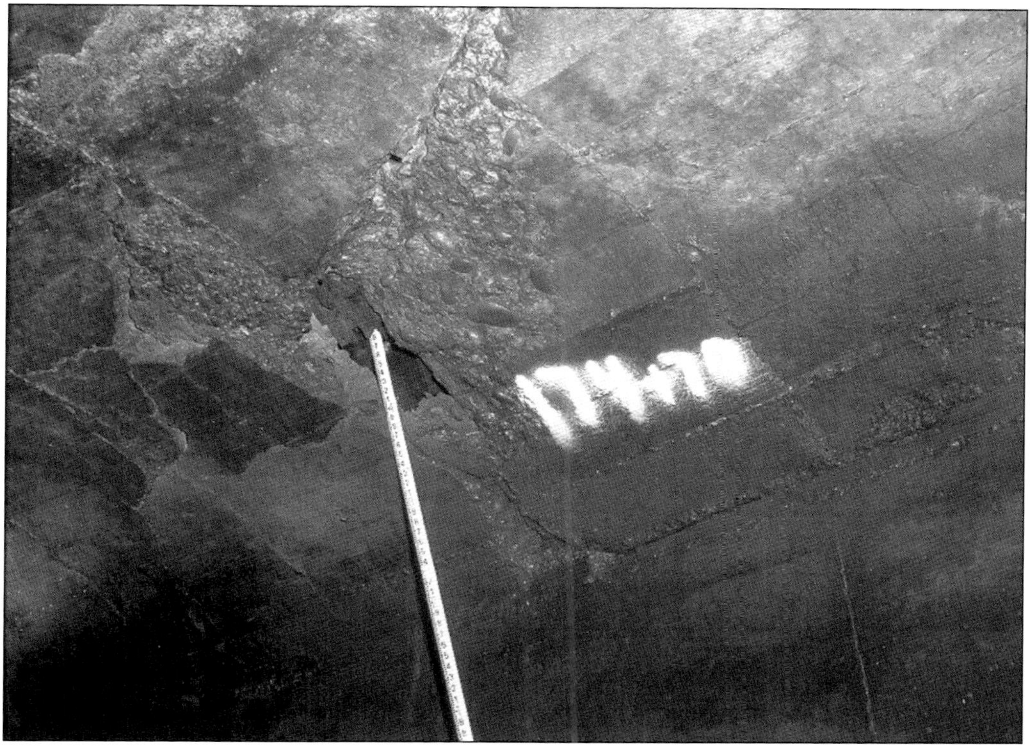

Tunnel inspectors mark the location of each damage site they find, numbering the spots in bright paint.

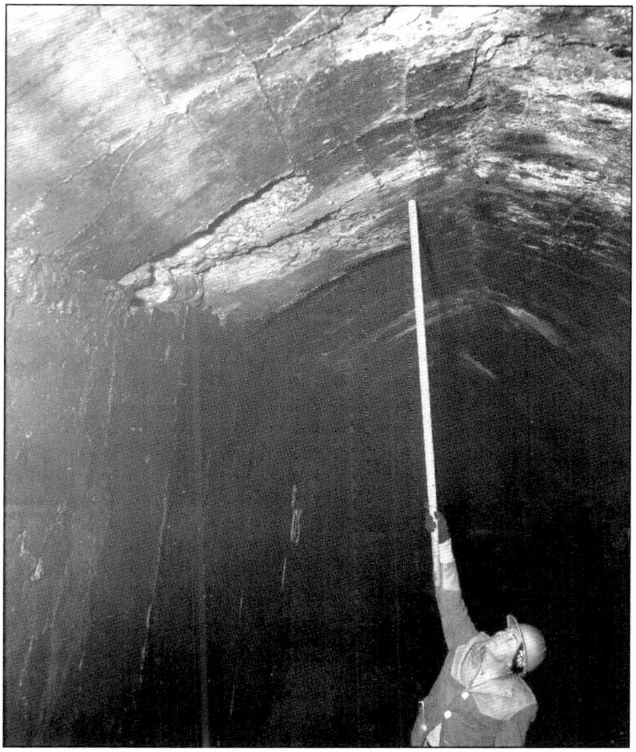

The Gunnison Tunnel requires constant maintenance. Here an inspector examines a spot where the concrete has eroded away to the depth of the original arch timbers.

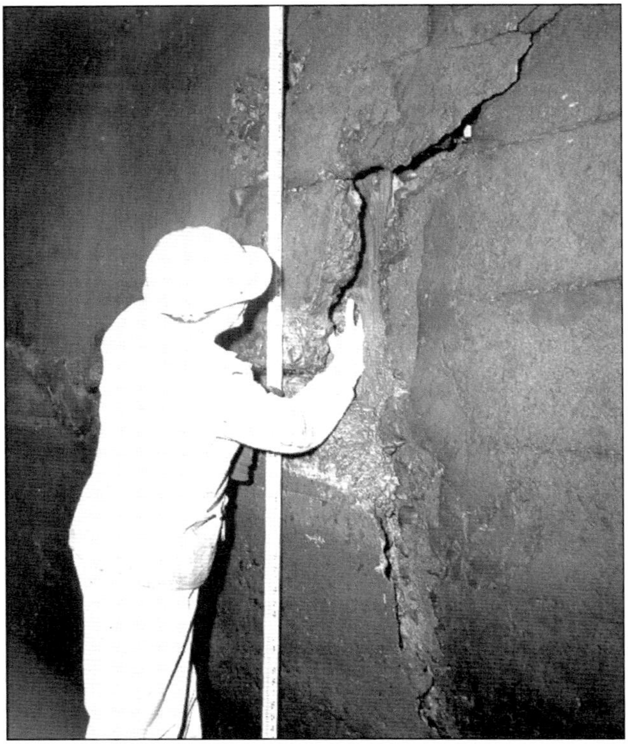

Reviews of the tunnel in the mid-1960s not only revealed roof damage but cracked walls due to shifting. Some of these cracks could be easily filled with concrete joints. Other wall shifting, such as that shown here (exposing the original timbers), required more extensive repairs. (Photograph by Vern Jetly.)

During the inspections and repairs of 1967 and 1968, not only had the water traveling through the Gunnison Tunnel taken its toll on the walls and roof of the structure, it had affected the tunnel floor, too. The inspector below is looking at the exposed ties in the tunnel's floor.

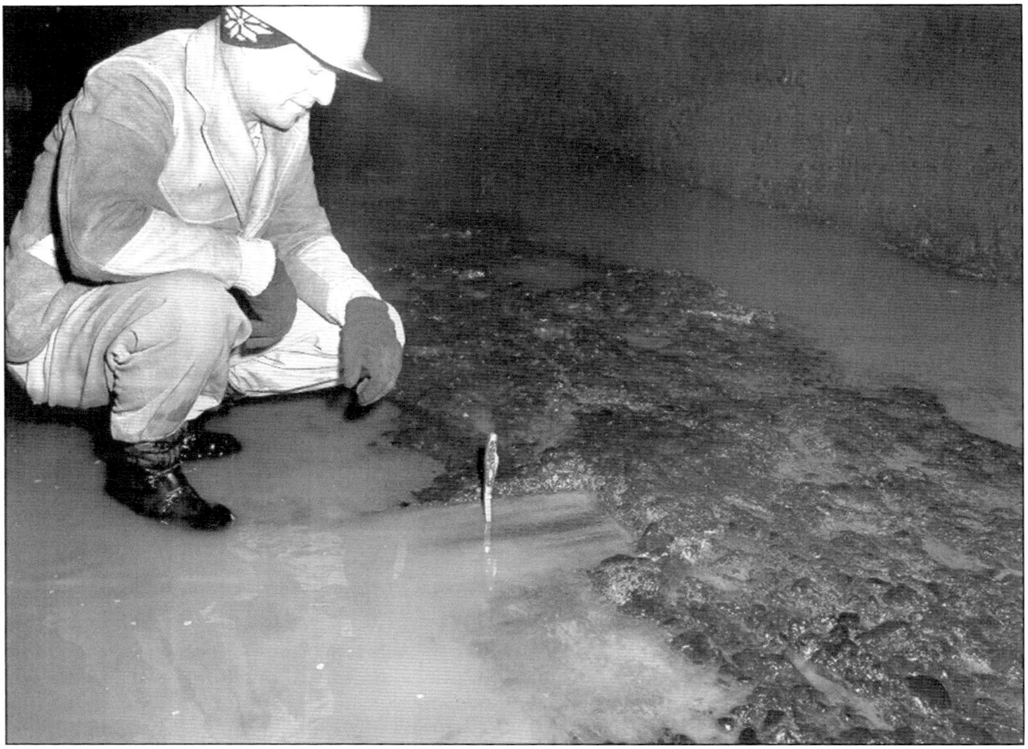

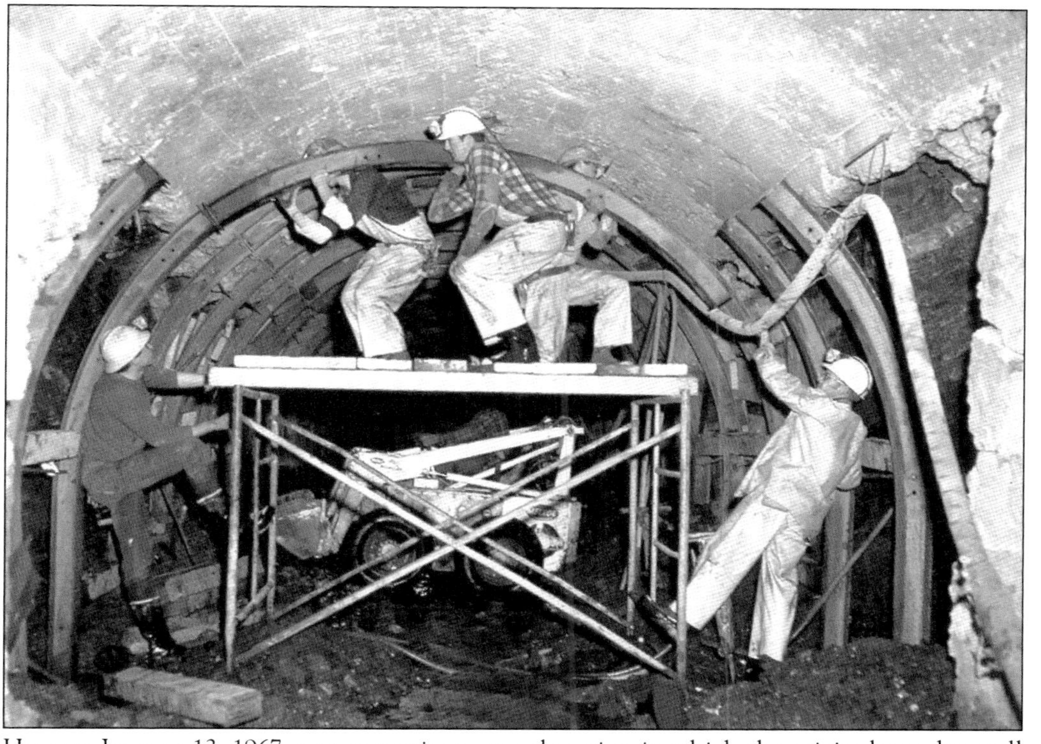

Here on January 13, 1967, a crew repairs a tunnel section in which the original wooden wall timbers have been exposed. When repaired, wooden supports were replaced with steel beams.

Workers are seen here during the 1967 and 1968 repairs, manually tearing out the tunnel's old walls and roof. The demolished roof lies on the tunnel floor. The removal of the walls was done manually to prevent any unnecessary disturbance to the earth surrounding the tunnel.

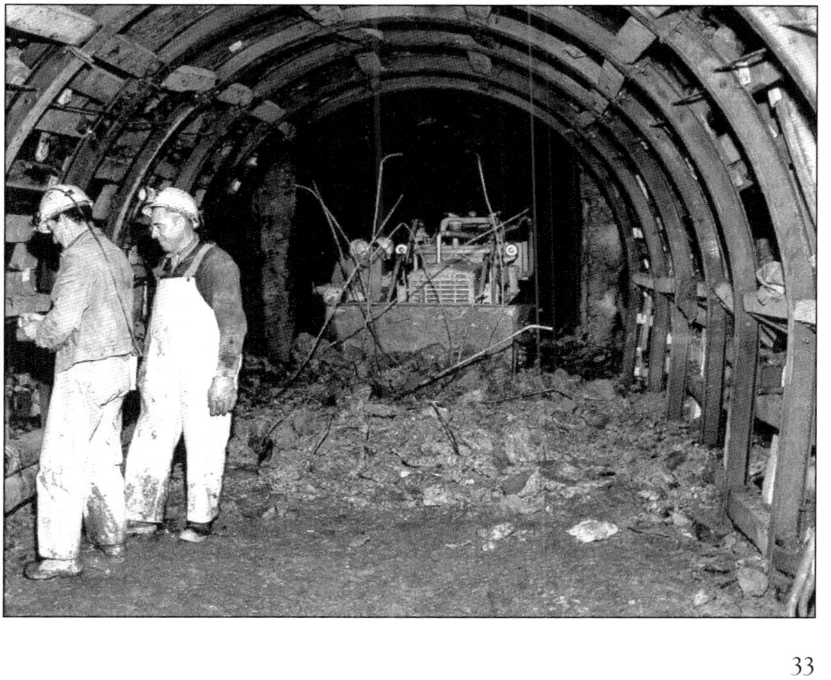

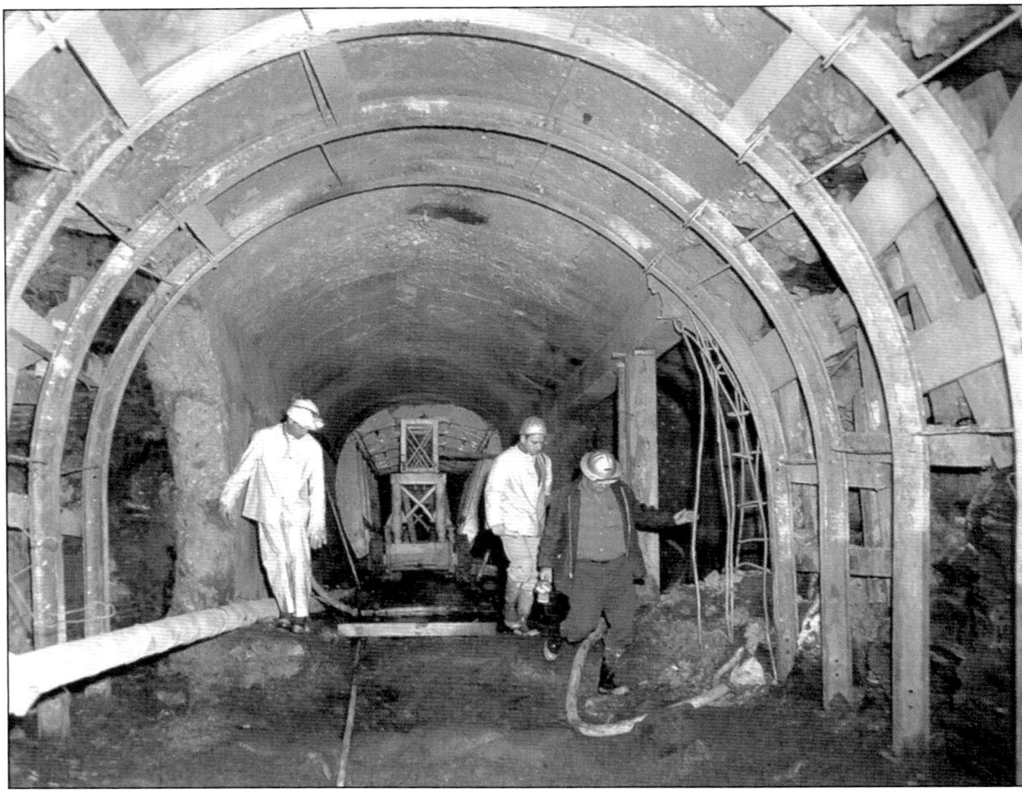

Here on January 26, 1967, workers are installing steel sets on 4-foot centers after excavation of the sidewalls. The crews of men wearing waterproof boots and hard hats are inspecting the steel framework to ensure that the cement will be properly supported.

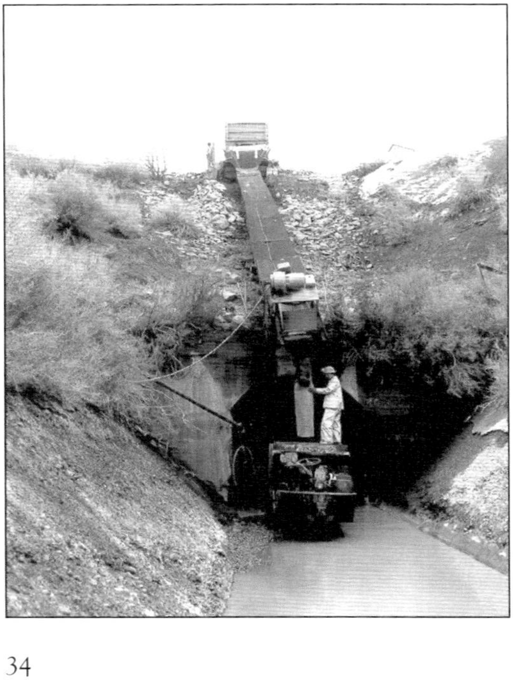

This 1967 view at the tunnel's portal shows dry-mix concrete being loaded into a tunnel buggy. The distance to the area where the tunnel was being relined was so far from the tunnel opening that the dry concrete had to be transported by vehicle to the mixer (which had itself been specially fabricated to fit into the tunnel). The water was then added and the concrete pumped into the forms. The bed of the dump truck atop the tunnel was divided into sections so that operators could dump one batch of concrete at a time.

This 1960s photograph shows crews working with premix, which goes into the concrete mixer via conveyor belt. Though there appears to be lighting in the tunnel, men wear lights on their helmets. Their heavy work clothes suggest that this part of the tunnel is chilly.

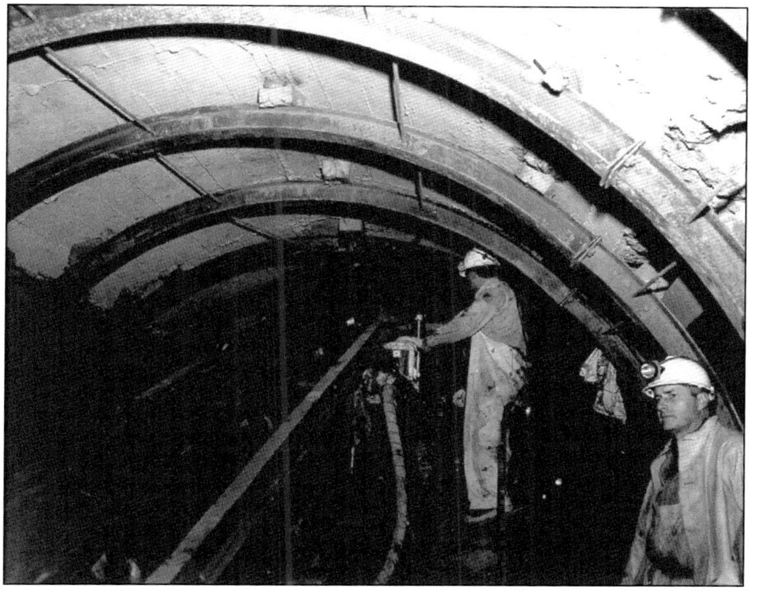

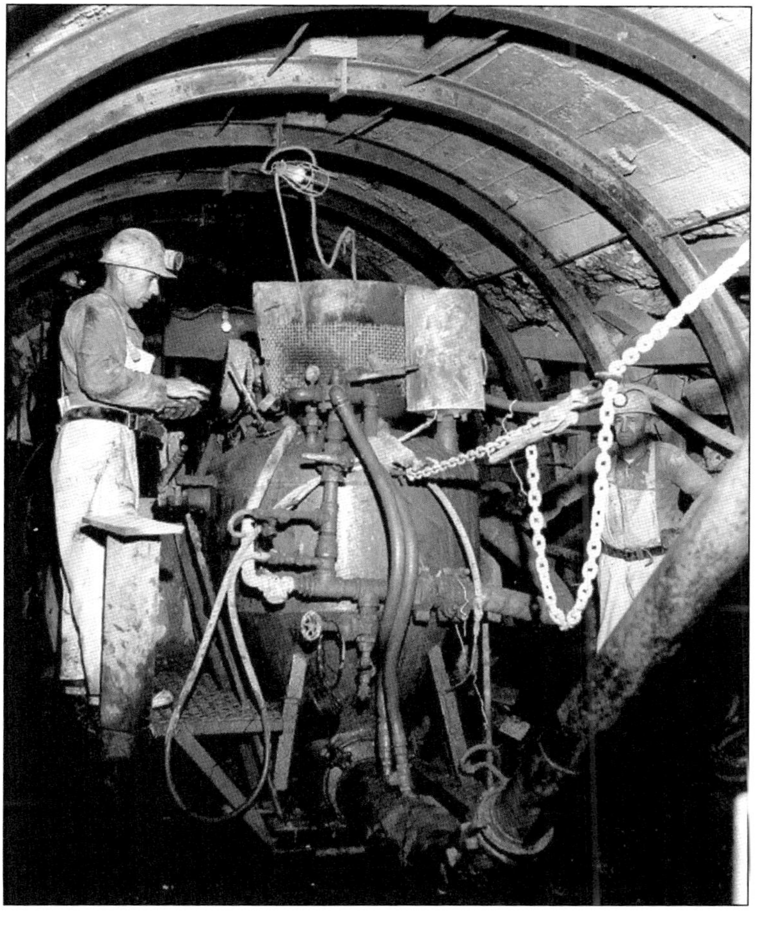

The machine seen here is called a concrete air-placement machine, which allowed for the concrete to be pumped down and placed overhead on the tunnel walls. Eagle Construction built the concrete mixing plant that was used in the re-lining of the tunnel. On January 23, 1968, after the job was complete, the plant was turned over to the Uncompahgre Valley Water Users Association. (Photograph by V. Jetly.)

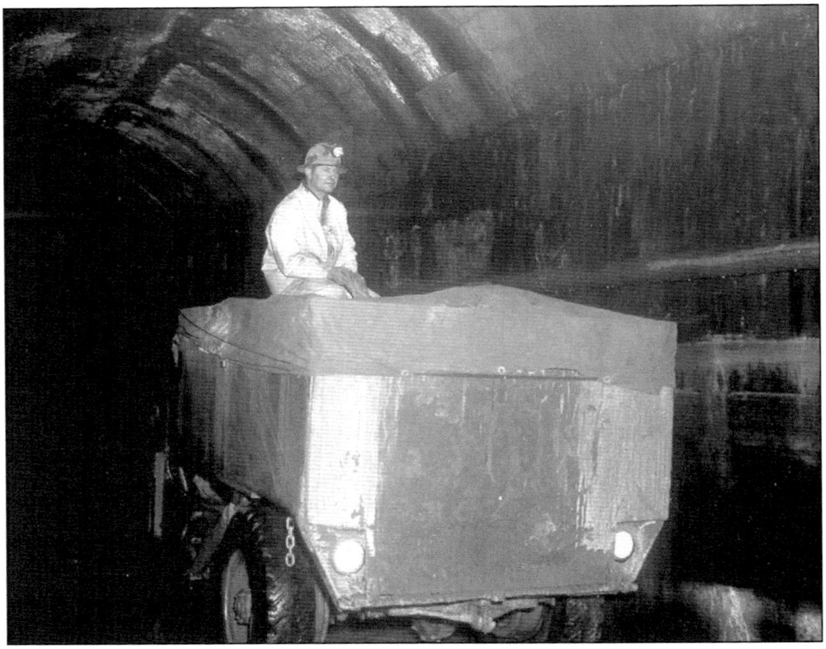

Here on February 23, 1968, ditch rider Jesse Jenkins is seen driving a tunnel buggy. The cart is filled with concrete to be used in filling holes in the tunnel. Perhaps his day is just beginning, or he may be simply starting out with another load.

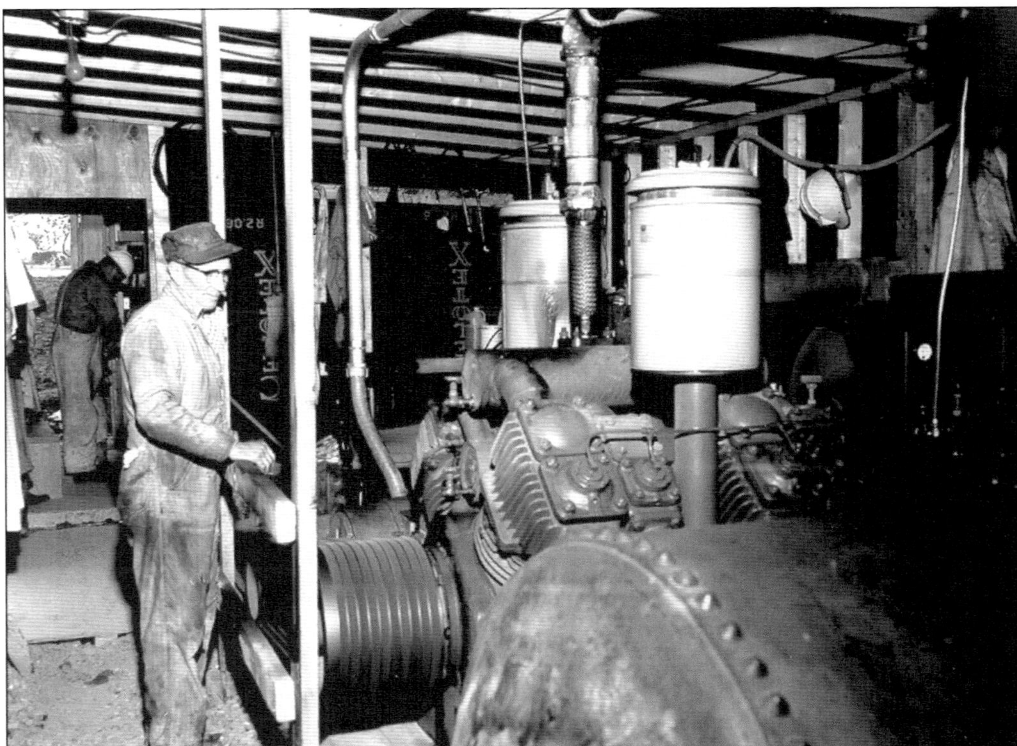

In this 1960s photograph, Carl Button Sr. is seen in the compressor house surveying the massive machinery. His vocation was to make certain that the equipment kept in good running order.

Carl Raish was president of the UVWUA. Carl's father, George Raish, had the hauling contract for all of the coal and machinery sent to the two portals during the building of the tunnel.

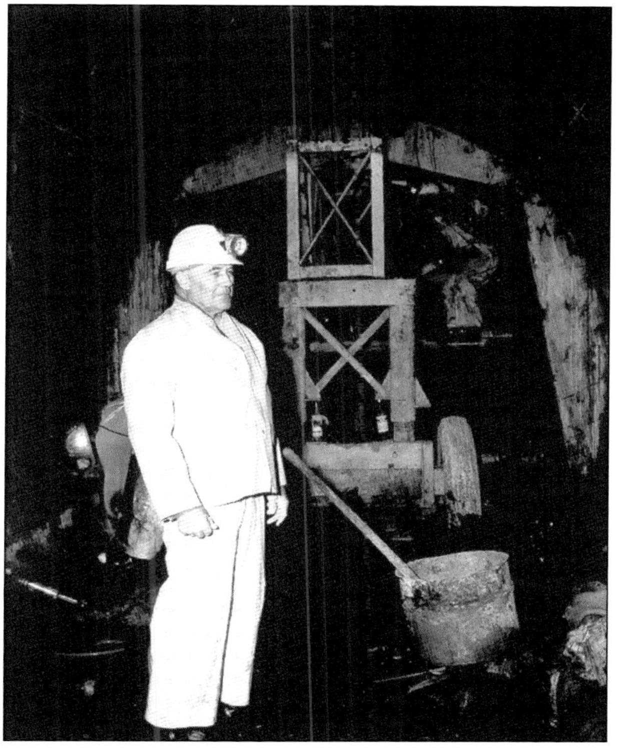

The tunnel repair crew here is ready to begin a big job. On the left is Tom Roy. Sitting on top near the front are Carl Raish (left) and Harold Anderson. The other two men are unidentified.

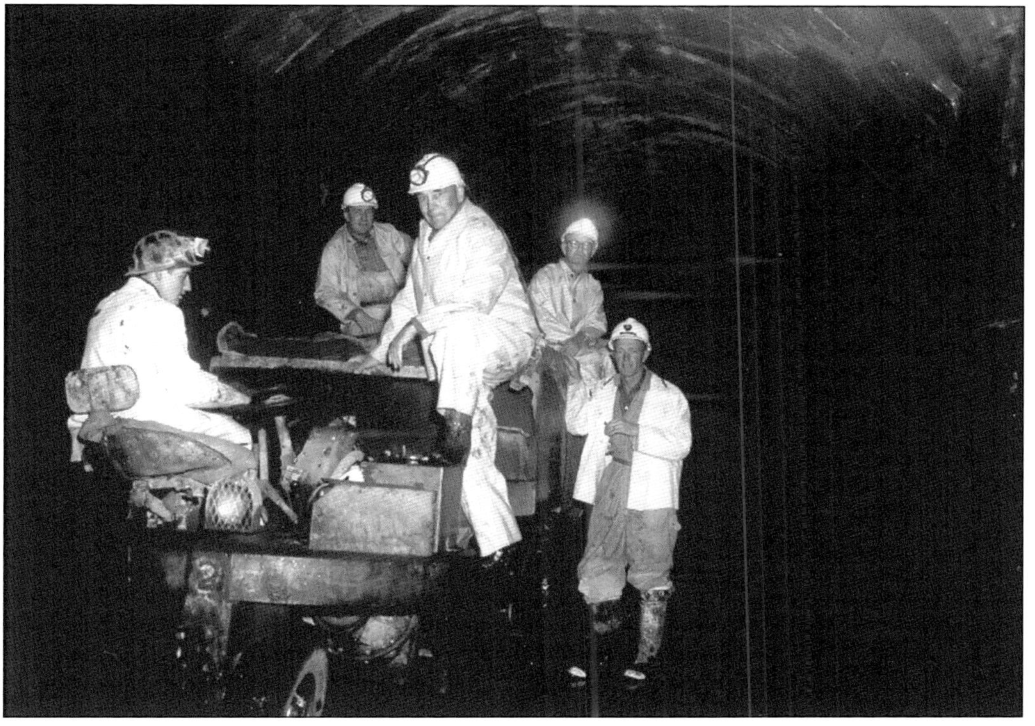

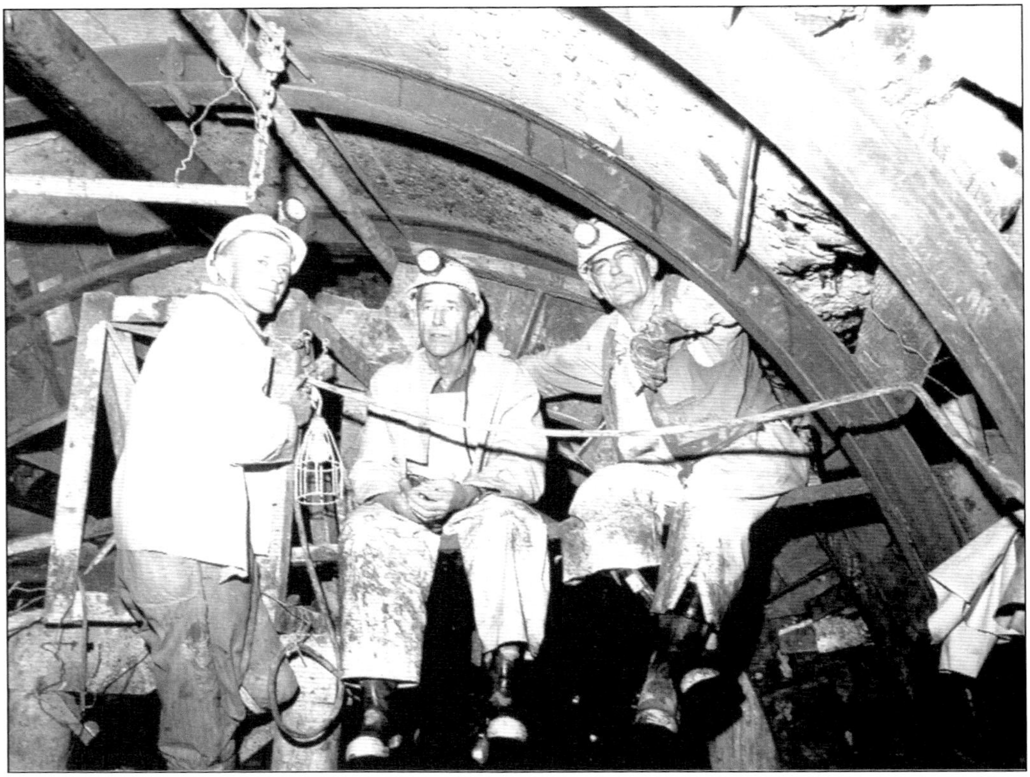

Pictured here on February 23, 1968, these three men were in charge of tunnel repairs. From left to right are Harold Anderson (manager of the Uncompahgre Valley Water Users Association), Bill Hoarad (shift foreman), and Charles Malin (job superintendent). (Photograph by Vern Jetly.)

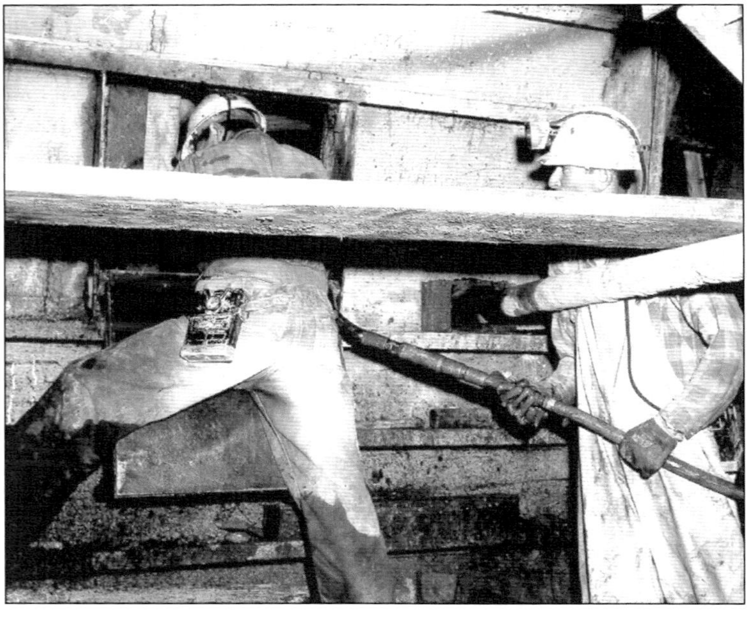

These two men are working through the form window with a vibrating machine designed to work air pockets out of the freshly poured cement. The long hours spent stretched and bent with this bone-rattling equipment was very strenuous but extremely crucial to the project.

The tunnel's maintenance was an ongoing process. Workers used scaffolds and concrete to hand-patch simple cracks in the tunnel's roof and walls. This photograph shows men performing a repair on a replacement wall from the late 1960s, when the original timber supports were replaced with steel and new concrete.

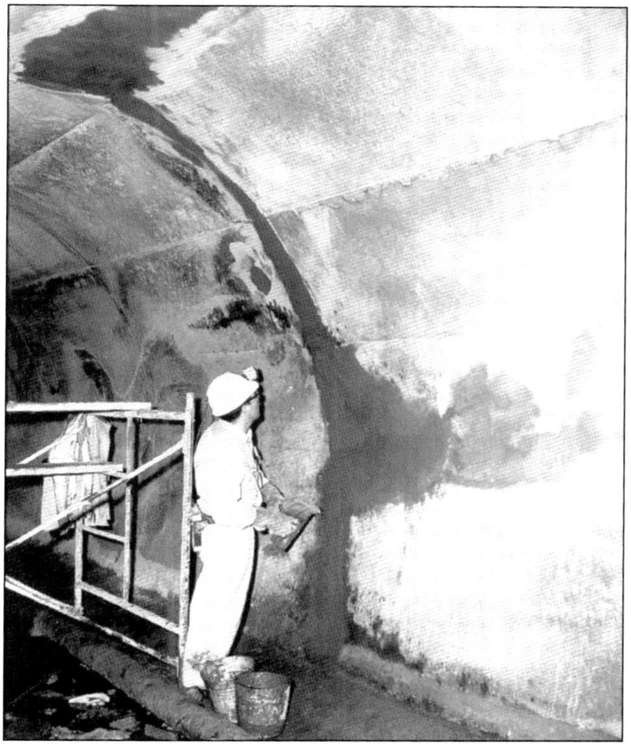

The two men seen here are in the Gunnison Tunnel looking downstream. This photograph provides a view of the tunnel lining and the tunnel forms. Hours spent trudging through cold water while dragging heavy forms in a tunnel snaked with white hoses was just another day on the job for these workers.

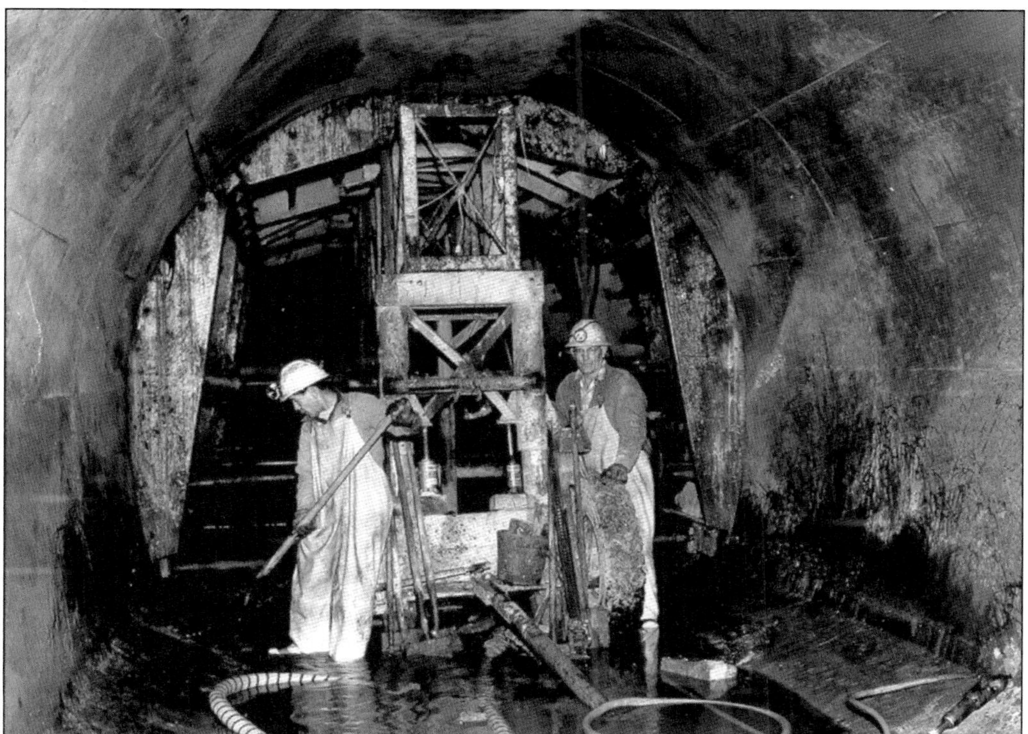

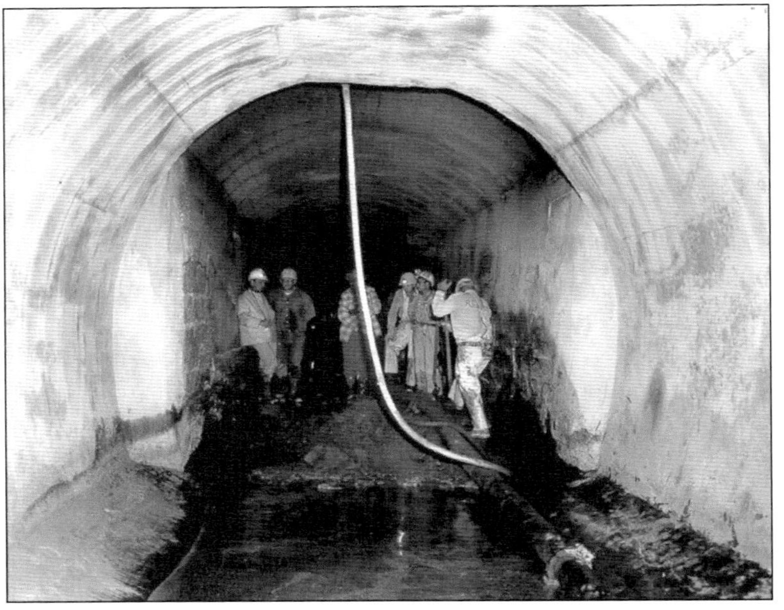

In this late-1960s image, repairs are being inspected by the work crews. In the photograph's foreground, the new walls meet the old wall. Using the improved technology of the times, workers were able to make the new replacement walls fully curved. The old roof in the background has more of an angle as it meets the side walls.

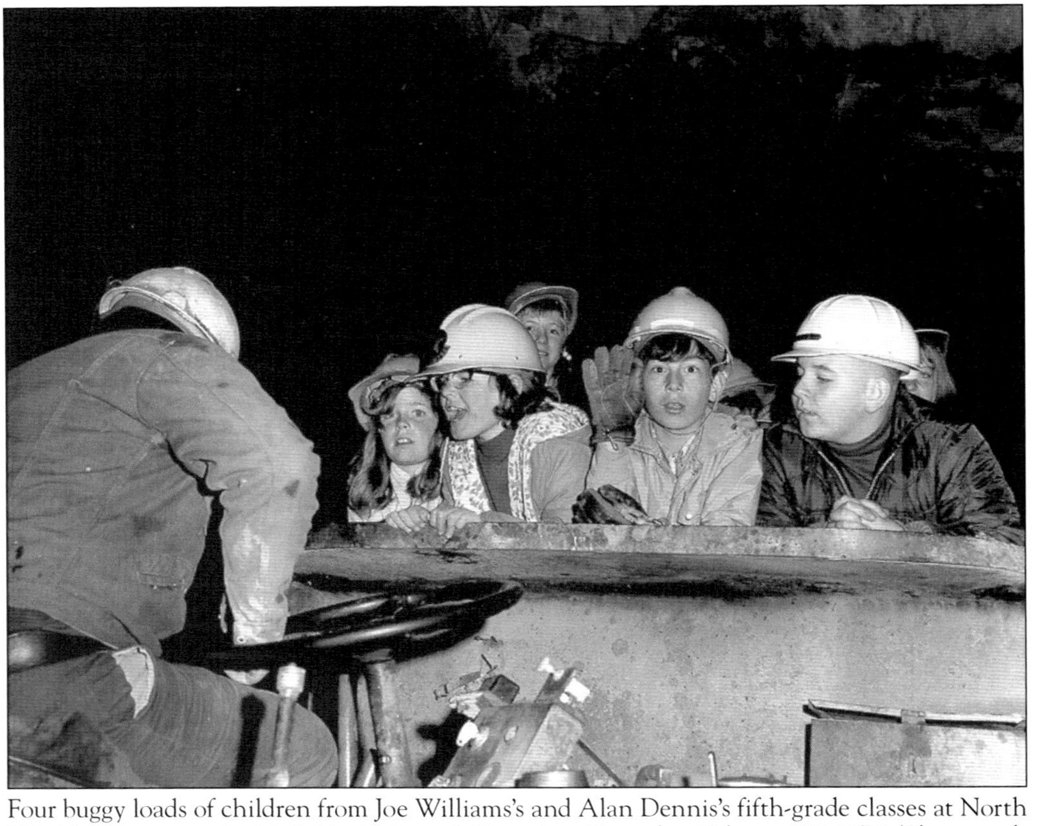

Four buggy loads of children from Joe Williams's and Alan Dennis's fifth-grade classes at North Side Elementary made this field trip through Gunnison Tunnel on February 18, 1970. (Photograph by Vern Jetly.)

Two

VALLEY AGRICULTURAL RICHES

From the beginning of its settlement, the Uncompahgre Valley has yielded record crops of all types. Three mountain ranges surround the valley, and warm and cold winds swirl over the peaks to the fertile valley floor, creating an environment well suited to growing such staple crops as corn, potatoes, onions, and wheat. But the valley, with its unique climate and rich soils, was at its most productive growing fruit. The juiciness, rich flavor, and superb coloring of the valley's fruit, combined with the sheer enormity of its yields, made Uncompahgre Valley apples, apricots, peaches, and grapes very desirable to grocers and vintners. In Delta, the produce and fruit borne by this land has been plentiful. Also enormous, at times, was the size of the valley's produce. Over the years, proud Uncompahgre Valley farmers have won countless ribbons, trophies, and awards at state and local fairs. The Department of Agriculture declared that an 11-pound potato pulled from the valley's verdant soils was the largest on record.

The prize vegetables and fruits produced by the valley were joined by prize livestock. In the spring, summer, and early fall, the vast open range in the Uncompahgre Valley filled with lush green vegetation The valley was prime land for raising cattle and, later, sheep. At the start of the 20th century, such a lush valley was a rarity in the arid West. The Uncompahgre Valley remains a major food producer to this day.

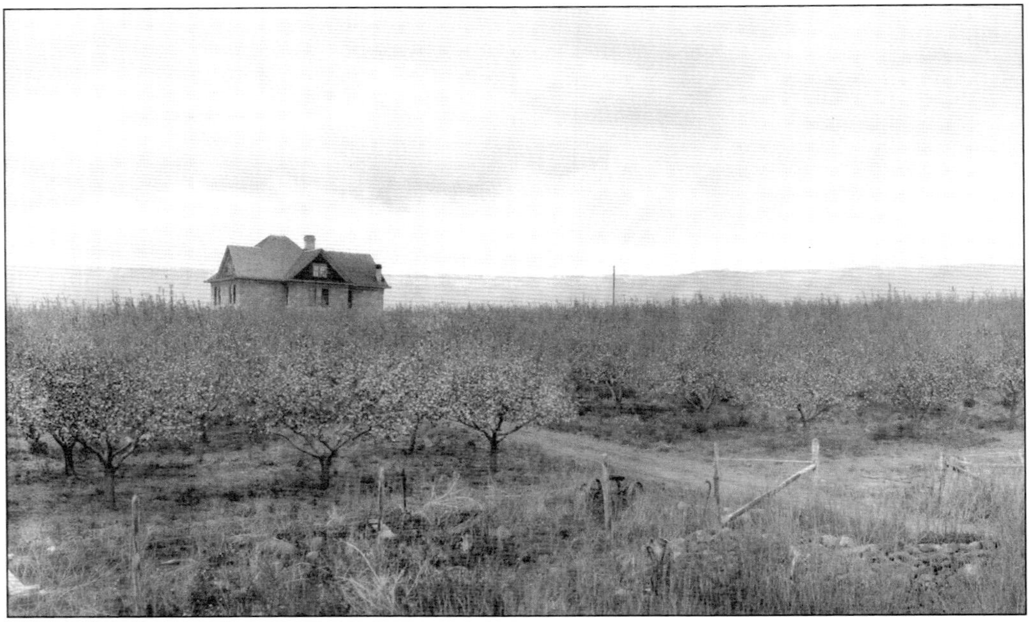

Stolte Orchard was located north of Cedaredge in an area known as the Surface Creek Valley. Henry Stolte and J. H. Wetterrich set out orchards in this area in 1895. In 1909, Stolte built a packing shed on his property. It was known as the Cedaredge Growers Exchange.

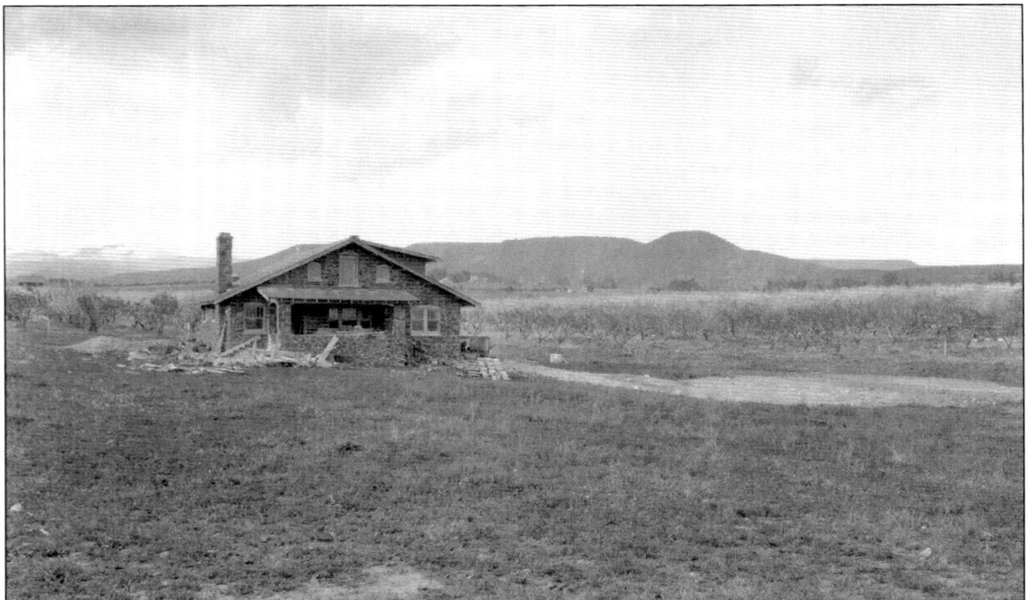

In 1919, Edward H. and Josephine Divelbliss established a peach orchard known as the Silver Spruce Orchards on Rogers Mesa near the town of Hotchkiss. Edward was Delta County's first extension agent, making contributions in the fields of education, agriculture, and horticulture. Edward worked for the establishment of the Leroux Creek Water Users System and many service organizations. The mother of two children, Josephine was one of Delta County's first 4-H leaders, vice chairman of the Republican Party, and a supporter of several service organizations.

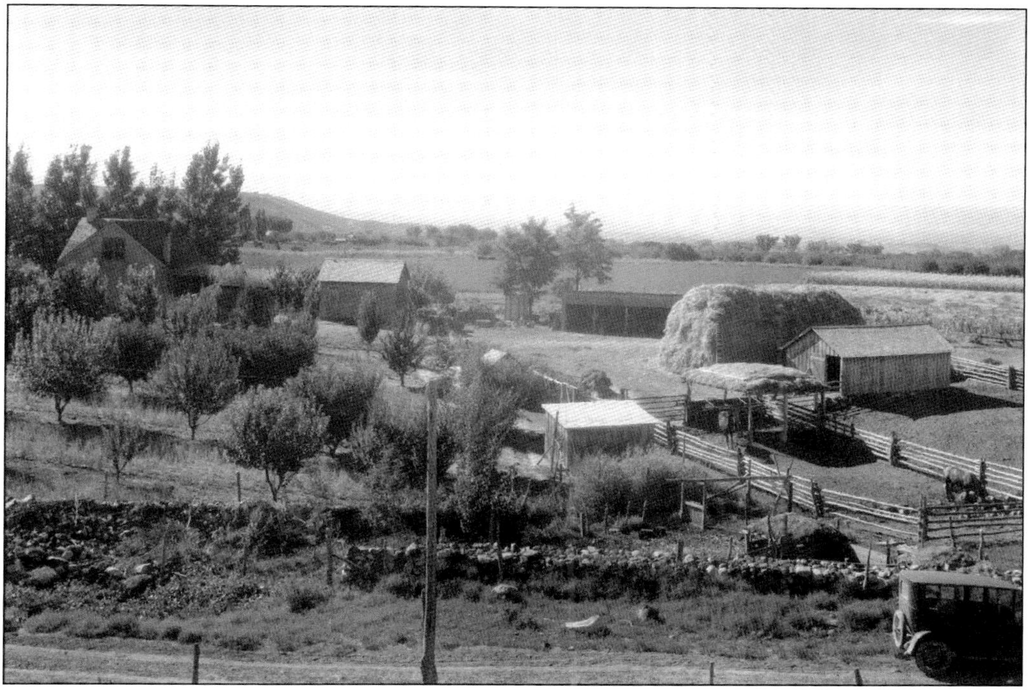

The Bailey Ranch was located in the small, unincorporated area of Eckert, Colorado, in the early 1900s. To the left in this picture is the farmhouse and a couple of small outbuildings. On the right is a haystack taller than the barn it stands beside. Also visible is the Bailey horse corral, and, in the background, the family's cornfields.

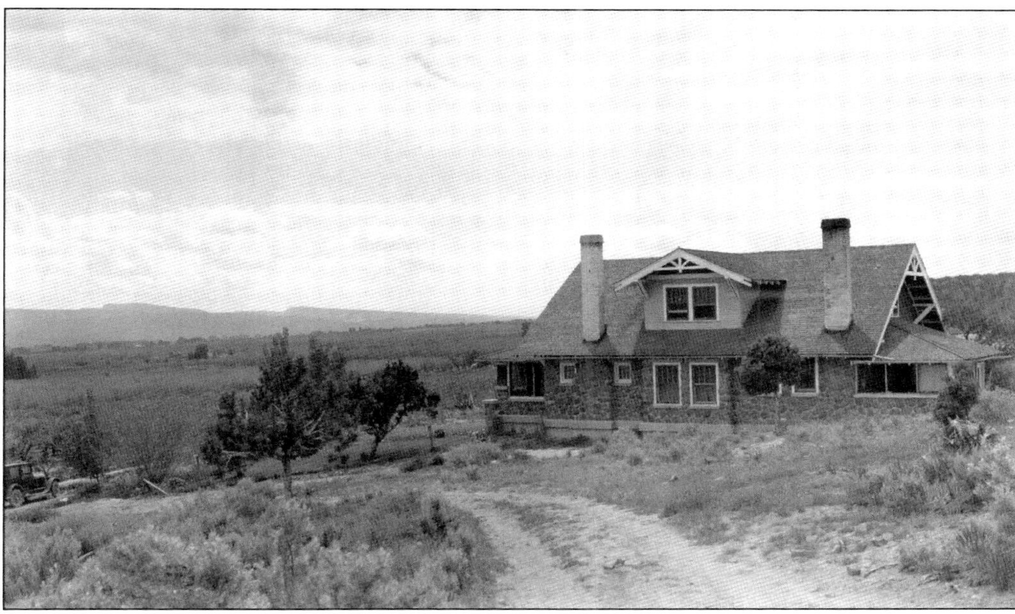

In the early 1900s, the valley was already home to numerous farms, but after the Gunnison Tunnel was built, many more were begun. This ranch house was located in the North Fork Valley. To the right and back of the photograph is a vast orchard of fruit trees.

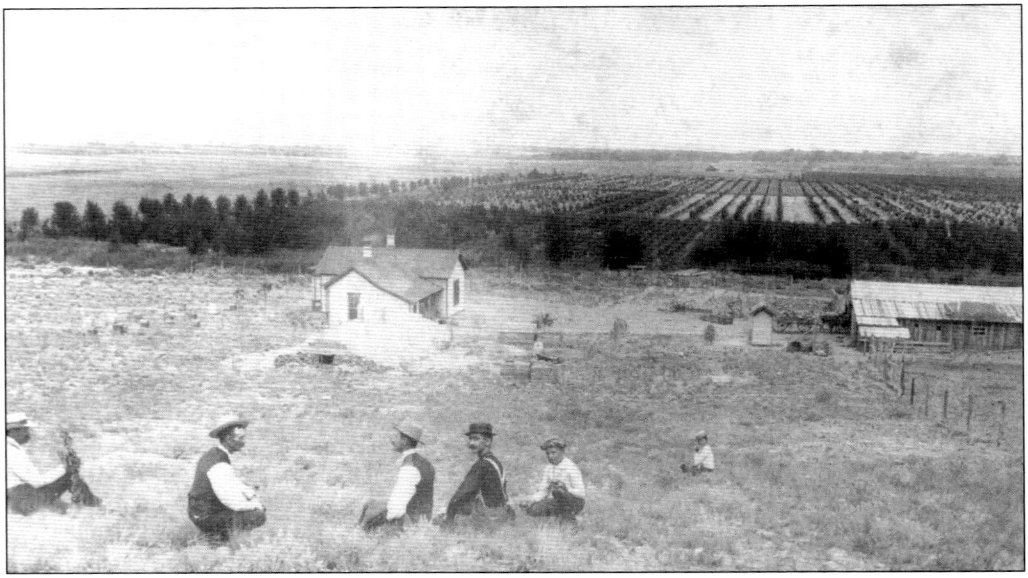

This Garnet Mesa farmhouse was built in 1885 by George Blair McGranahan. It can still be found today, at the end of the Seventh Street extension.

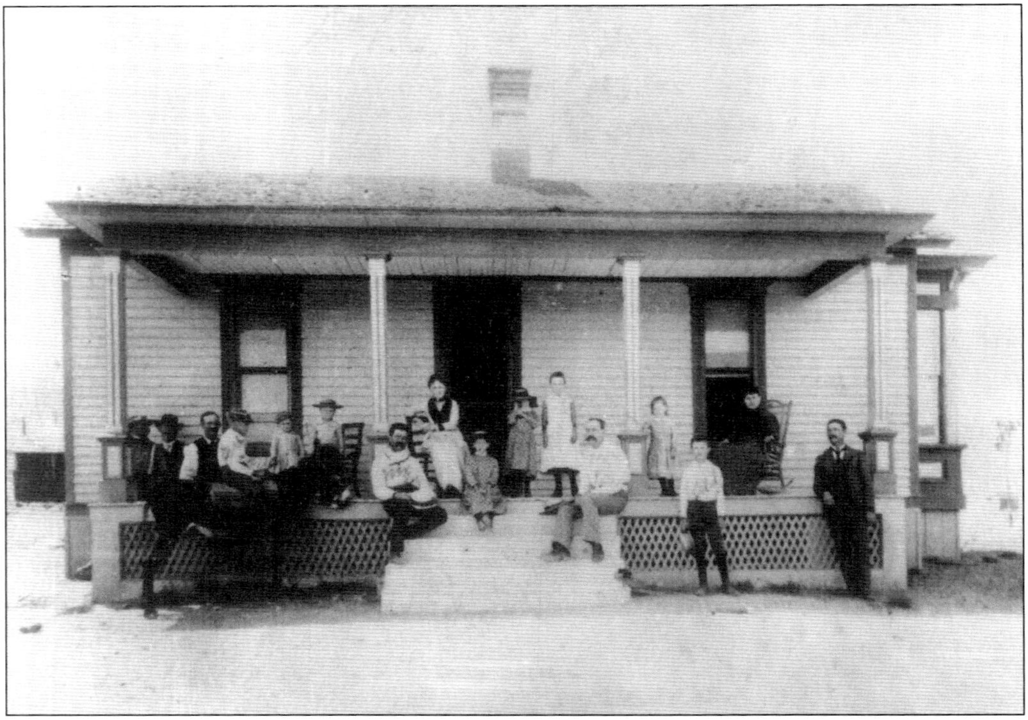

This image shows an 1883 gathering at the McGranahan home. In this photograph, George is the man wearing a vest and standing behind the mule, which is being ridden by Guy James, a relative of George's wife. Moving left to right, the rest of the people shown in this photograph are Butler McGranahan, Harvey McGranahan, unidentified, Abe Butler, Mildred McGranahan, Ed James, Mrs. James (mother of the James children), and Will James (their father).

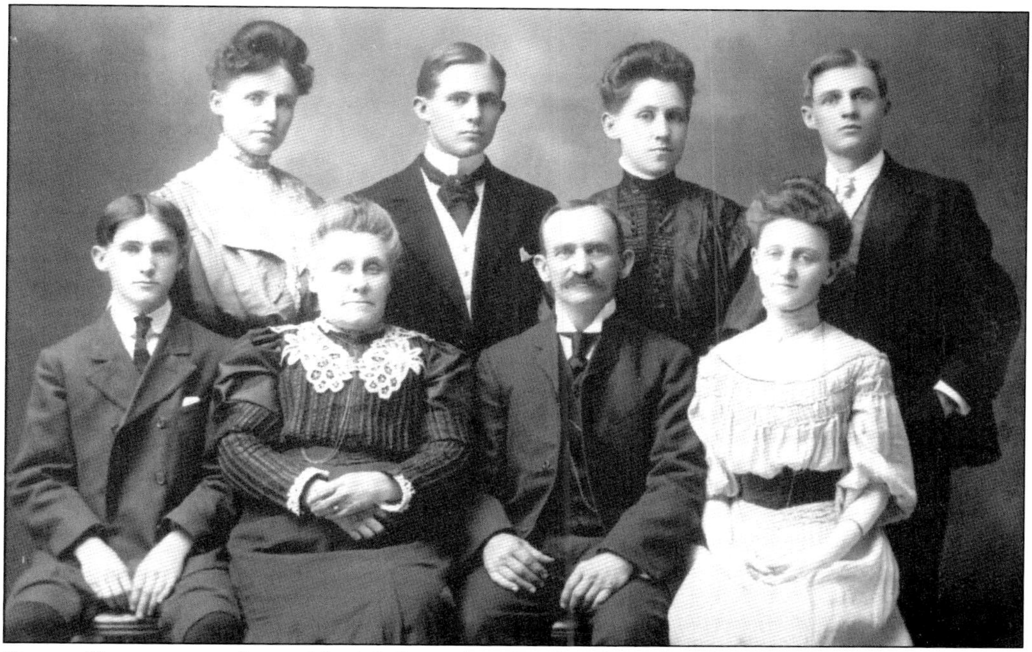

Pictured here are members of the McGranahan family, whose farmhouse is also in this collection of pictures. George McGranahan pioneered the Delta area in 1881. From left to right, pictured here are (first row) High Emmett, Harriet James, George Blair, and Margaret Jane; (second row) Mildred McGranahan, George Butler, Charlotte May, and Harvey Paul.

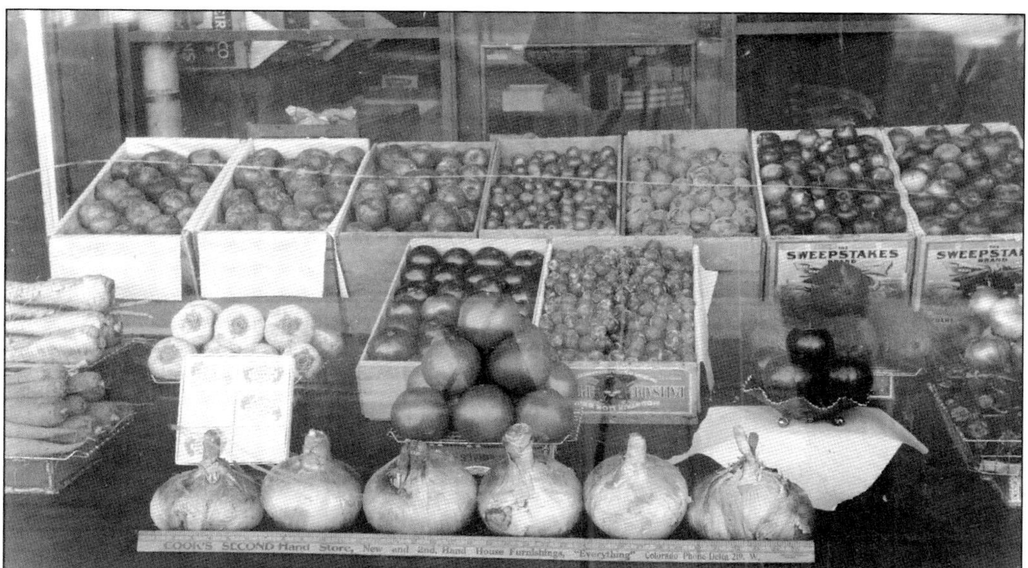

The fruit and vegetables grown in the valley are desired from coast to coast. Apples, pears, peppers, plums, carrots, and onions are some of the produce shown here. Notice that the six onions on the first row span the entire length of a yardstick, meaning that they were each an average of 6 inches in width.

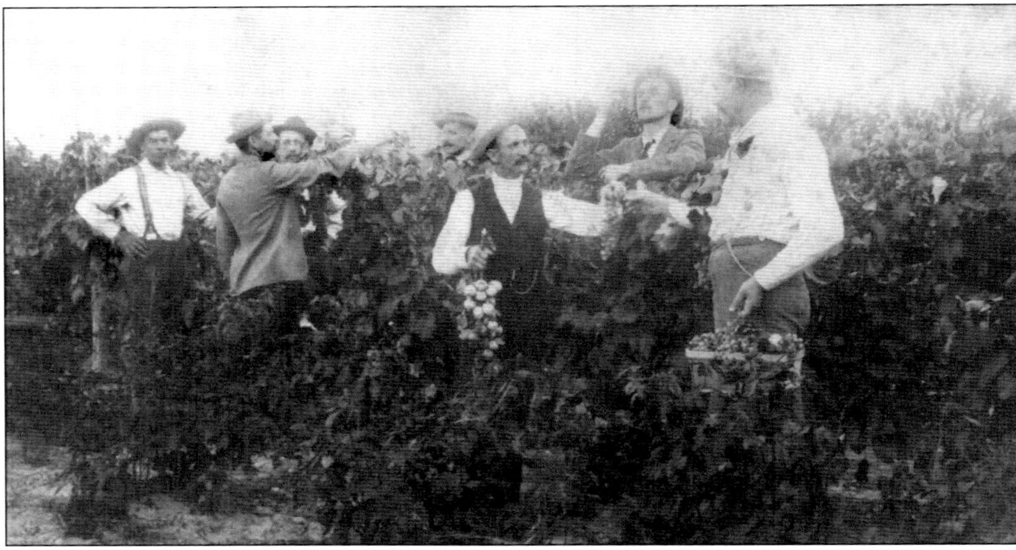

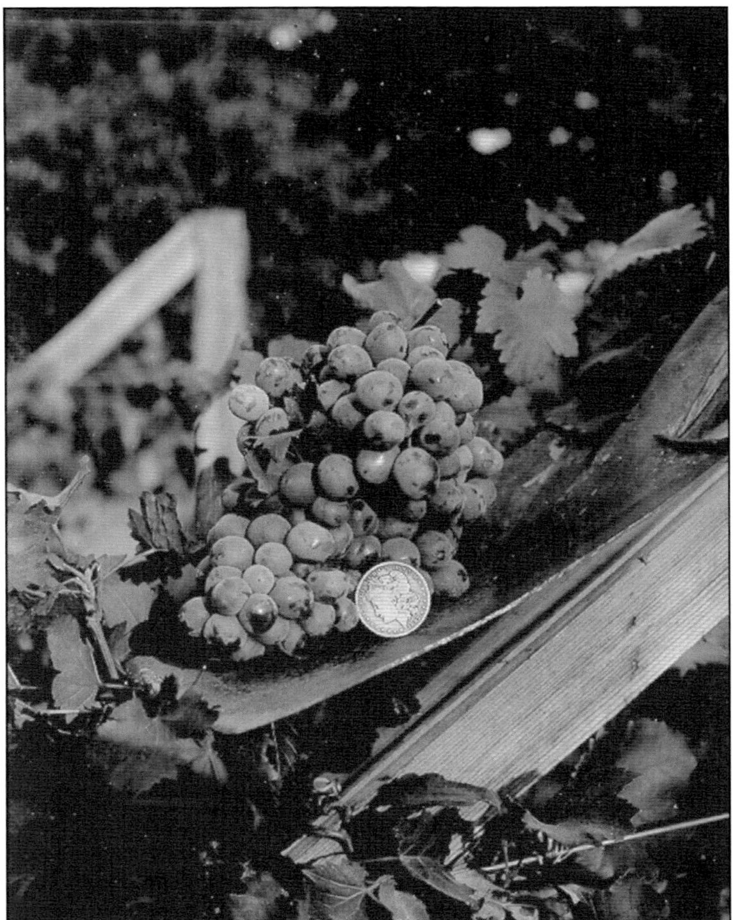

The *c.* 1900 photograph above was taken in a vineyard on the McGranahan Farm on Garnet Mesa. George Stephan is second from left, with his back to the camera. Abe Butler is third from right, holding grapes. Judging from the expressions of these men, the harvest is a good one.

Note the size of the grapes in this photograph, shown here with a silver dollar to provide a sense of scale. They testify to the richness of the soils found in the Uncompahgre Valley.

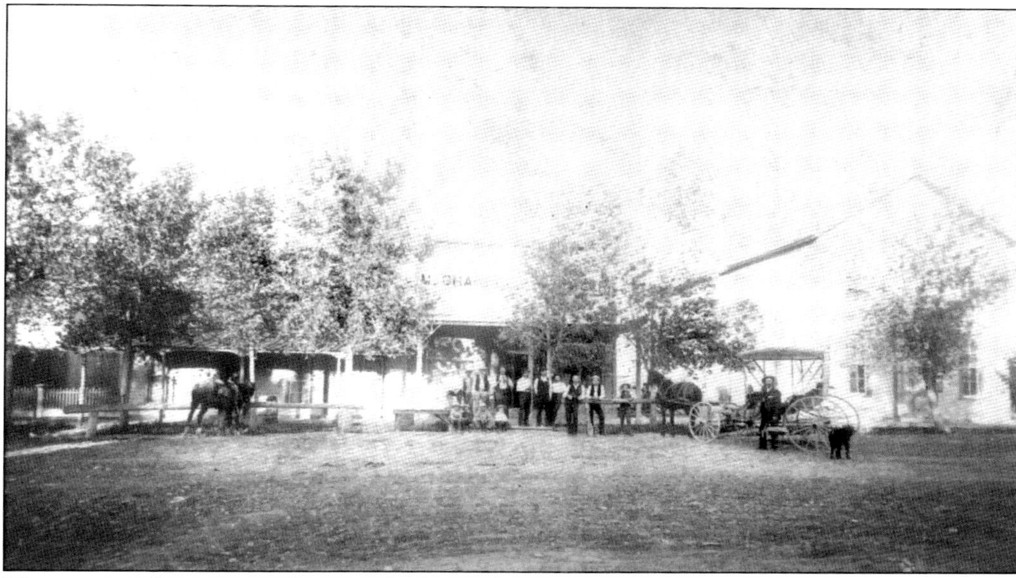

This turn-of-the-century photograph shows the McGranahan Brothers Store and Warehouse, beside the courthouse on the right. From the late 1800s through the early 1900s, the McGranahan name dominated Delta-area agriculture.

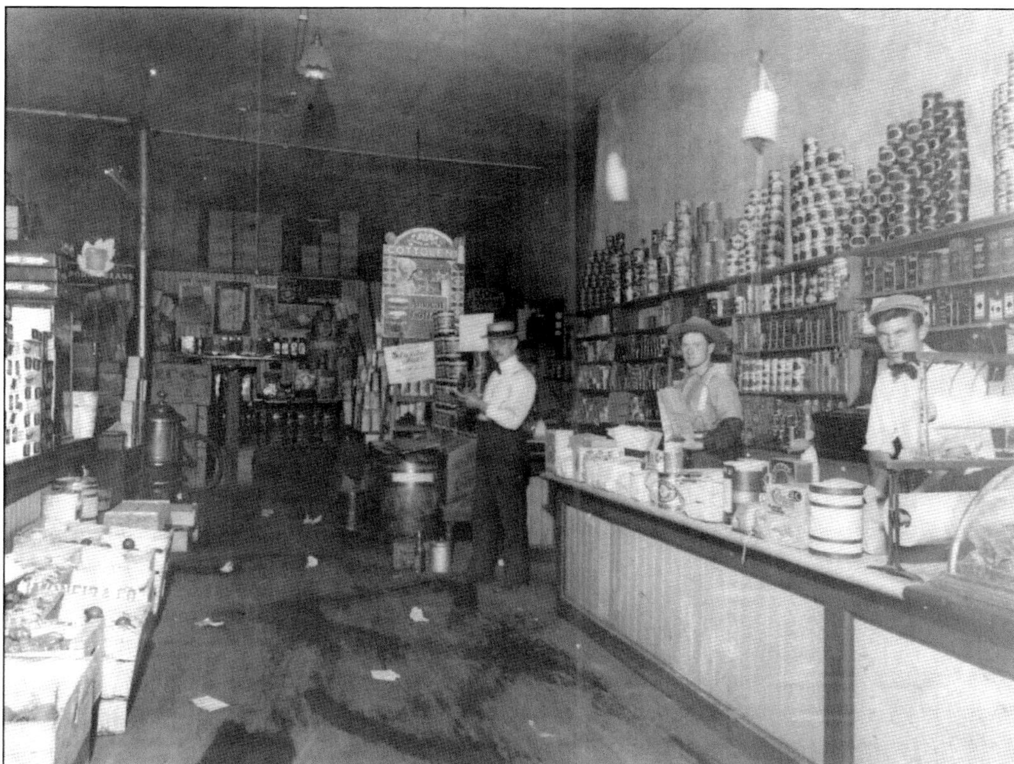

This photograph shows the interior of the McGranahan Brothers Store around 1882. Here at the center of the store, three salesmen wait to attend to the needs of customers.

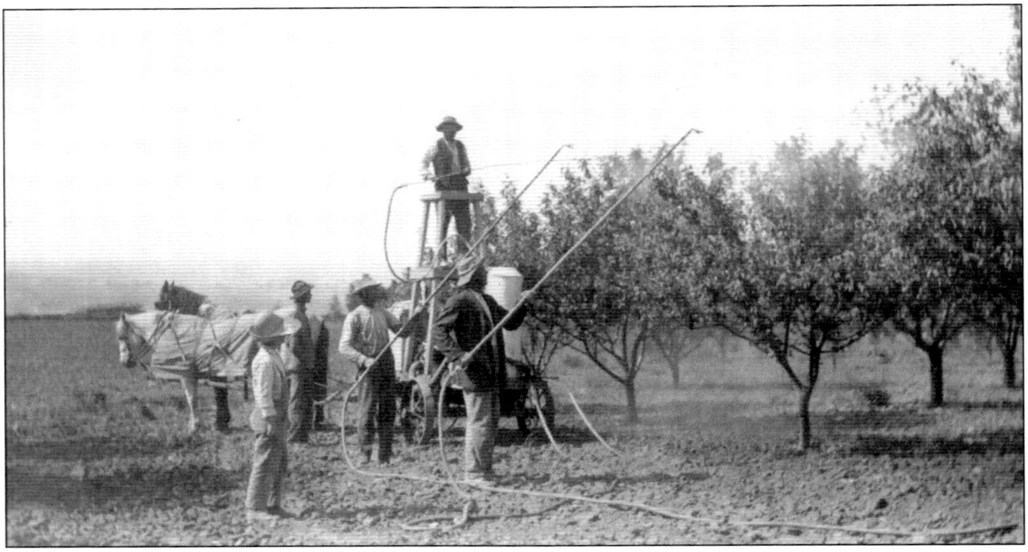

Using two horses to pull their equipment, these five men are spraying orchards in Hotchkiss, Colorado. Roy E. Dickson is the younger child in the straw hat.

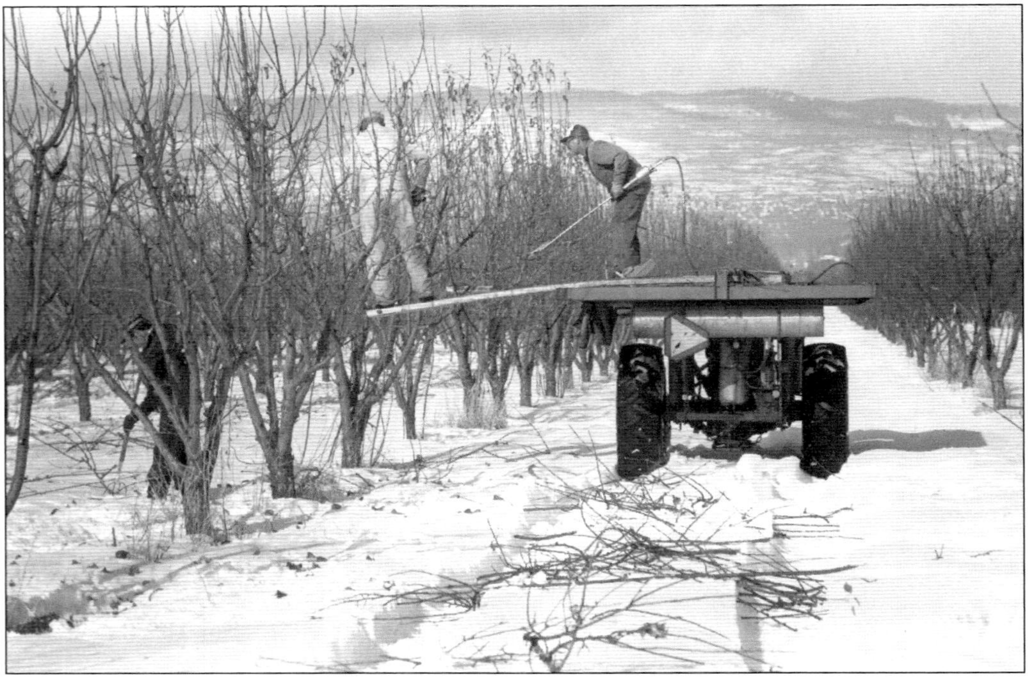

Arnold Dailey and a partner are pruning trees with a pneumatic device and a tractor with an extension that helps remove all of the necessary branches. This type of work normally takes place during the winter months when the trees are dormant. The men are working on Steve Palmer's Orchard. There are a few inches of snow on the ground, and a beautiful mountain view in the background.

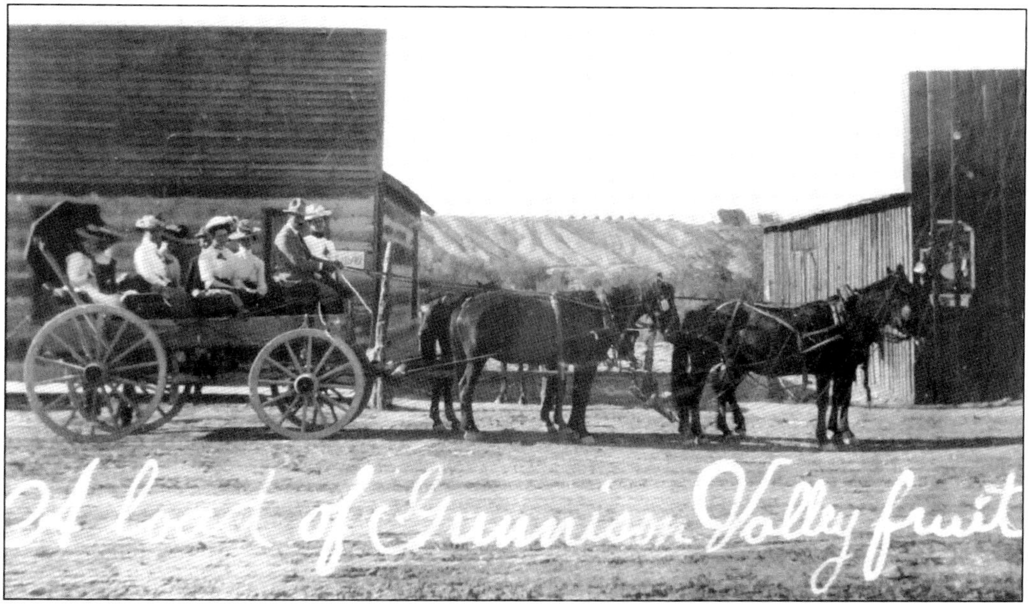

In 1899, a team of horses pulls a wagonload of smiling passengers to explore packing sheds or perhaps a local fruit co-op. Judging from the way they are dressed, this appears to have been a warm, lovely day, perfect for using a parasol and sporting the latest styles in sunbonnets. Seated in the second row here are Jessie Gallup Carlson and Minnie Cope Smith.

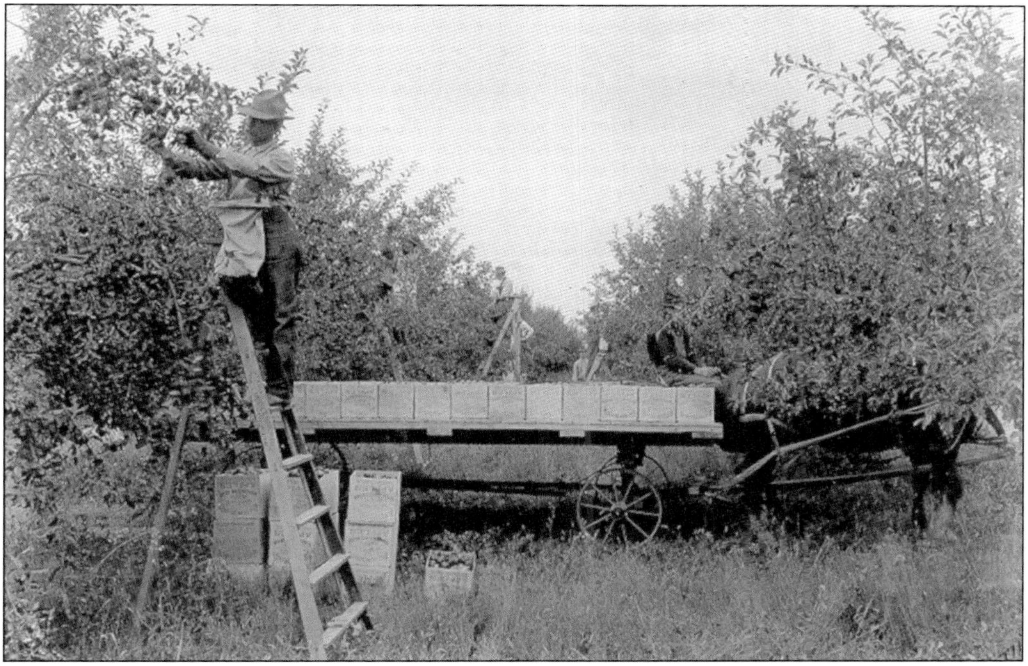

These men at Lake View Apple Orchards quickly fill the wooden crates that wait to be loaded into the nearby wagon. The apples in this area were well known for their taste and quality and would bring a fair price in the markets. Apples are still one of the leading crops in the valley and are likely to remain so for years to come.

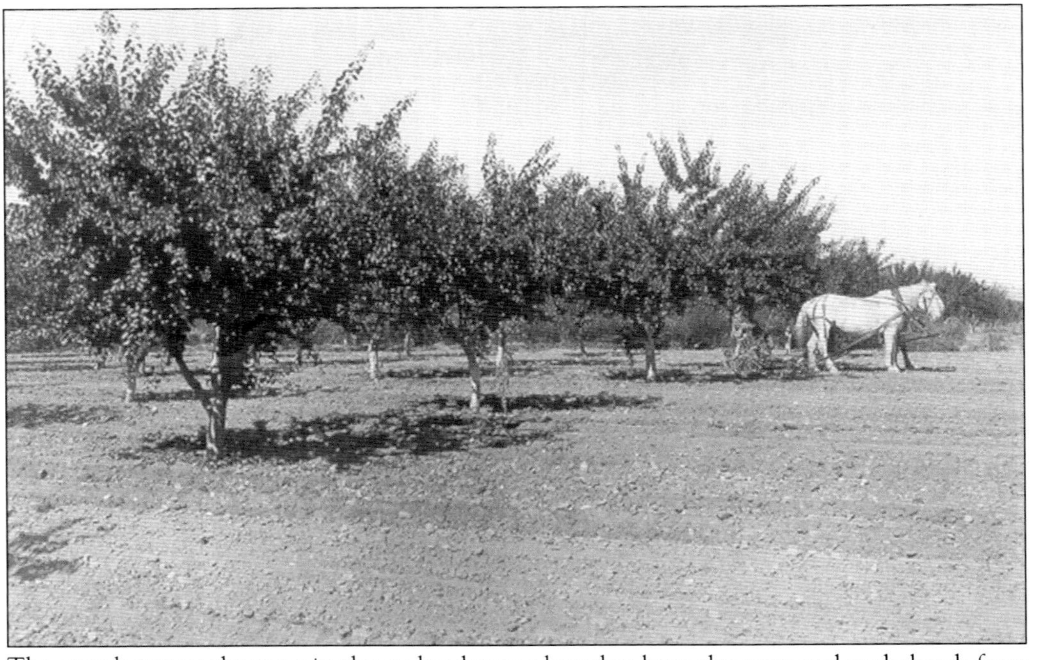

The rows between the trees in the orchard were plowed to keep the grass and underbrush from sprouting under the trees and impeding their growth, as well as the harvesting process. From the late 1800s to the early 1900s, most of this clearing was done with a horse-drawn plow.

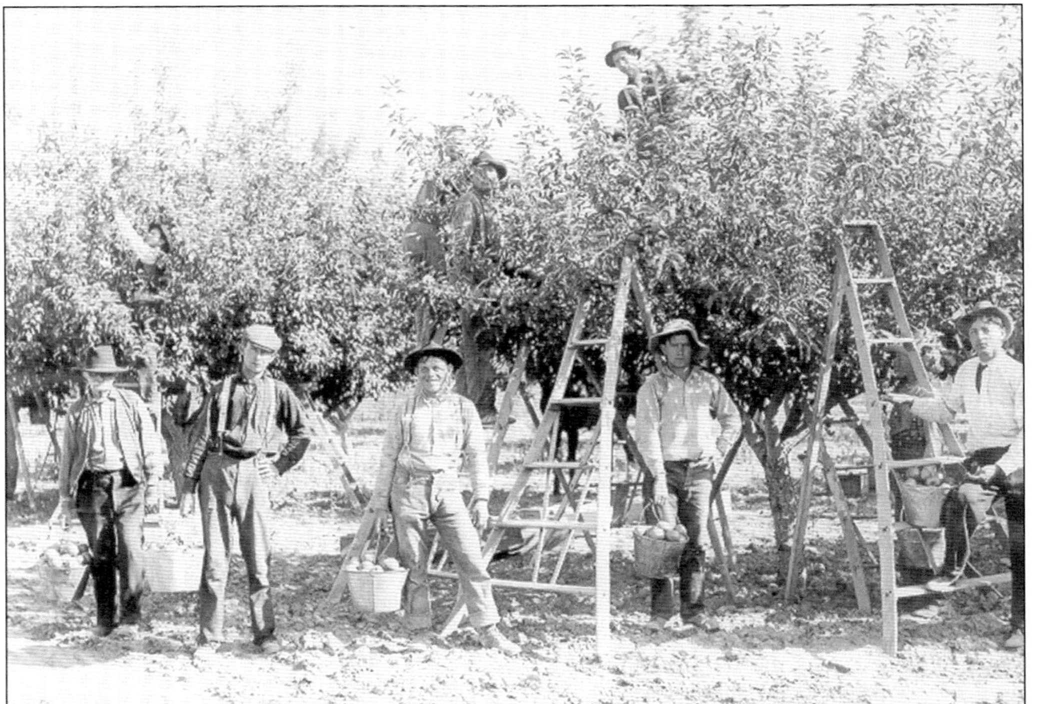

This group of men is picking some rather large apples around 1900.

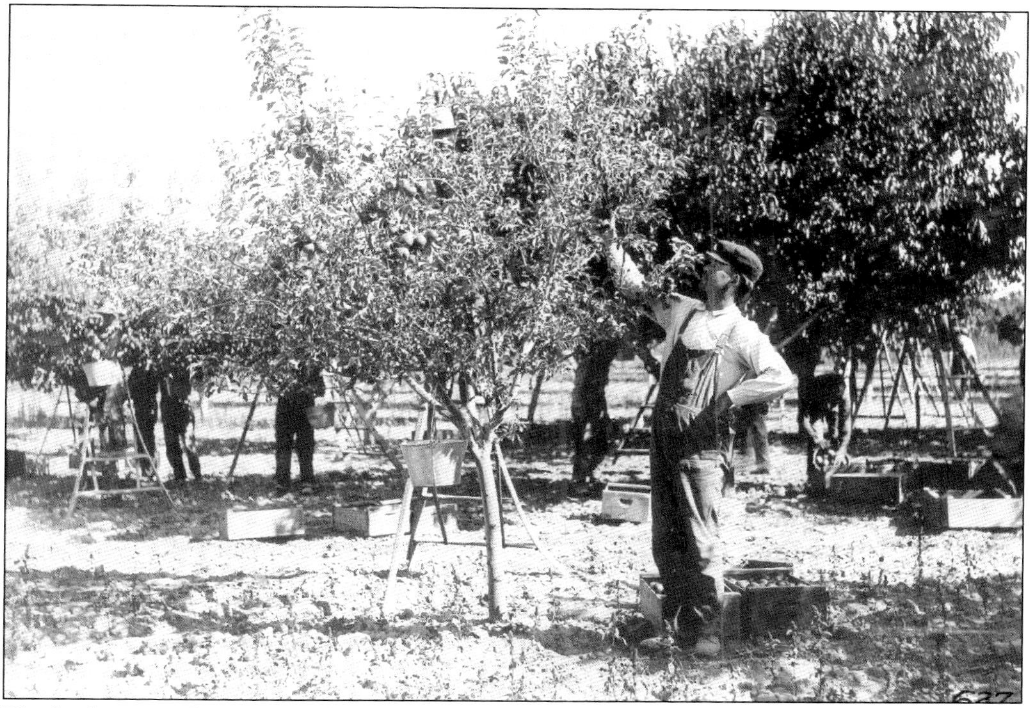

The buckets seen hanging on the trees were the first stop for newly picked apples. When a bucket was full, its apples would be dumped into a crate like those seen on the ground in this photograph. Though here they seem largely to have been an ergonomic convenience, when the trees were larger and the fruit pickers were standing high atop ladders, these buckets were essential.

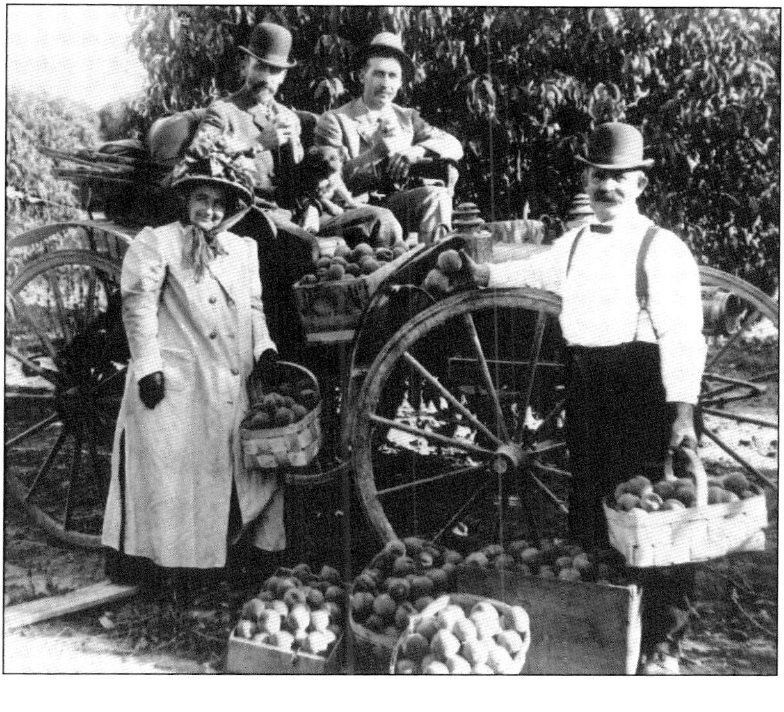

These local growers-turned-motorists, dressed in their Sunday best, pose proudly with their orchard's bountiful harvest of peaches.

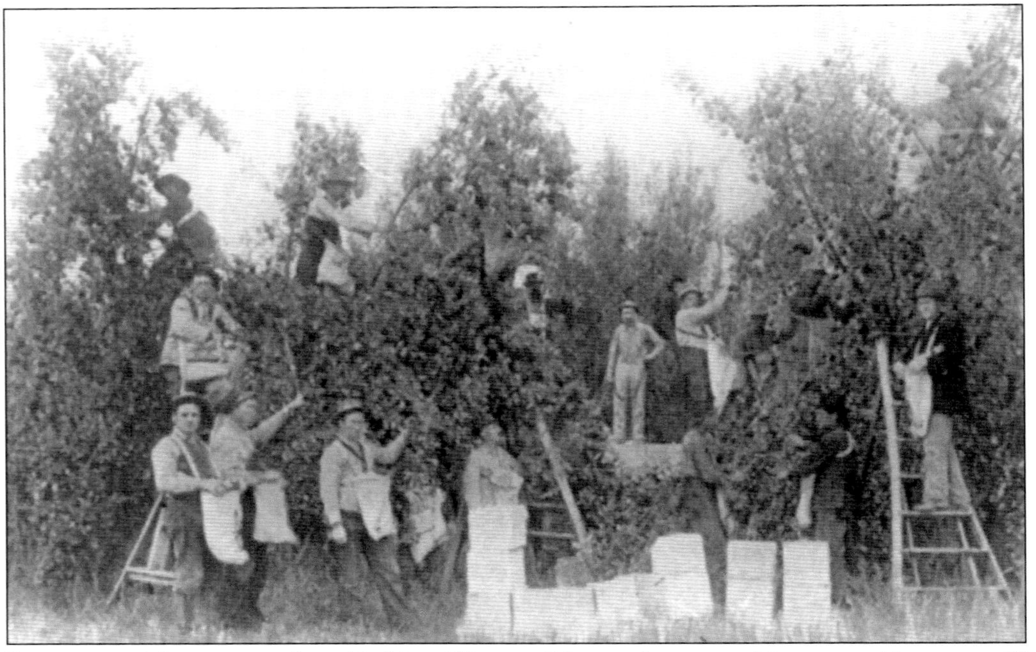

Sometimes pickers outnumbered ladders. The sensible men here are taking turns. One man will climb up the ladder, fill the bag hung around his neck with fruit, and then climb down to dump the fruit into a crate as another man scrambles up the ladder in his place. When full, these crates will be loaded onto wagons, taken to the packinghouse, and shipped to market.

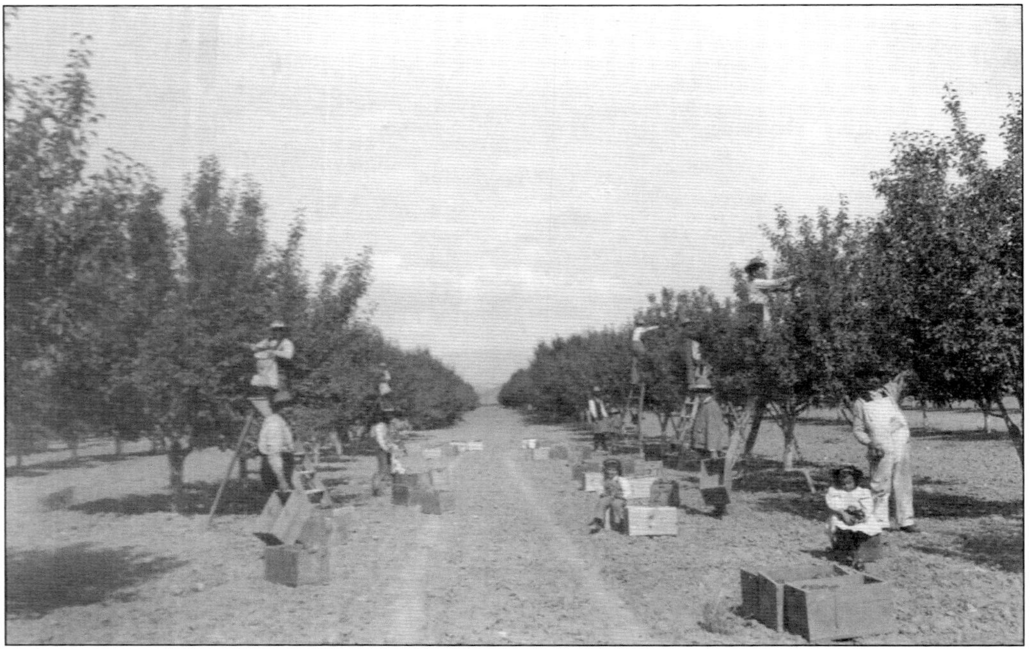

In this photograph, a few of the men picking fruit have their children with them. Though their long-sleeved shirts provided shelter from the summer sun, the men here must have been sweltering from the heat. (One man is even wearing a jacket.)

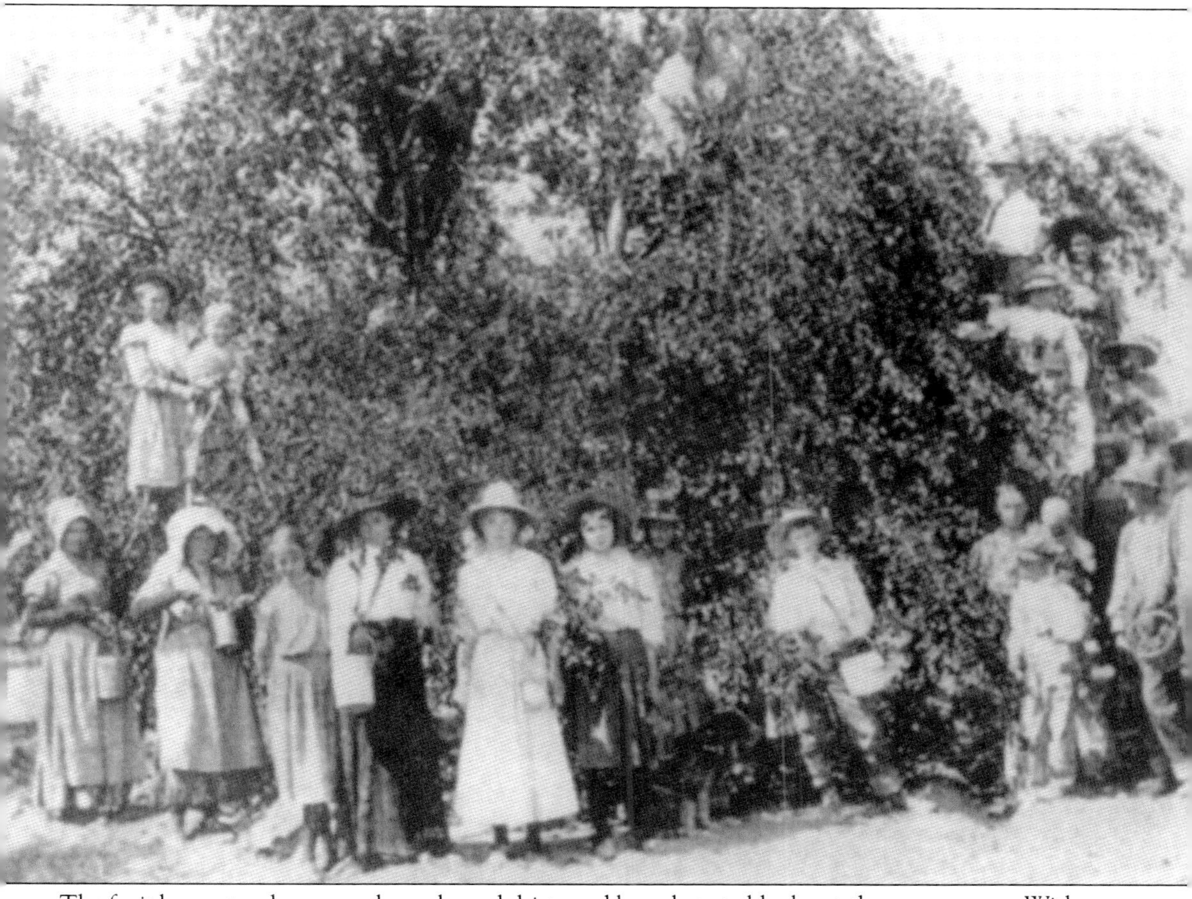

The fruit harvesters here wear long-sleeved shirts and large hats to block out the summer sun. With a few exceptions, the pails they hold are not for carrying fruit, but for carrying their lunches.

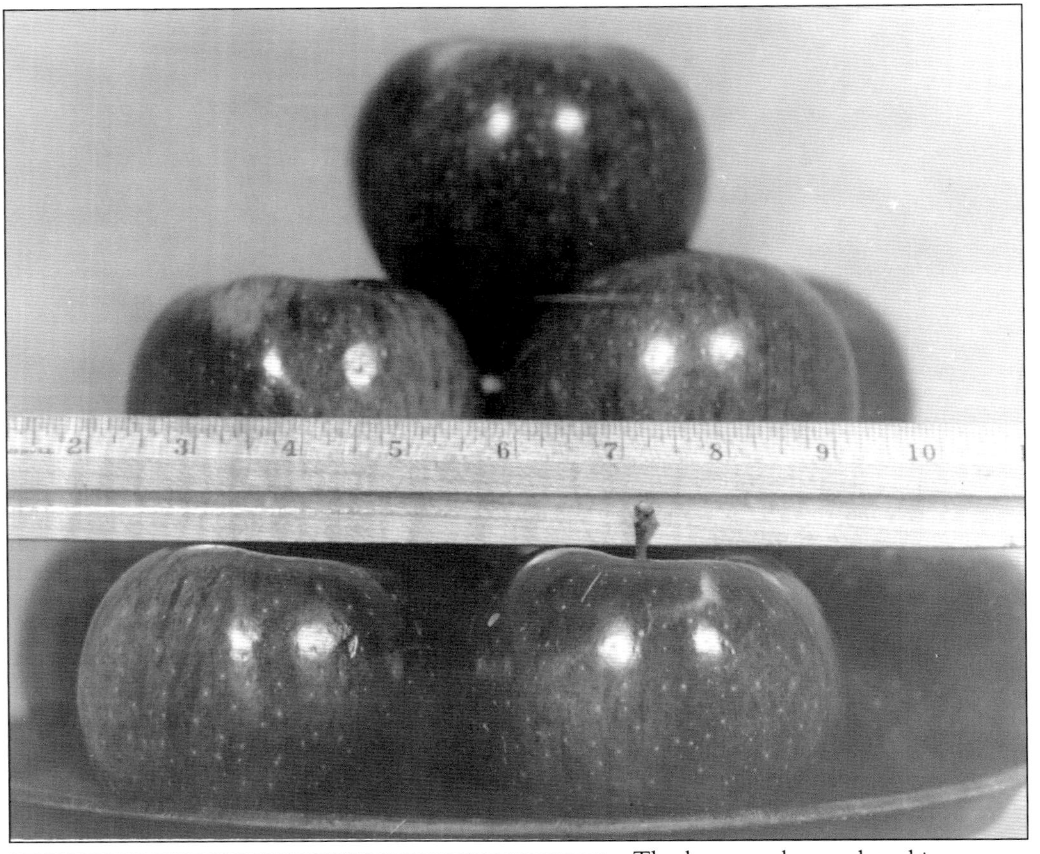

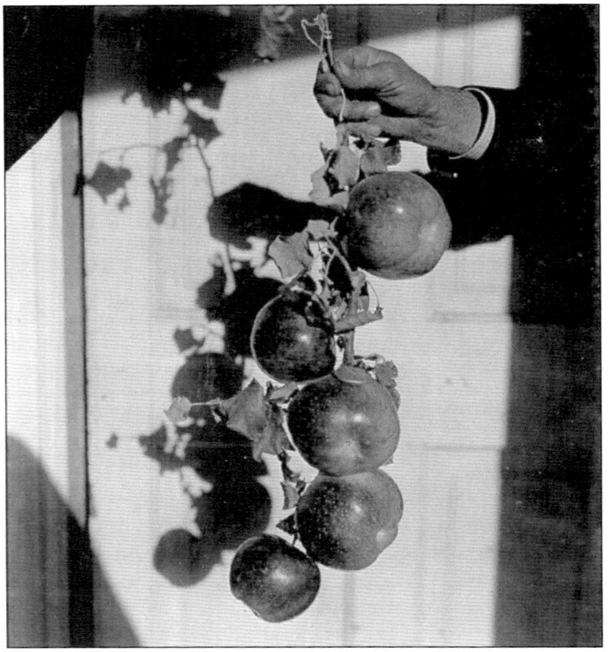

The large apples produced in the valley—especially in the Cedaredge area—were highly desired in the market. Shown here are red apples measuring an average of 3.25 inches in width.

These apples, displayed at the Western Slope Fair in 1914, were especially well formed, plump, and colorful. Apples remain a major cash crop in the Uncompahgre Valley and continue to do well in both local and statewide competitions.

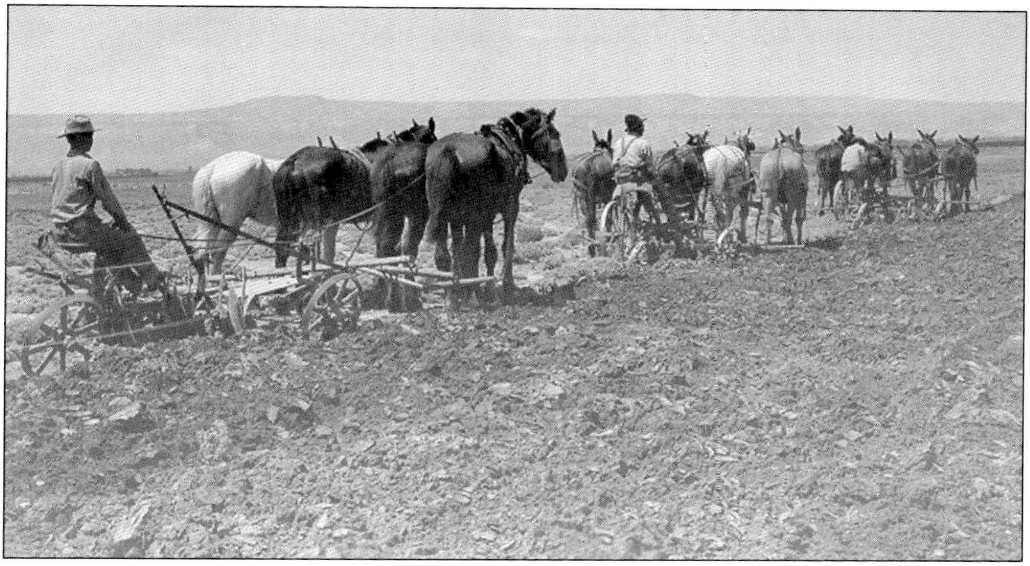

In 1905, government teams plow the desert valley, preparing for the crops that will be grown to feed construction and road crews on the River Portal and in Lujane. Shortly after moving the reservation for the Ute Indians, the area opened to settlers who would farm the rich soils, enjoying the milder winter and a long growing season.

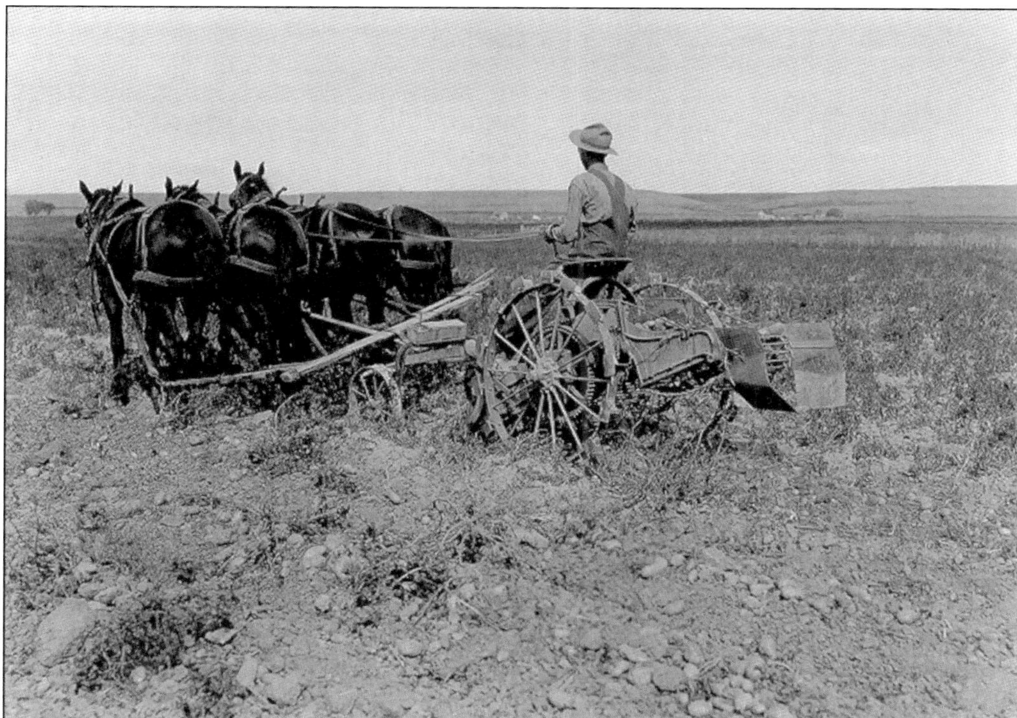

In this c. 1900 photograph, a man and his team of horses are digging up potatoes at a place known as Pepper's Gardens. They appear to have a lot of work left to do, but the year's crop looks like a good one.

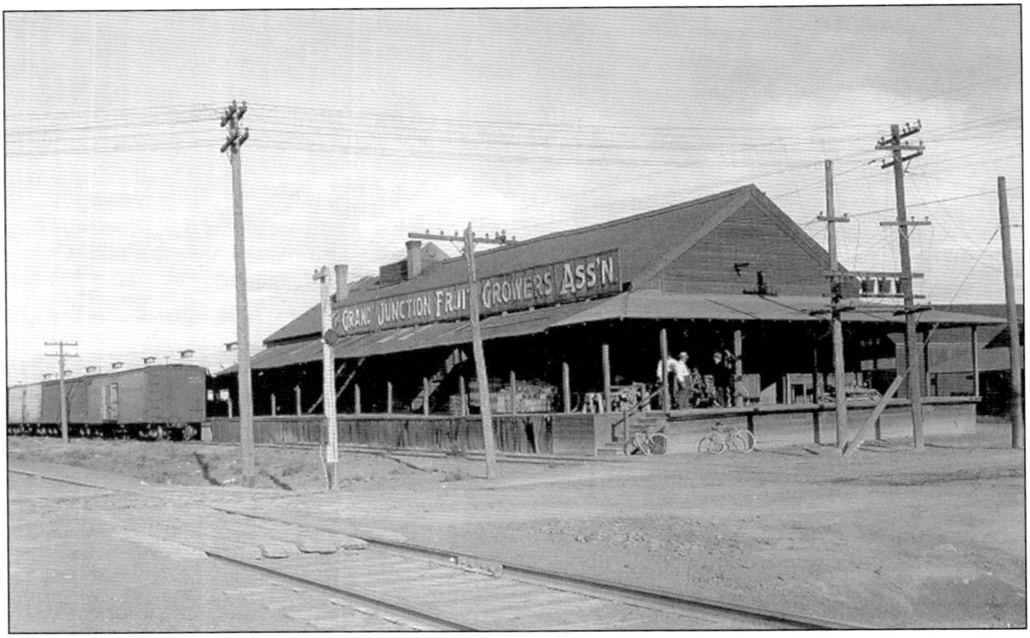

At the Grand Junction Fruit Growers Association railroad depot loading platform, local produce could be easily transported from the valley's rich farm country to the hungry world beyond the mountains. This scene illustrates the buzz of local activity in the early years of the 20th century. The preferred mode of transportation seems to have been the bicycle—at least on sunny days such as the one pictured here.

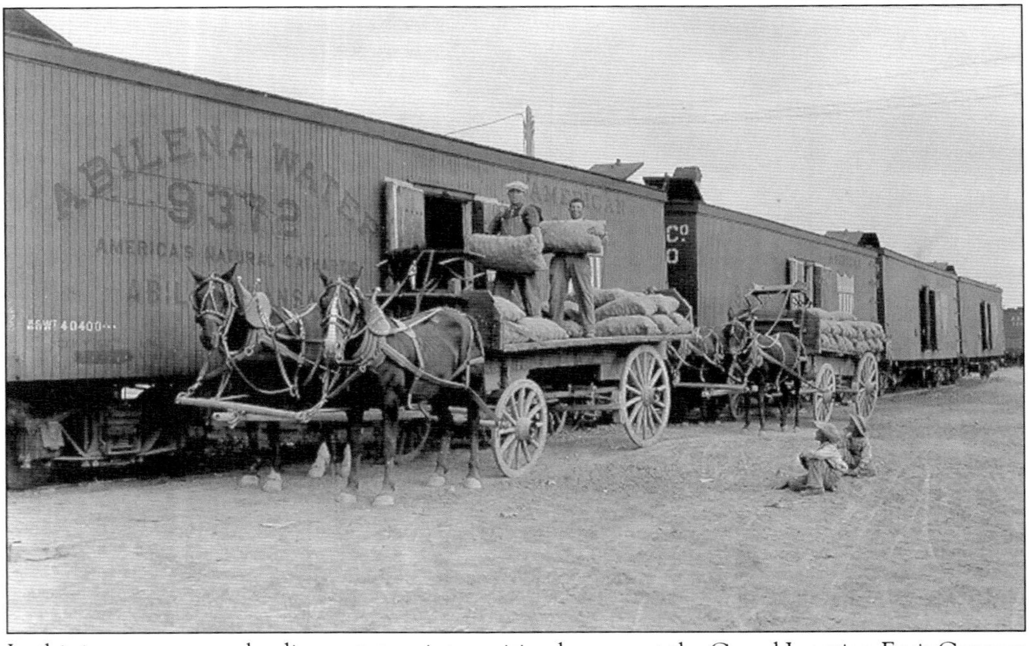

In this image, men are loading potatoes into waiting boxcars at the Grand Junction Fruit Growers Association platform as young children watch nearby. Notice the big smile on the second man's face.

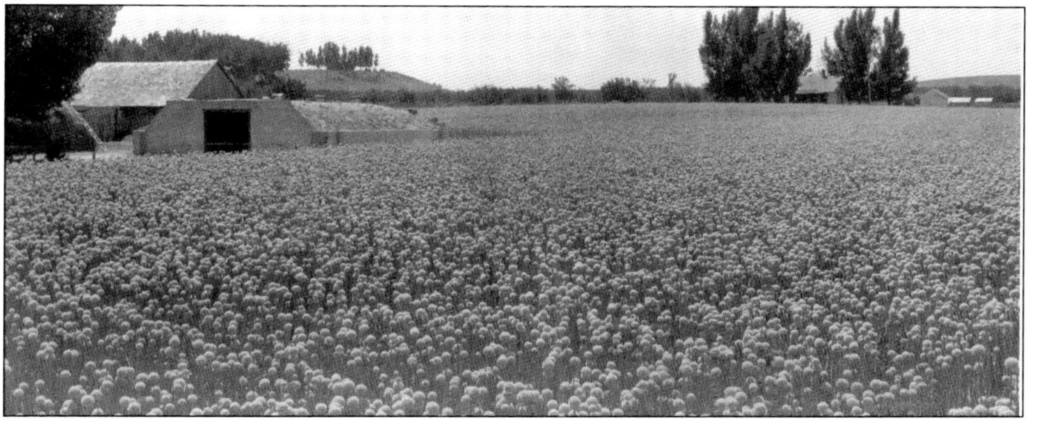

In the early 1900s around Delta, hundreds of acres might be nothing but onion fields. Onions were a great crop to grow, because they did not require constant crop rotation; the same type of onions could be planted year after year in the same soil without a drop in quality. Onions grew best with cool, moist-to-dry conditions in the early part of their growing cycle and hot, dry conditions during their maturity—and this was exactly what the Uncompahgre Valley offered.

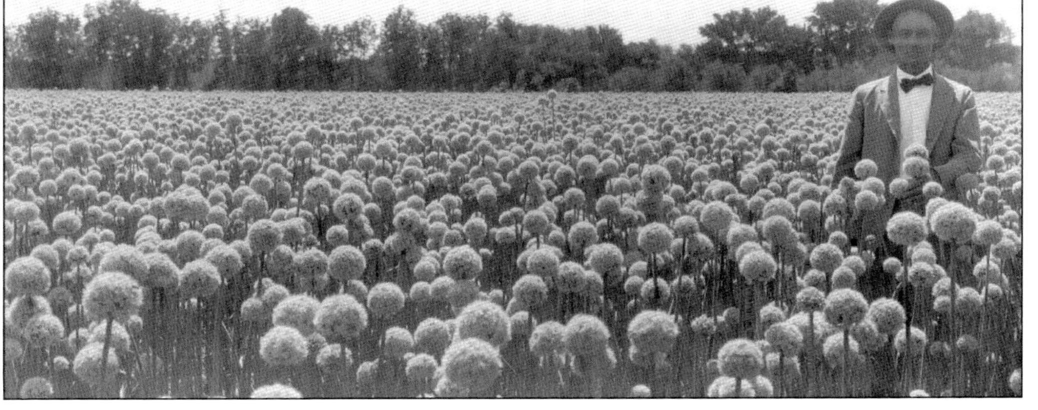

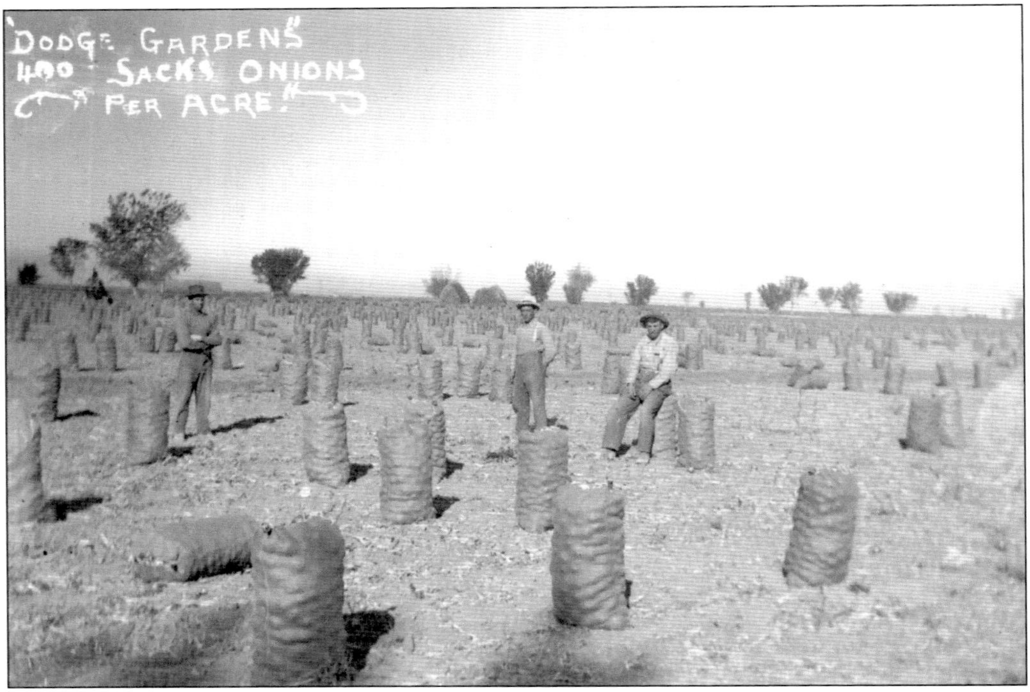

In this picture taken at the Dodge Gardens, men pose next to large sacks of onions. The harvest in this particular year produced 400 sacks of onions per acre; undoubtedly, the men here were proud to pose with the products of their hard work.

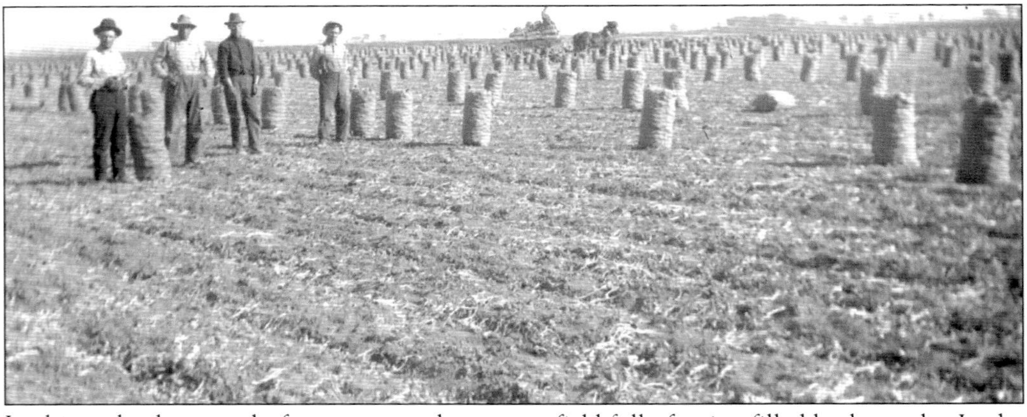

In this early photograph, four men stand next to a field full of onion-filled burlap sacks. In the background, a horse or a mule pulls a wagon already laden with produce. Judging from the numbers of bulging, waist-high bags, this may have been a profitable season.

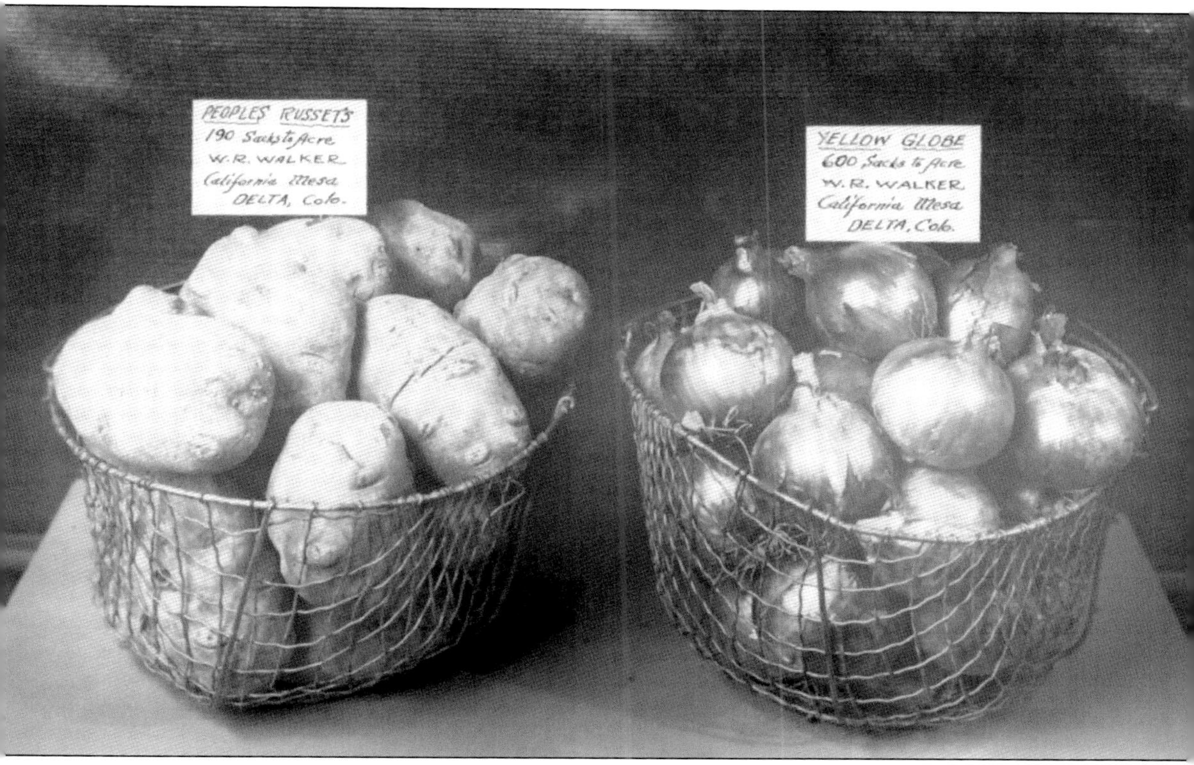

The per-acre yield for many of the valley's crops, especially in the Delta area, was enormous and full of variety. The People's Russet Potatoes grown by W. R. Walker on the California Mesa yielded 190 sacks per acre. Walker's fields of Yellow Globe Onions yielded 600 sacks an acre.

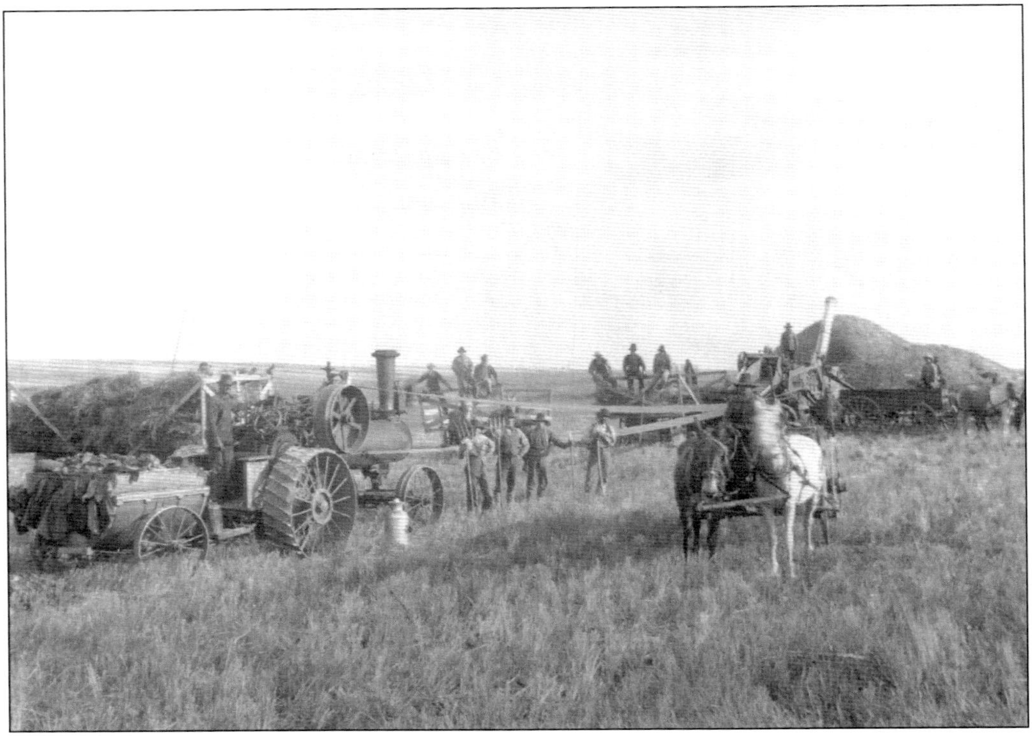

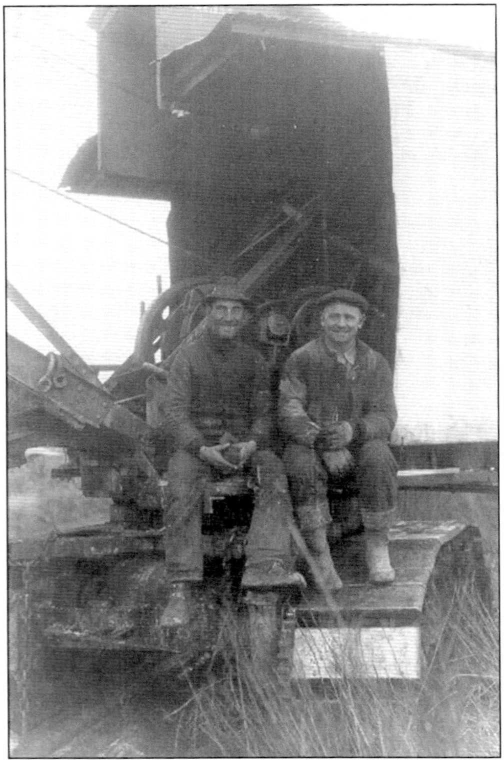

In the 1912 photograph above, the wheat harvest appears to be moving along smoothly thanks to the aid of J. I. Case's tractor, which is furnishing the power for a grain separator. Huge mounds of grain are ready to haul away. M. H. Patnode is the man nearest to the front of the tractor wheel.

Two Uncompahgre Valley farm workers are pictured in the early 1900s sitting on a hay thrasher. The thrasher had metal tracks like a bulldozer, which allowed for better traction in the type of dirt found in hay fields. Before the motor-powered thrasher was invented, workers cut hay by hand.

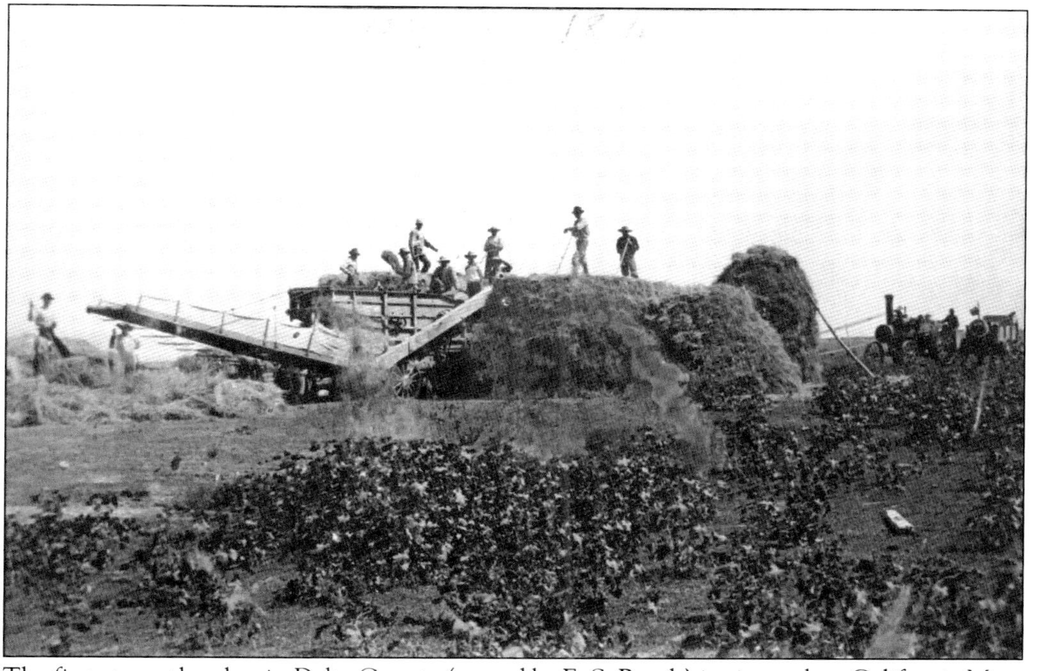

The first steam thrasher in Delta County (owned by E. S. Beach) is pictured on California Mesa in 1891. The introduction of modern equipment streamlined the harvest and allowed for greater production and better profits.

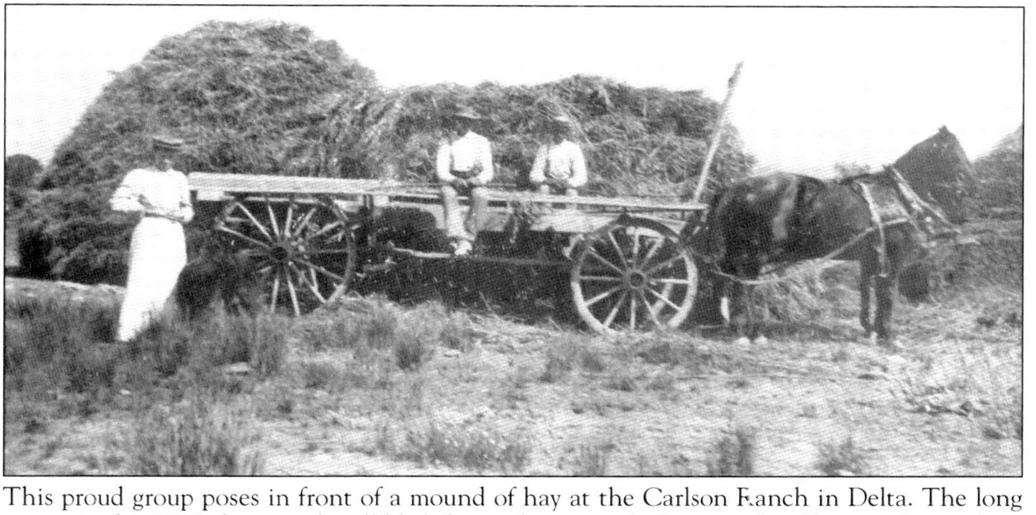

This proud group poses in front of a mound of hay at the Carlson Ranch in Delta. The long wagon in this 1898 photograph will likely be used to carry the huge stacks of hay to a barn where it will be stored for feeding livestock in the winter months, or the hay may be sold and hauled off by steam train to distant markets.

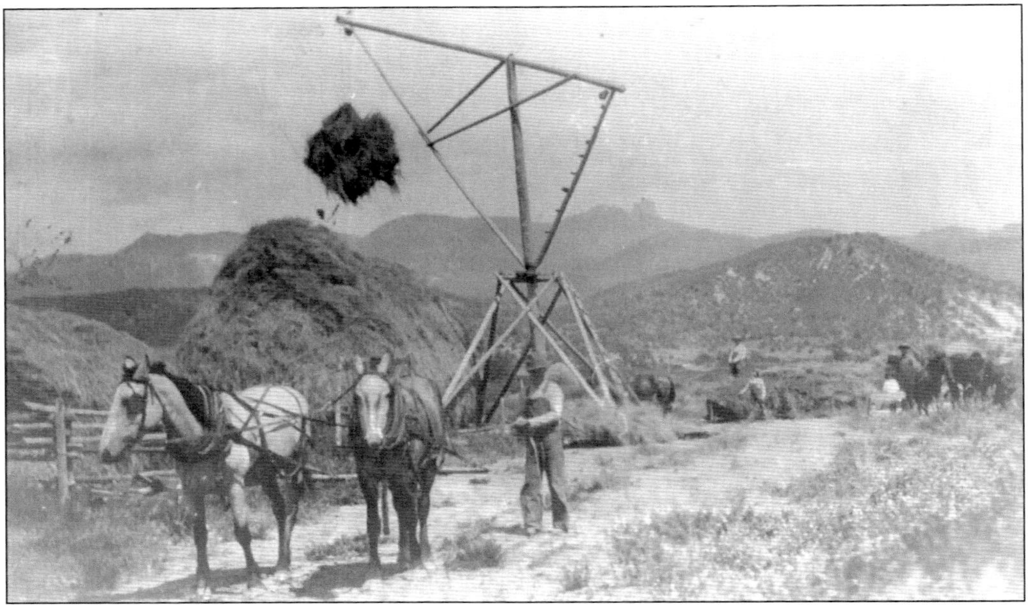

At the turn of the century, the Will Fluke Ranch lay at the foot of Cathedral Rock in Crawford. This photograph shows Reuben Fluke driving a team of mules or horses. Brison Fluke is on the stack of hay, guiding more into place, as Will Fluke and his daughter Ruby J. Fluke observe. Will was 34 years old at the time, and Ruby was 3.

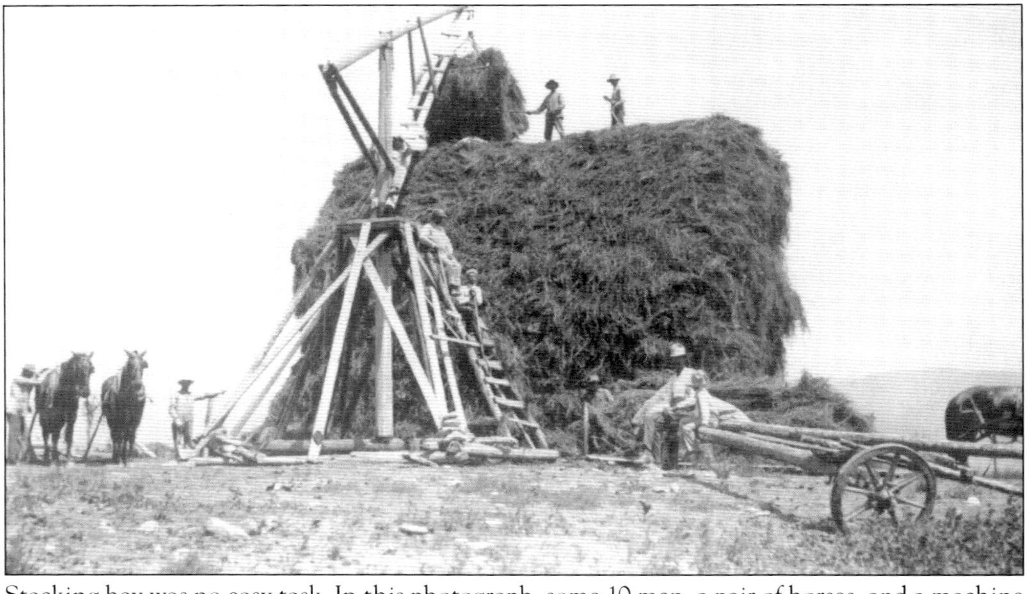

Stacking hay was no easy task. In this photograph, some 10 men, a pair of horses, and a machine are all laboring to get the job done. Roy E. Dickson and Mr. Zimmerman are taking a rest on the log in the right corner of the photograph.

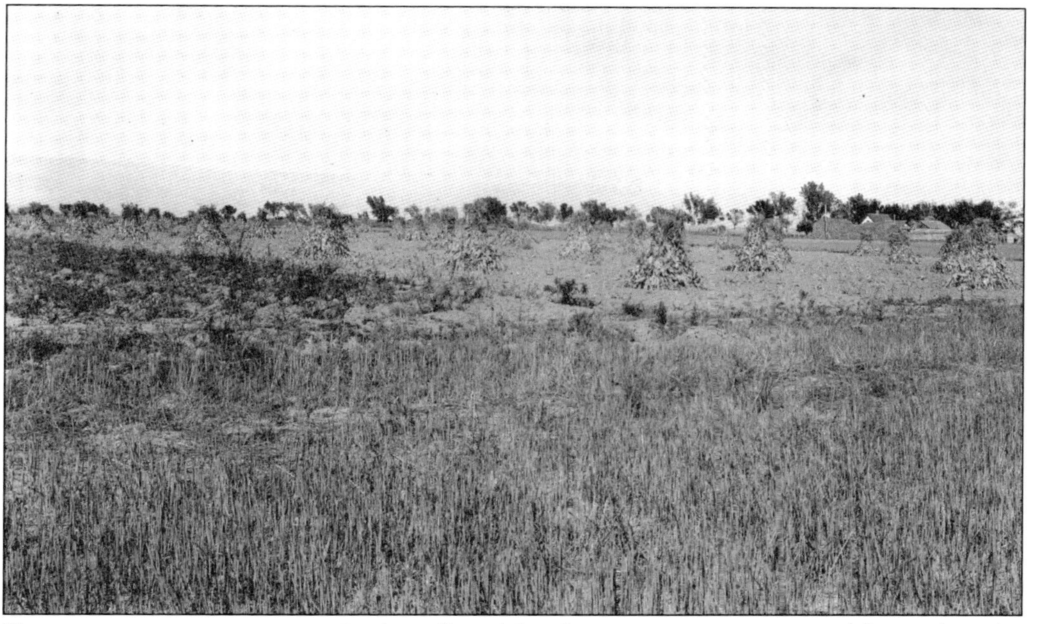

Corn was a very common crop in the valley. After the corn ears were removed for market, the farmers would pull the corn stalks and stand them up to dry them out. Hay would be grown in the fields next to the corn. The hay would be cut dried and piled high for the winter to feed the livestock. In the top right of the photograph, hay is piled up in front of the farmhouse as high as the eaves of the roof.

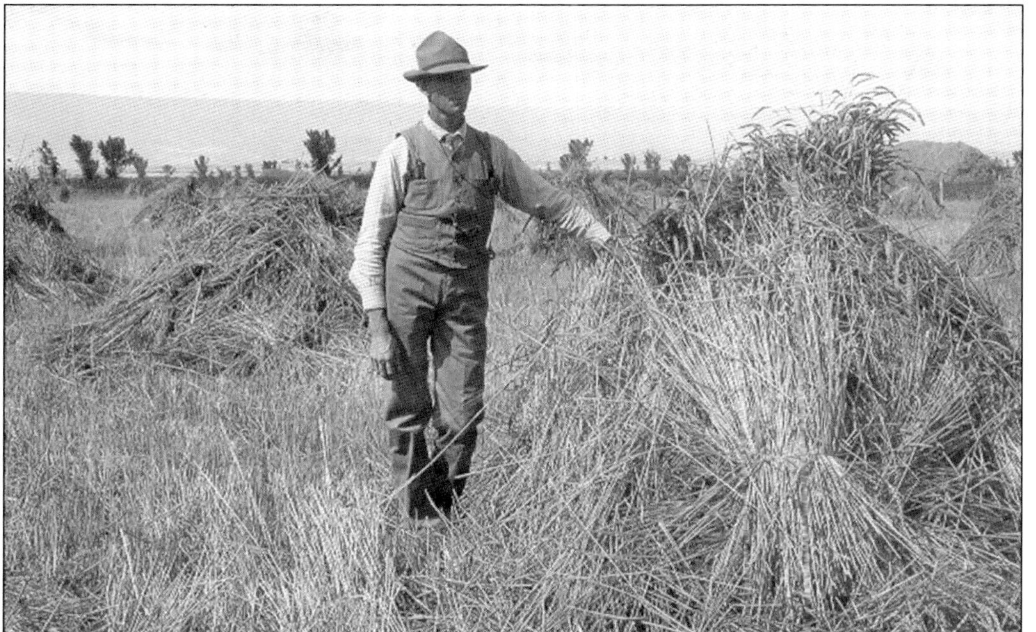

A man poses next to wheat in a shock on the Brandy Ranch, which was located 5 miles south of Delta in August 1904. The silhouette of the Grand Mesa can be seen in the background as well as a large heap of the golden crop.

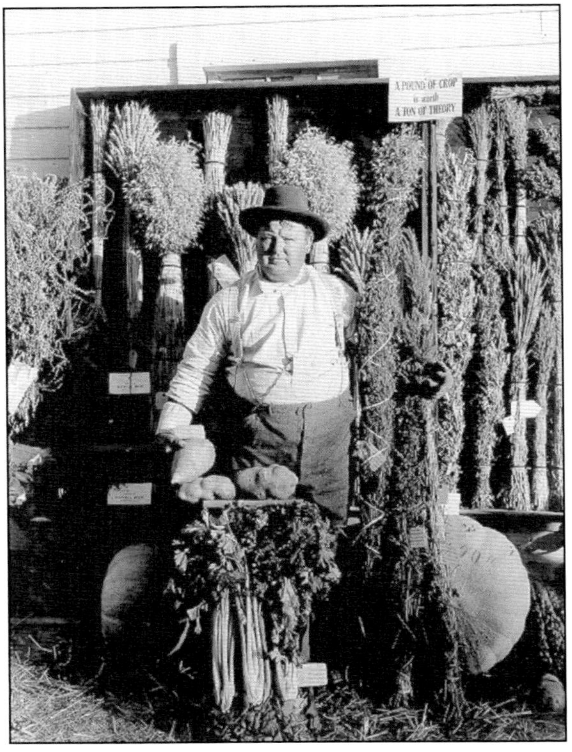

Here in September 1914, this proud farmer at the Western Slope Fair at the Montrose Fairgrounds poses in front of his booth brimming with giant vegetables and superior-looking grains. Planters quickly discovered that the area's rich soils produced remarkably high yields. A sign at the top of the farmer's booth makes this point: "A pound of crop is worth a ton of theory."

The men harvesting the huge valley pumpkins below placed a hat nearby to show just how big they really are.

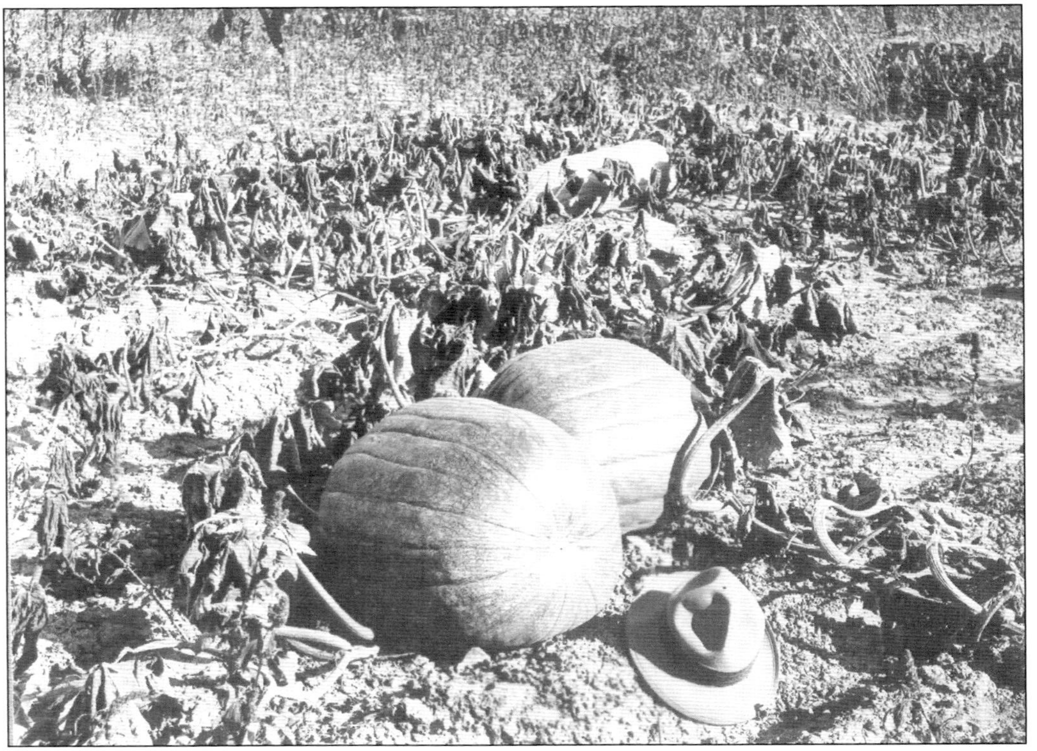

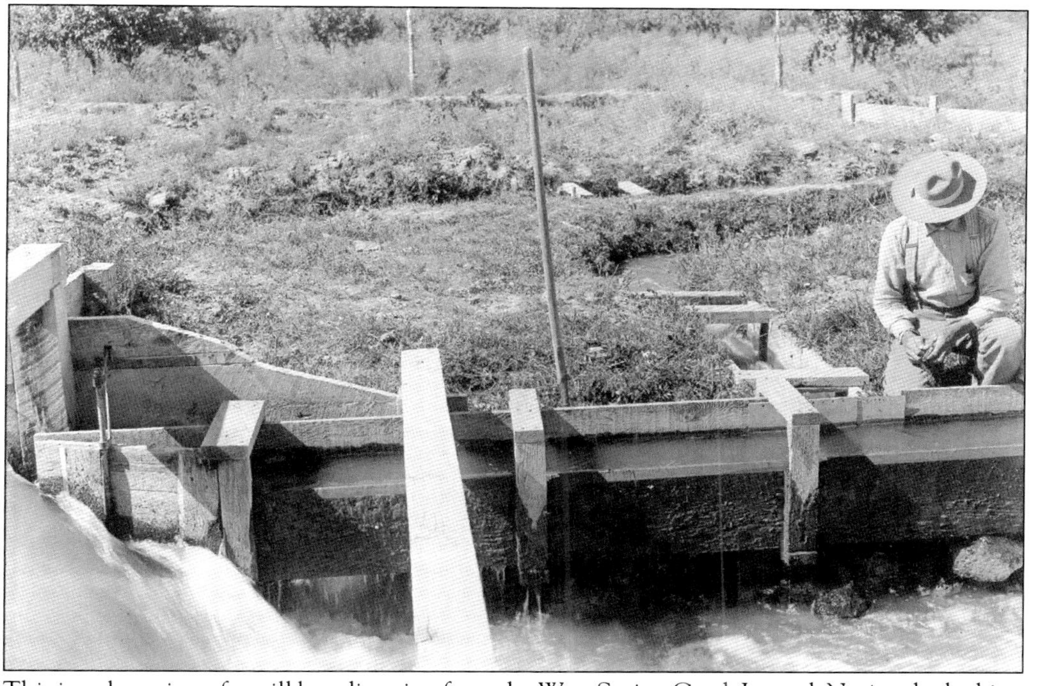

This is a close view of a spill box diversion from the West Spring Creek Lateral. Notice the locking irons in the far left of the photograph. The ditch rider has unlocked the metal spill box opening to provide water to the trees in the distant orchard.

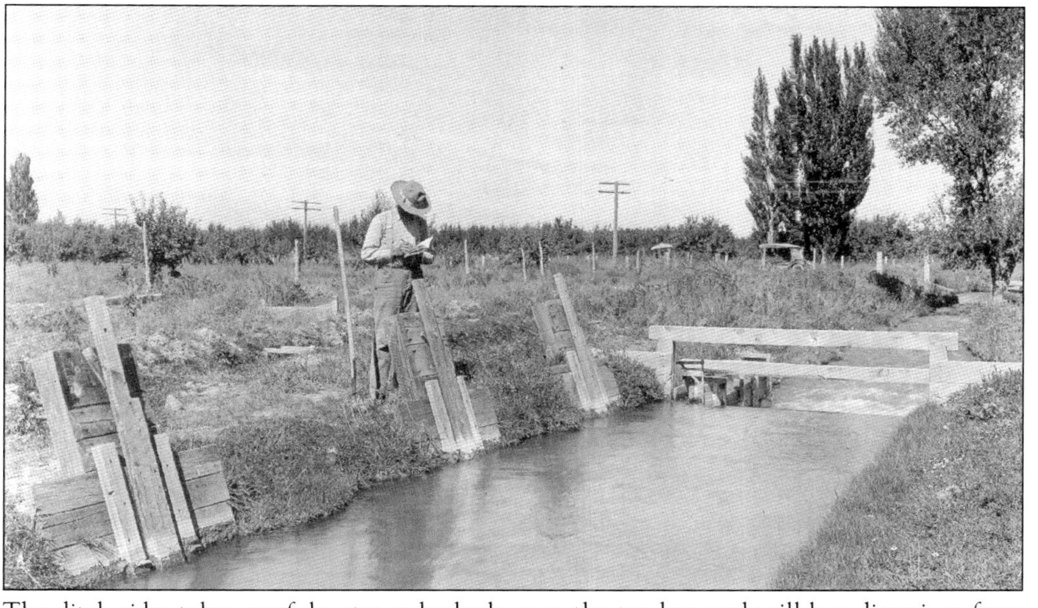

The ditch rider takes careful notes as he looks over the tap box and spill box diversions from the West Spring Creek Lateral. The wooden tap boxes line the left side of the ditch. When the tap boxes are closed, this part of the ditch nearly overflows its banks, and the excess water flows over the spill box, which serves to dam the water, creating an easy flow through the tap boxes, if desired.

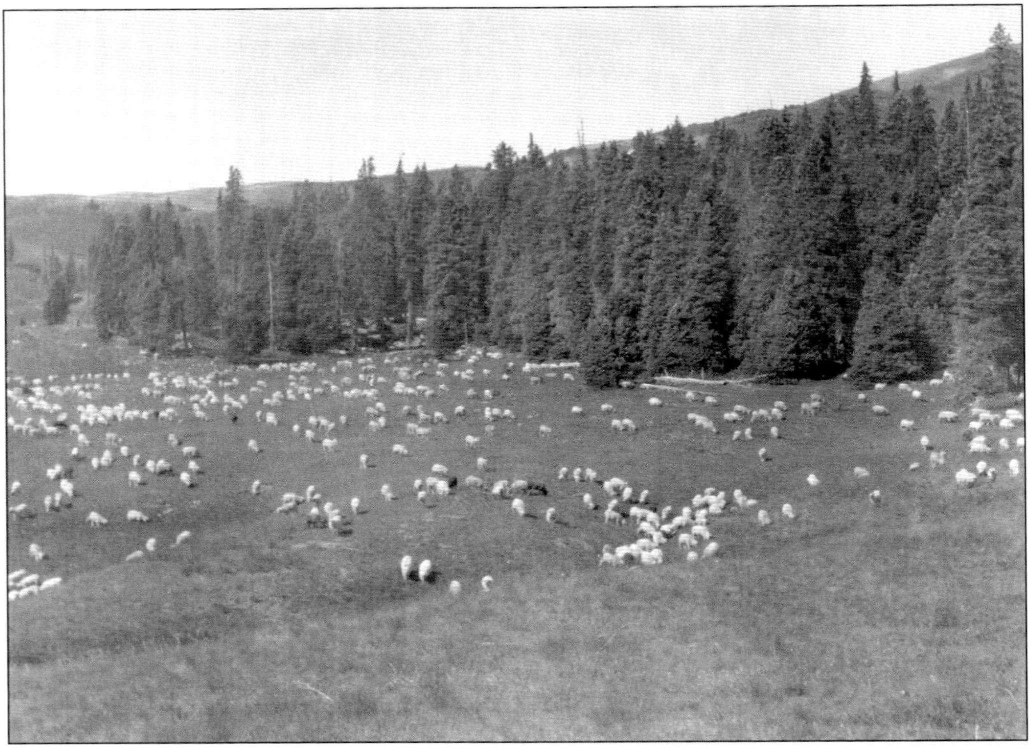

Taking advantage of the valley's wide open ranges of prime mesa land, the thoroughbred long-leg sheep industry was introduced to the valley. In the early years, controversy arose between the cattle ranchers and the sheepherders, but over time they learned to share the land. The sheep produced very well here. In this picture, a herd of several hundred grazes on the rich grassland.

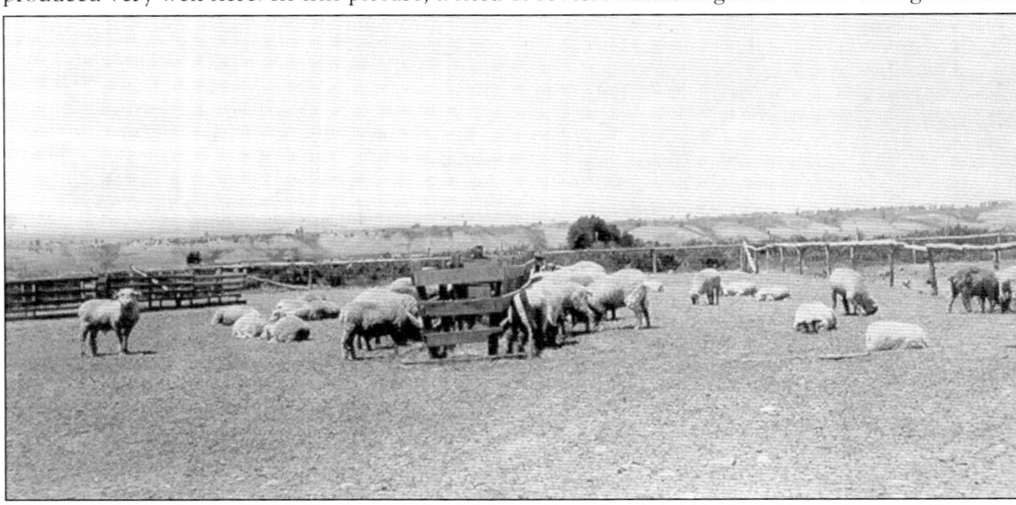

On a bright July day in 1908, these sheep are being raised in the Uncompahgre Valley near Montrose. Sheep ranchers were not welcomed by local cattle ranchers because of the flocks' grazing habits. This became the source of strong debate, resulting in the deaths of hundreds of sheep and a few cowboys. In the end, however, the two groups managed to settle their differences, coexist, and thrive.

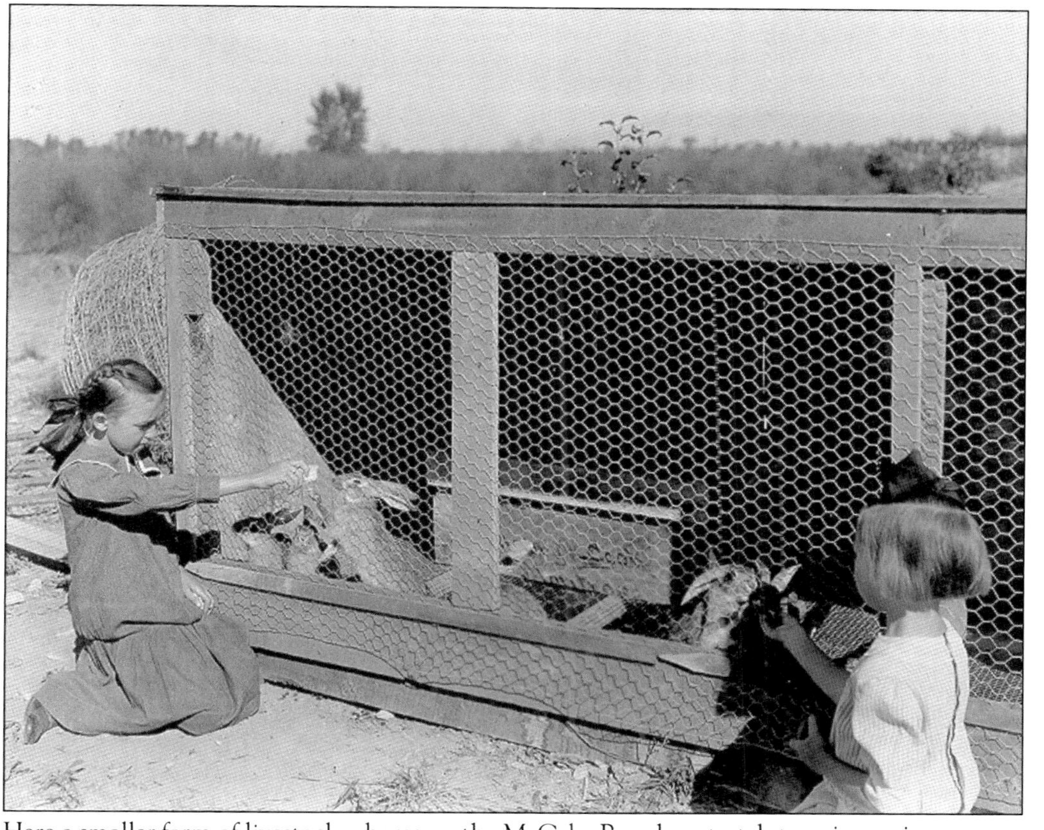

Here a smaller form of livestock—hares on the McCabe Ranch—stretch to enjoy a nice summer snack. The two girls dressed in c. 1900 finery (complete with satin bows) seem to be enjoying this particular chore.

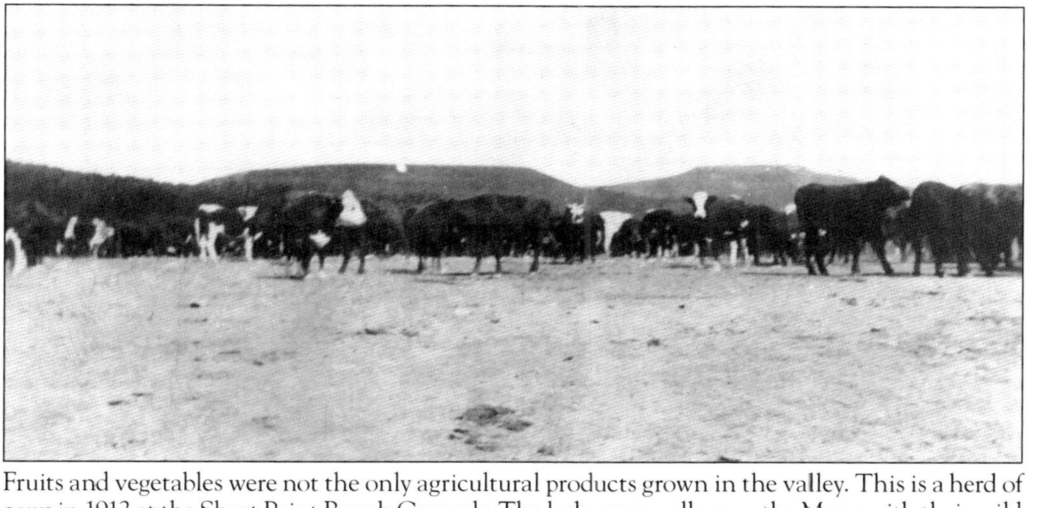

Fruits and vegetables were not the only agricultural products grown in the valley. This is a herd of cows in 1912 at the Short Point Bunch Grounds. The lush green valleys on the Mesas with their mild winters allowed for fat and healthy livestock. (Photograph courtesy of the Calhoun family.)

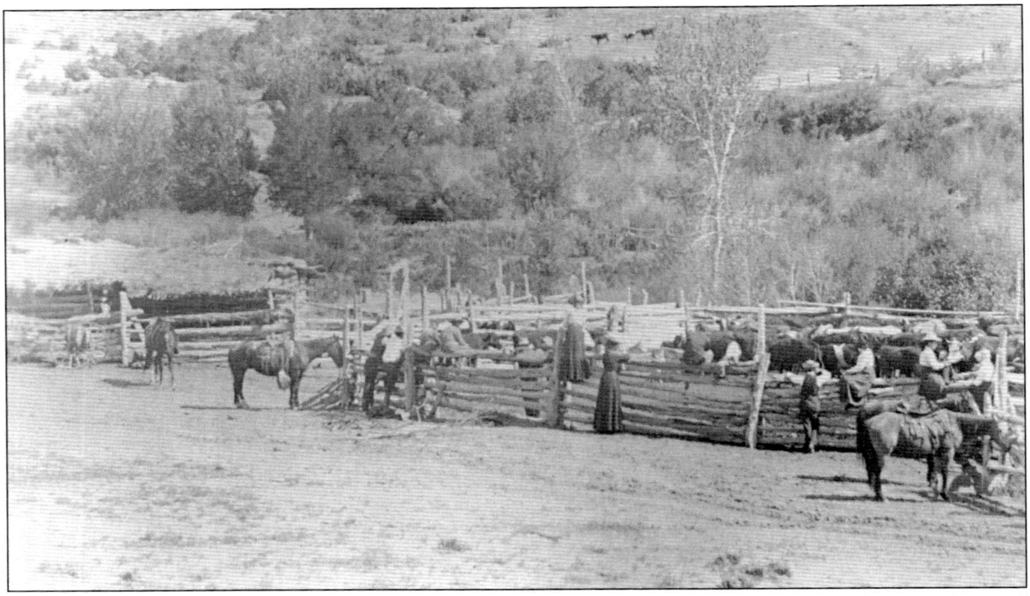

Note the mix of men and women here at the Clough Corral. The women wear their traditional dark skirts and white blouses along with their hats. In the left corner of this photograph stand the livestock shelters (made of wood, mud, and grass) that help keep the horses out of bad weather. In this photograph, the horses have been tied to the outside of the corral; apparently the cowboys are taking a break before beginning the hard work of branding the cattle.

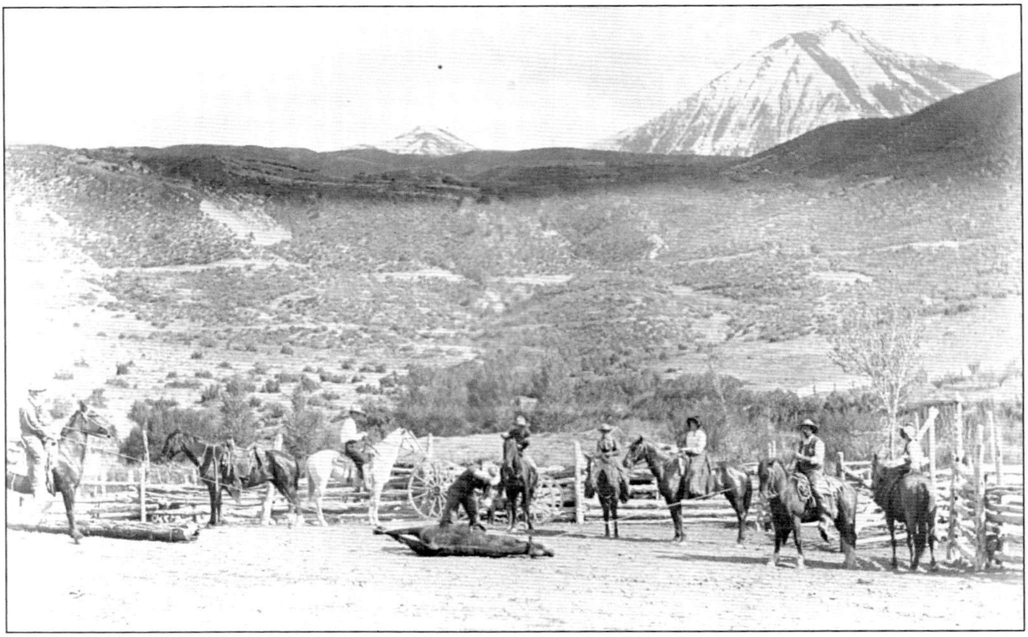

After rounding up all of the cattle, the branding process begins. The two men on horseback have each end of the cattle roped and stretched out. Another man on foot wields a hot iron with which he brands the cows. Other men and women stand by on horseback, waiting for any assistance that might be needed.

Three

Canneries, Packinghouses, and the Sugar Beet Industry

Before the addition of railroad service, Uncompahgre Valley farmers had to hustle to get their harvests to market before the fruit and vegetables started to rot. Their markets were limited to those within a short distance of the valley. The Denver and Rio Grande Railroad arrived in 1882 and gave the farmers easy access to the Denver and Salt Lake City markets. With the addition of refrigeration to the railroad cars and warehouses, both the East Coast and West Coast markets came within reach of the valley's farmers.

Throughout the 20th century, the valley's agricultural industry became increasingly mechanized. This assisted the farmers in raising bigger and better crops. A glut of canneries, packinghouses, and food processing plants opened in Delta. With the addition of railroads and canneries in the valley, the demand for Uncompahgre Valley produce rose to new heights. One of these newly profitable crops was sugar beets. They were introduced into the Uncompahgre Valley in 1904, and quickly became a staple. The average amount of saccharine matter in the valley's sugar beets was 16 to 19 percent. The Uncompahgre Valley held the record for producing the sweetest sugar beets grown anywhere in the United States. This allowed the sugar beet industry to quickly become one of the most important ones in the valley.

To process the beets, a sugar factory was located in Delta in 1906. Farmers planted more and more of the beets, which offered a speedy and guaranteed return on investments. Farmers could know when they planted beets in the spring that a market would be there for them in the fall. At the time, no other crop industry offered so little risk. The building of sugar beet canneries industrialized the fruit and vegetable agriculture industry in the valley.

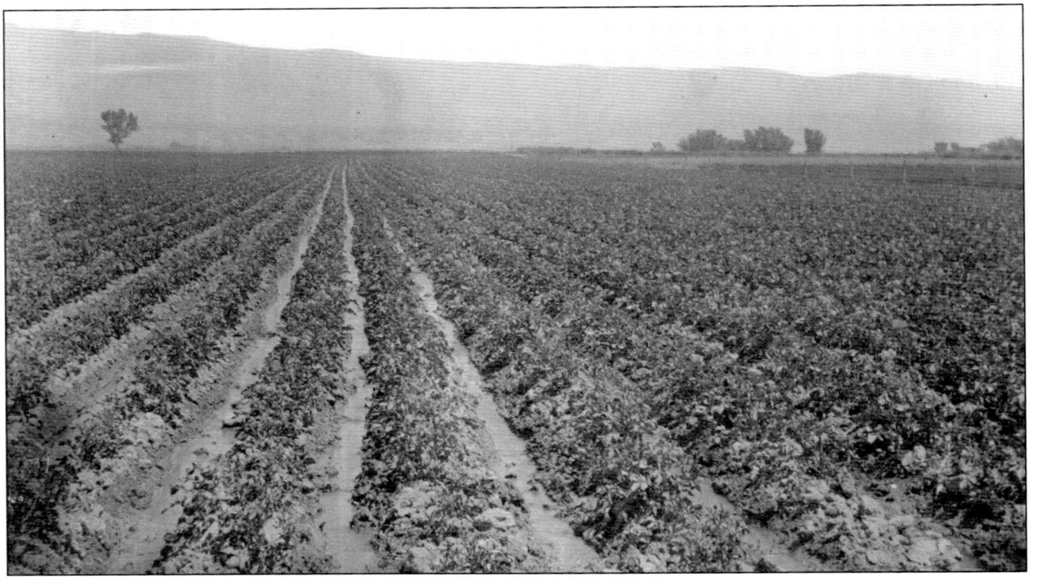

Sugar beets were introduced to the valley in the late 1800s and soon became a staple. The return on the crops had one of the highest yields and profit margin. The crops were planted in mounds; the beets were then watered by the irrigation ditches. Because the sugar beets were so profitable, farmers would plant acres and acres of them.

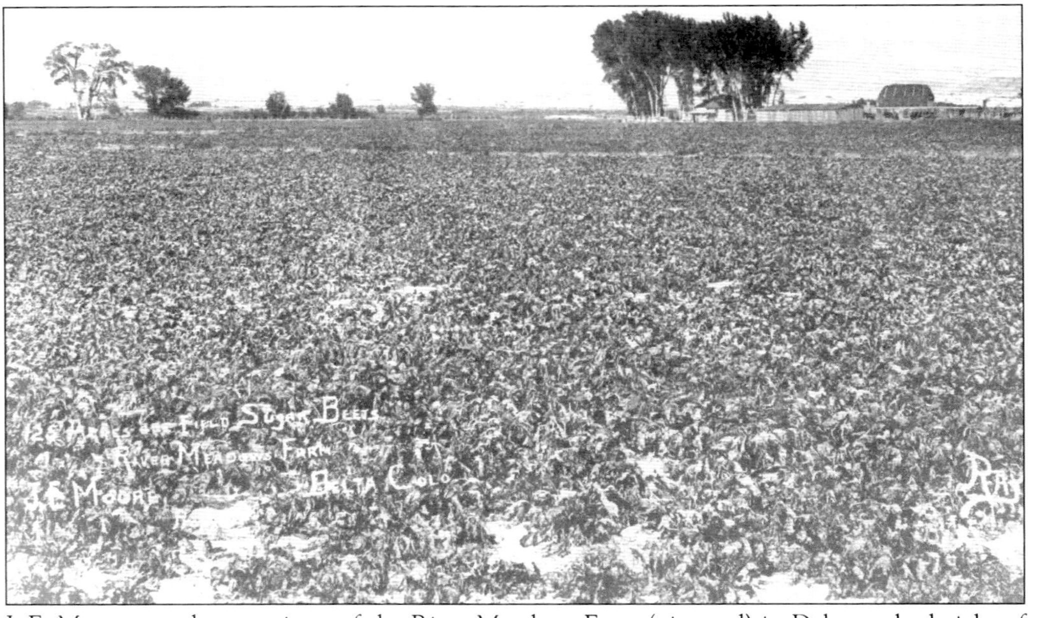

J. E. Moore was the proprietor of the River Meadows Farm (pictured) in Delta at the height of the valley's sugar beet boom. Just one of his fields of sugar beets covered 125 acres.

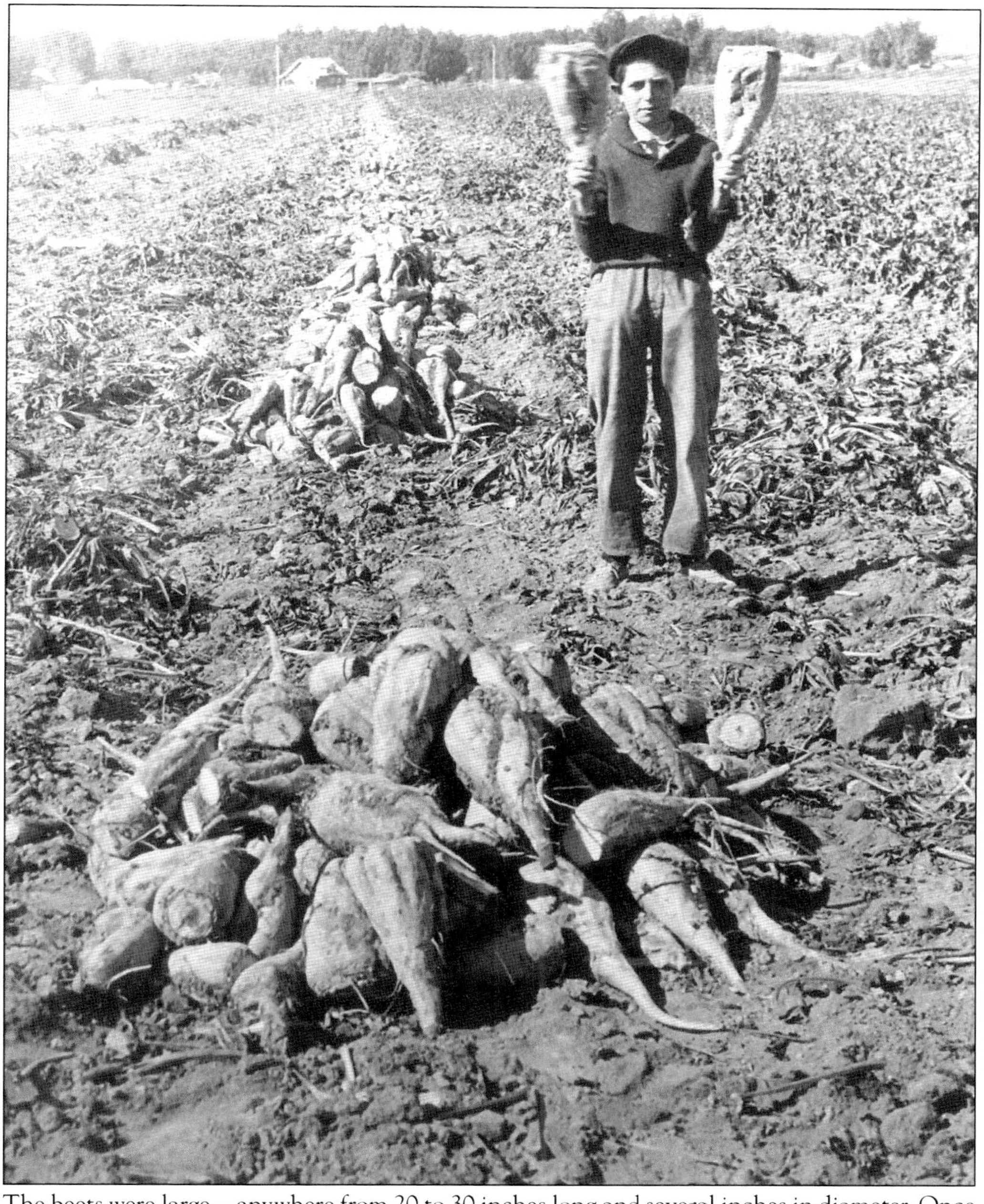

The beets were large—anywhere from 20 to 30 inches long and several inches in diameter. Once pulled from the soil, their tops were cut off, and they were placed in piles, then loaded and taken to the processing plant. Here a local boy holds up two beets that are about a quarter of his size. Their diameter matches that of his head.

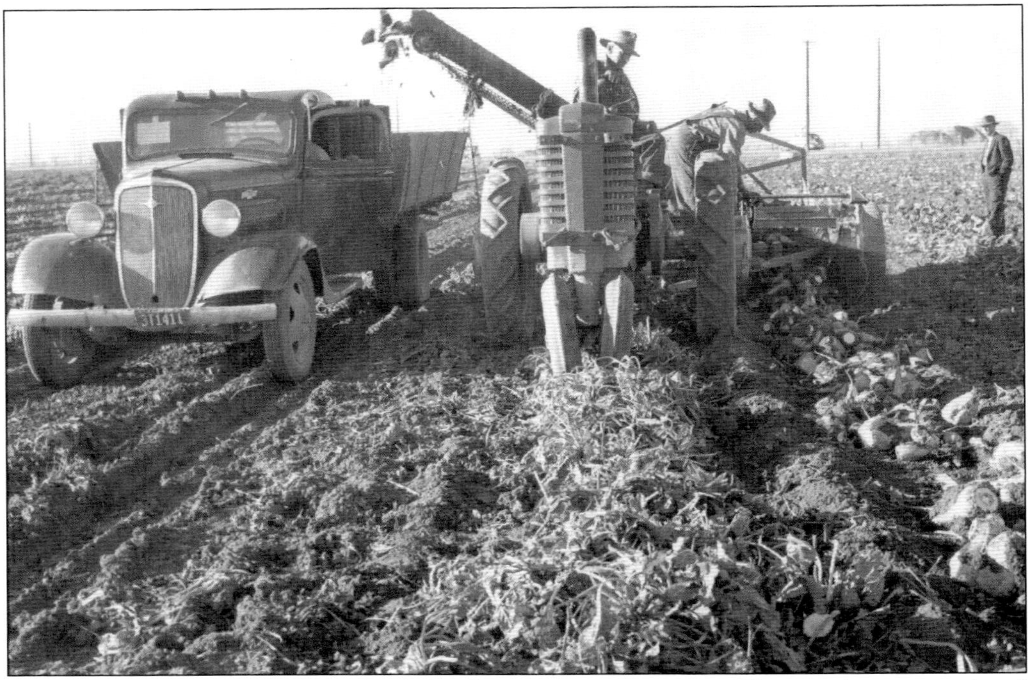

Shown here are sugar beets being loaded with pneumatic equipment. The sugar beets were placed in rows; the tractor moved alongside the crop, and paddles pulled the beets from the ground onto a conveyer belt. A truck with enclosed sides moved with the tractor through the field. The sugar beets would move along the conveyor belt and then over into the truck.

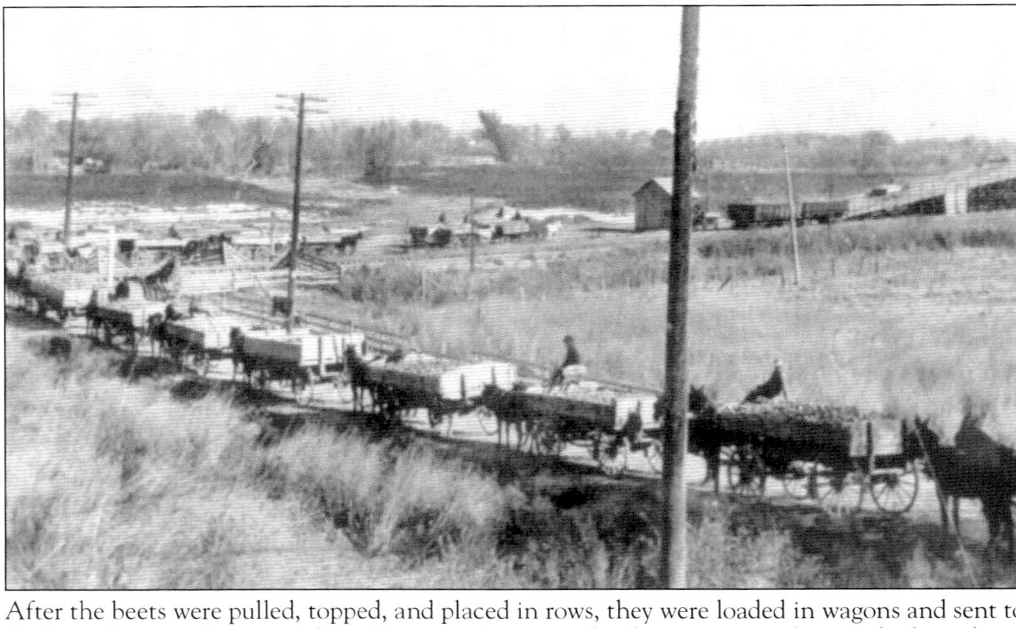

After the beets were pulled, topped, and placed in rows, they were loaded in wagons and sent to the beet dump at the sugar plant. Here are the wagon haulers waiting in line at the beet dump to deposit their loads. They would head up the ramp and dump the beets into waiting railcars. When full, the railcars would be hauled into the sugar plant.

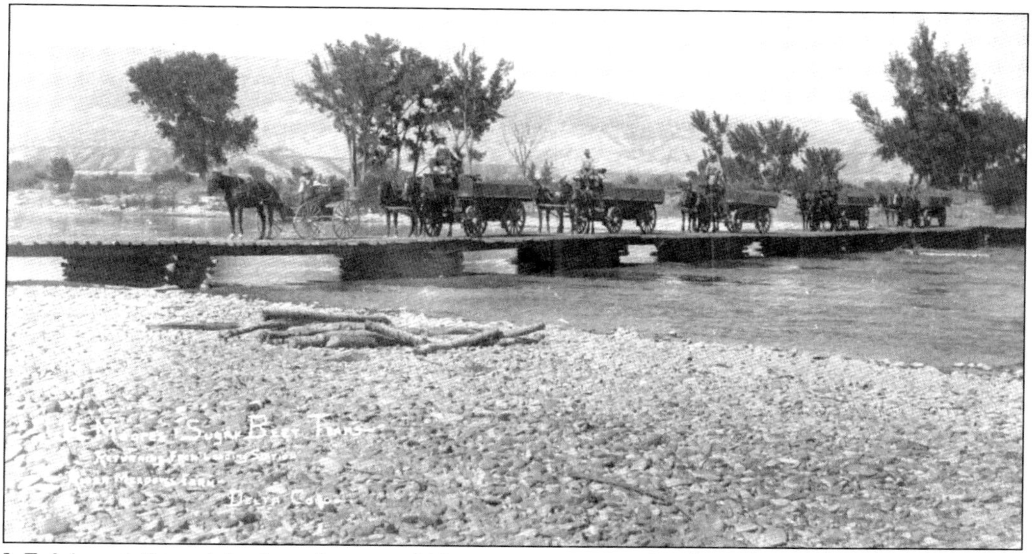

J. E. Moore's River Meadows farm would have many wagons hauling the crops to the sugar beet dump. After they unloaded the crops, they would have to return to the farm. Shown here is Moore's wagon team returning from the beet dump.

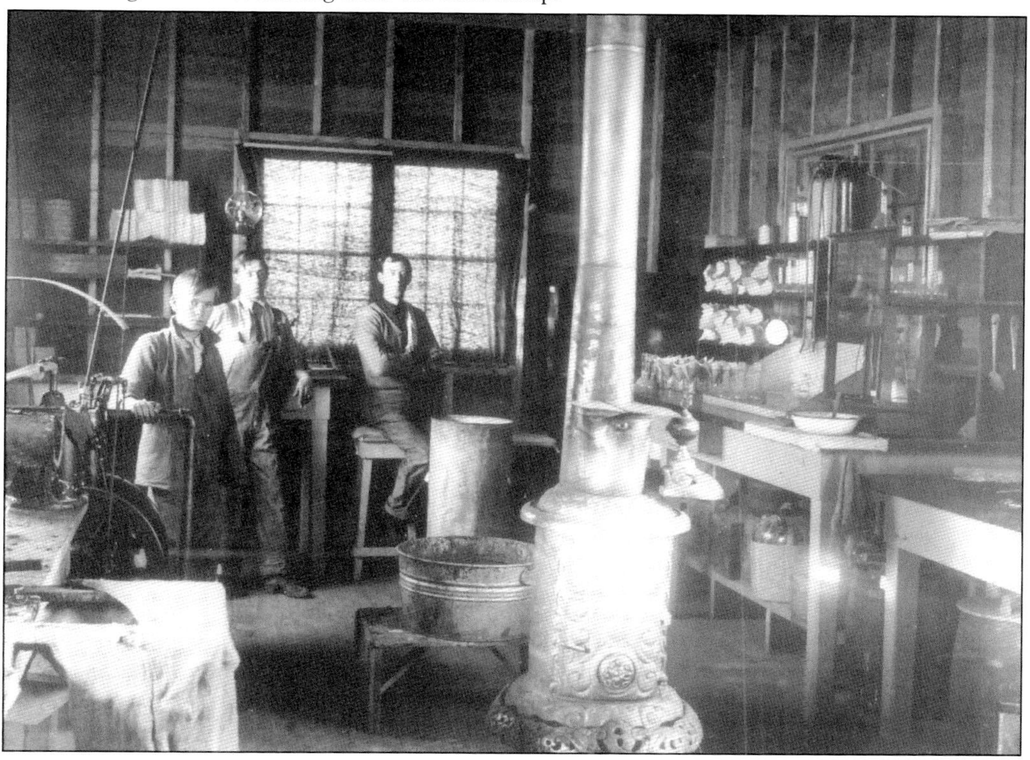

In 1910, the Holly Sugar Company maintained a laboratory at the beet dump. The job of the boy on the left was to select and wash beets at random. Lewis Seicrest (center) used the machinery to grind the beets to pulp. The chemist at the right measured the sugar content. The stove was used for heat. The lab operated until the factory went online in 1920.

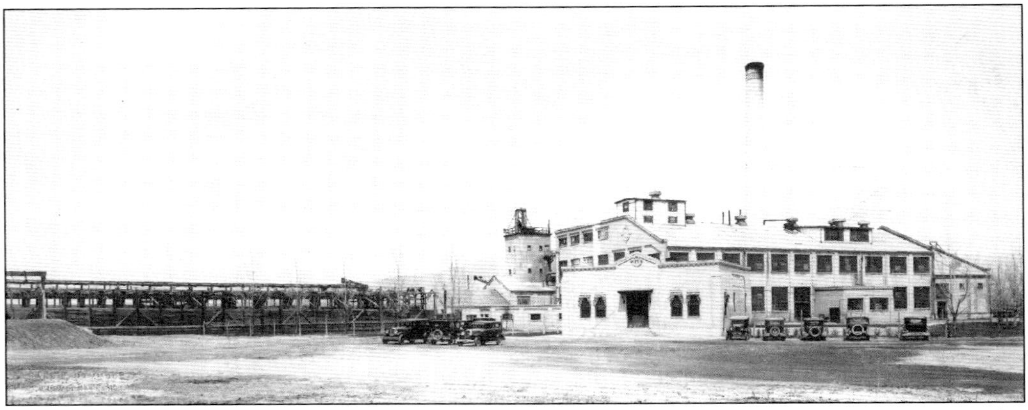

In 1898, a factory for sugar beets was built in Grand Junction. The first beets were sliced in the Uncompahgre Valley in 1899. In 1920, Delta finally got its first sugar beet plant when the Holly Sugar Corporation moved machinery there from a nonoperating plant in Glendale, Arizona. The factory had a smokestack for the processing. To the left in this photograph is the outline of the footer of the original offices. The Holly Sugar Corporation beet factory operated until 1976.

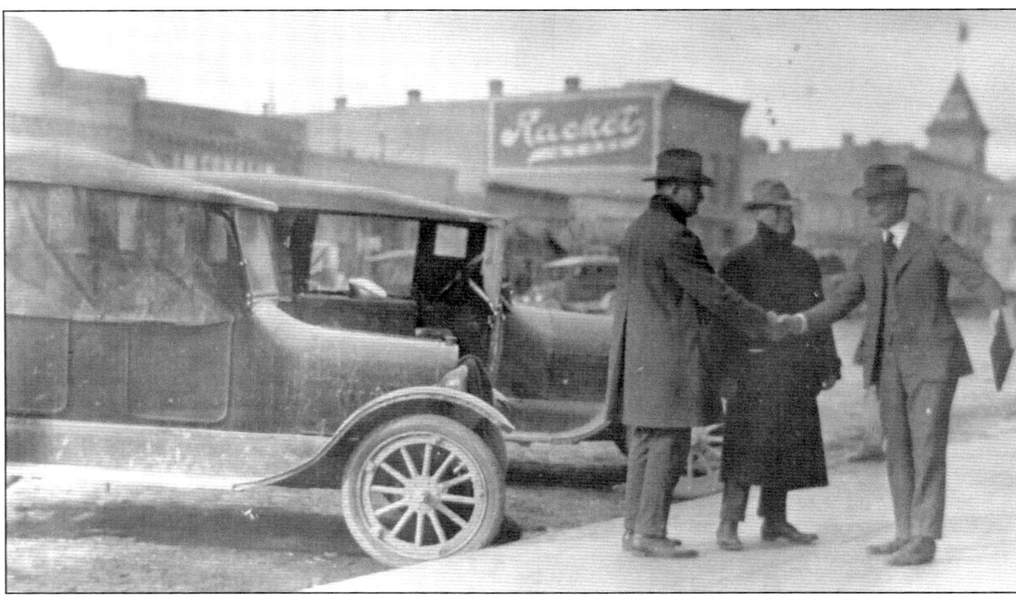

The superintendent at the Holly Sugar Corporation was Neal Draper. Neal is seen here shaking hands with Judge C. E. Blaine in front of the law offices of King and Blaine. This building was later torn down to make a drive-up area for the present Municipal Building on the corner of Fourth and Main Streets.

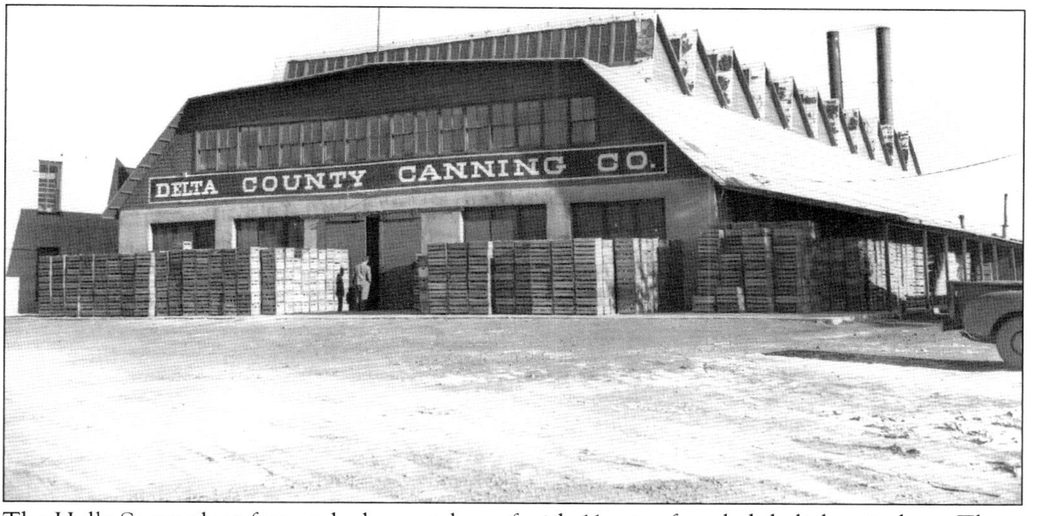

The Holly Sugar plant featured a barn-style roof with 11 sets of angled skylight windows. These early skylights allowed the inside of the massive factory to be well lit, with very little effort or expense. Two rows of windows across the end and a row down each side of the factory allowed light in from all angles. The factory also had three large smokestacks, which vented exhaust from the cookers inside the building.

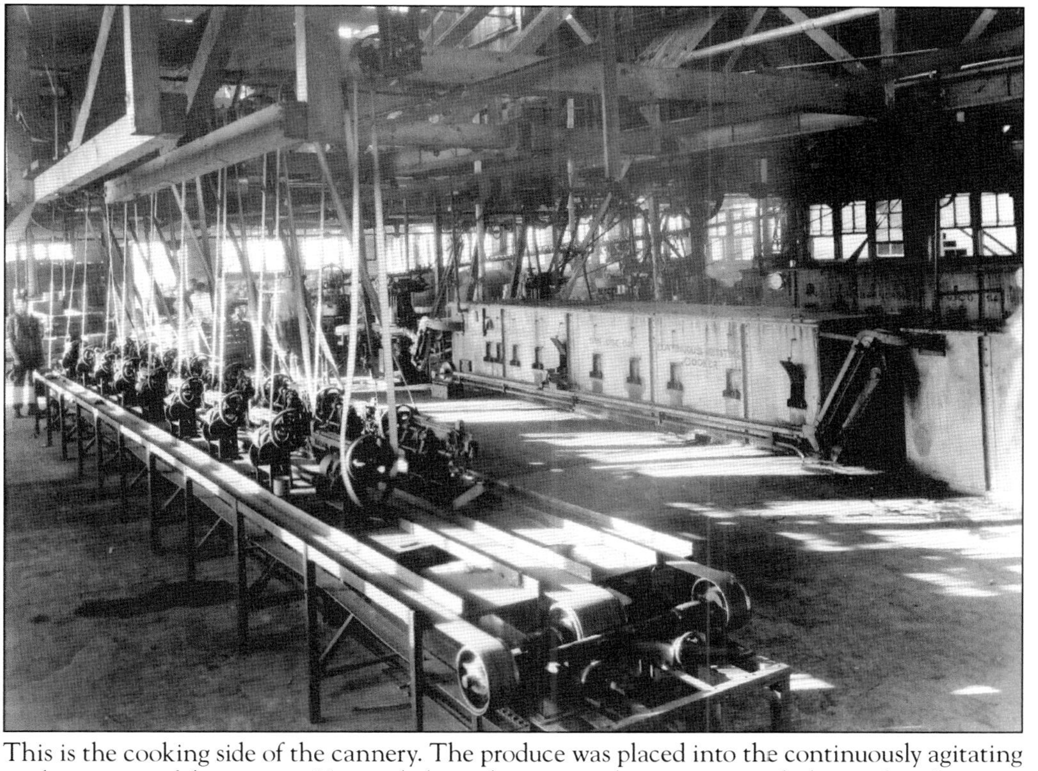

This is the cooking side of the cannery. The produce was placed into the continuously agitating cooker as part of the process. Various belts and motors with conveyors took the product from raw to cooked, to canned, to labeled, to packed. In this photograph, approximately 17 motors (with large belts connected to additional wheels in the ceiling) are powering the process.

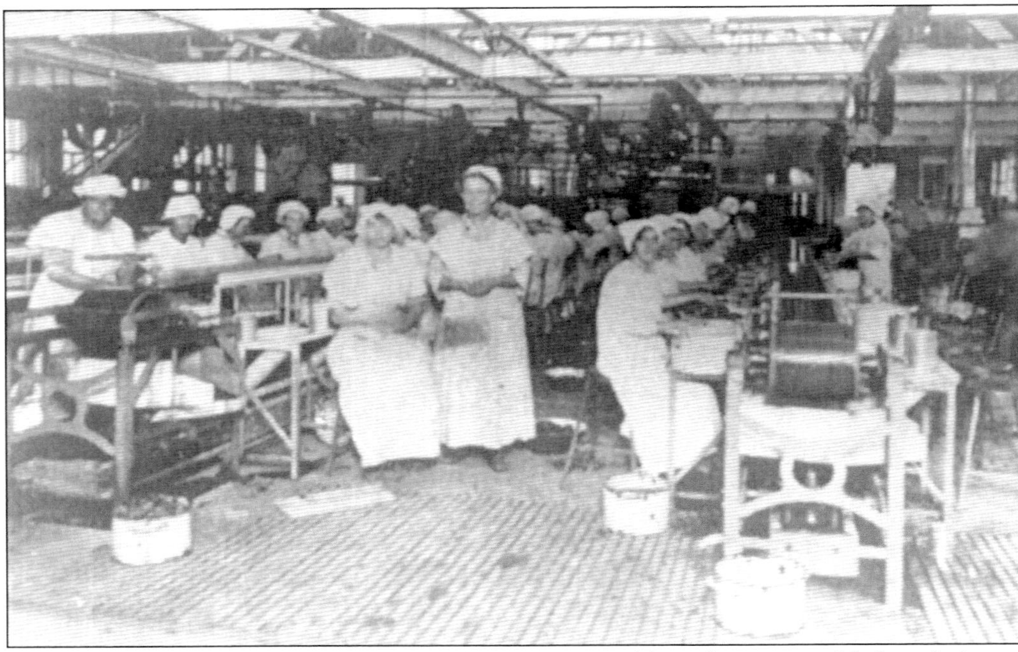

Mostly women were employed to work at the processing tables. They wore ankle-length dresses with a bonnet to keep their hair in place. Each preparer sat in front of an individual sink over which she would core and peel the produce, one at a time. The skinned beets would then travel down the conveyor belt in the large two-handled pots (seen below) to the plant's cookery section. Notice how the pots have been washed and turned upside down atop each other on the two rows of sinks. To the right in the image below stands another pyramid stack of these canning pots. At the end of each processing table were wooden slats on the floor with a trough underneath for drainage when the floors were washed down.

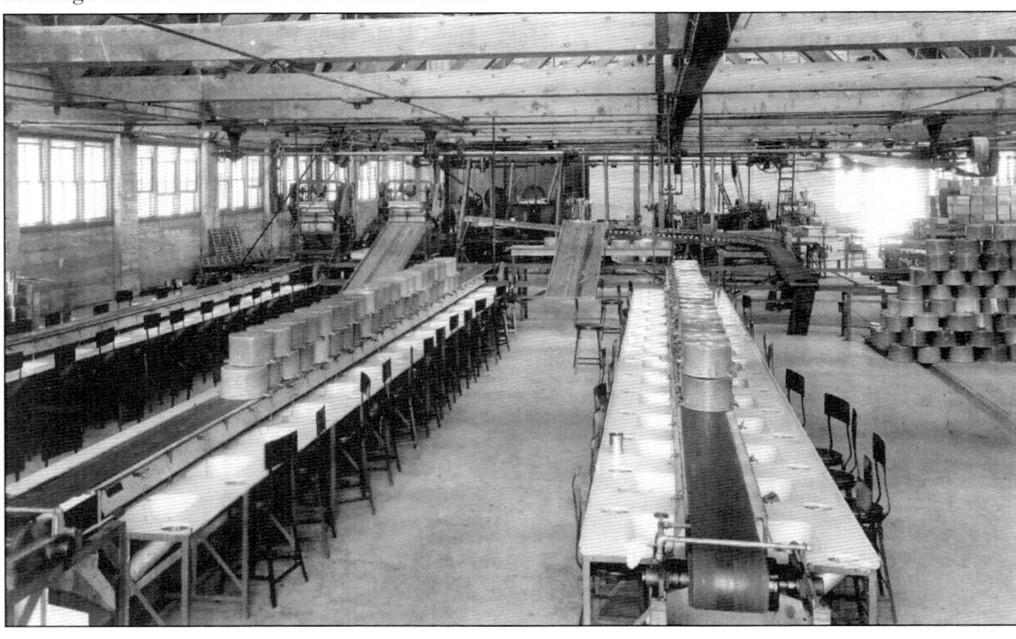

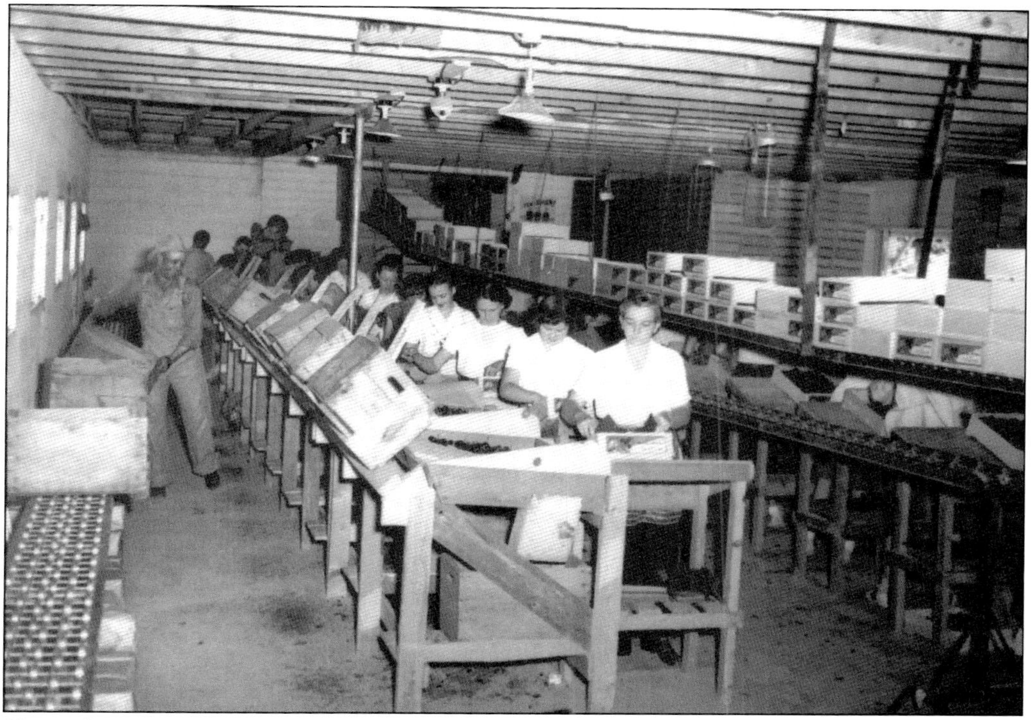

Shown here in 1946, the packers at the Girling Orchard's assembly line are still mostly women. The picked fruit would be brought in wooden crates placed on a manual roller line, and transferred over to the women at the seated packing line. They placed the fruit in labeled packing crates; when a crate was full, it was passed over to another manual roller line, then placed on a electric conveyor belt and sent out for shipping.

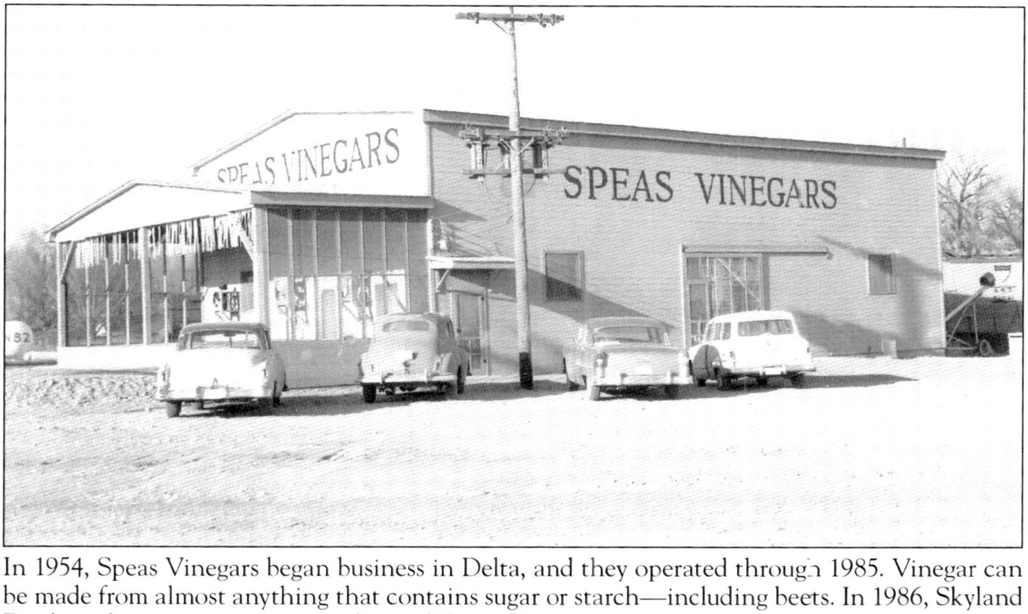

In 1954, Speas Vinegars began business in Delta, and they operated through 1985. Vinegar can be made from almost anything that contains sugar or starch—including beets. In 1986, Skyland Foods took over Speas Vinegars, but it did not take over the Delta operations.

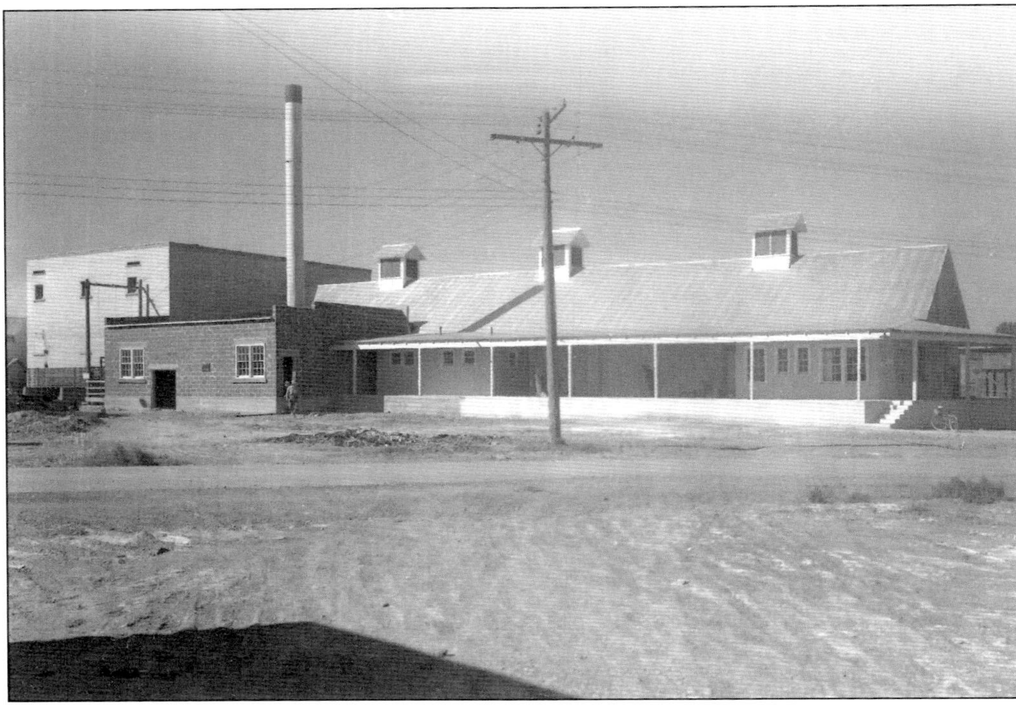

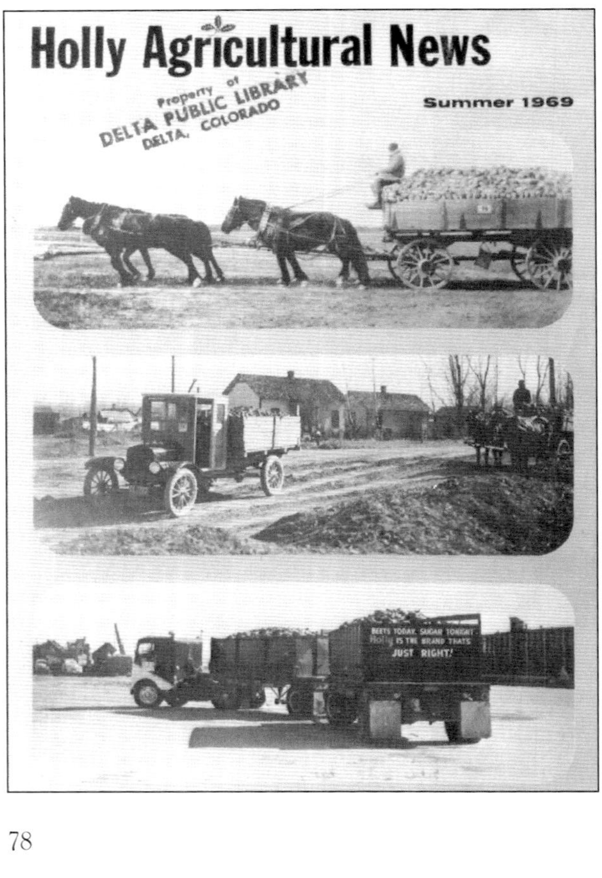

The building above was erected by L. W. Sweitzer, operator of L. W. Sweitzer Mercantile. In 1913, a group incorporated as the Delta County Farm Supply. In 1942, they became Fresh Frozen Foods. In April 1947, Fresh Frozen Foods became Skyland Food Corporation. In 1988, the organization became Whitehouse-Skyland Apple Products Company.

The Holly Sugar plant produced a newsletter, the *Holly Agricultural News*. The top photograph shows a horse-drawn wagon that would have been used around 1900. The center photograph shows an early 1900s truck. The bottom shows a new 18-wheel truck towing two trailers full of sugar beets to the factory in 1969. The caption on the tail of the truck reads, "Beets today, sugar tonight. Holly is the brand that's just right!"

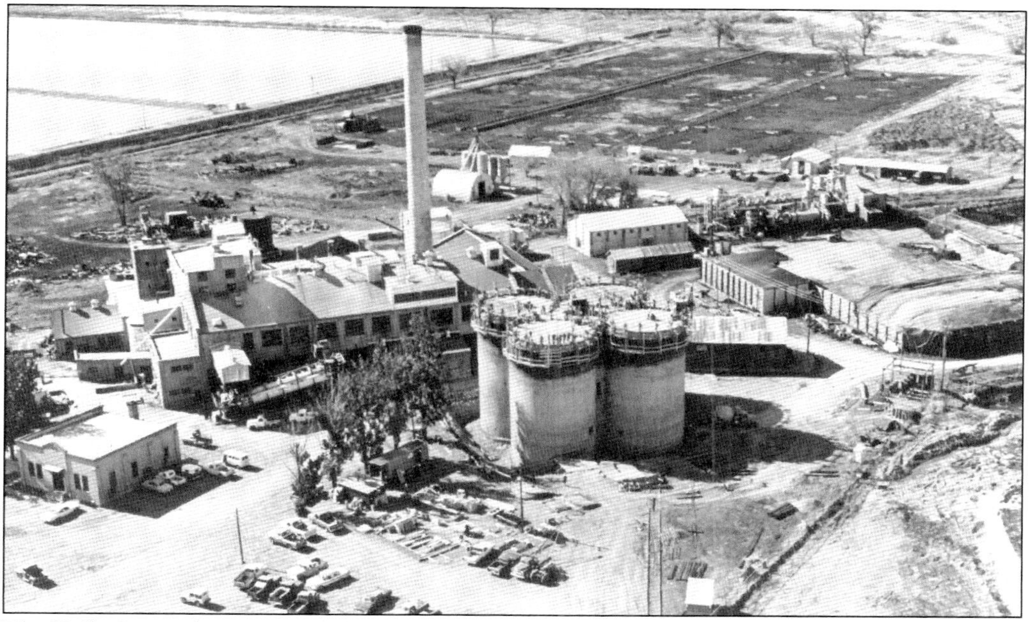

The Holly Sugar plant received their new storage silos in May 1969, built by the Jarvis International Construction Company of Salina, Kansas. The Delta Sand and Gravel Ready-mix plant supplied the estimated 5000 cubic yards of concrete needed for the project. The inside walls of the silos received a special slick finish on them, which was required to properly store bulk sugar. Jarvis International was able to complete the construction of the massive silos in just two weeks.

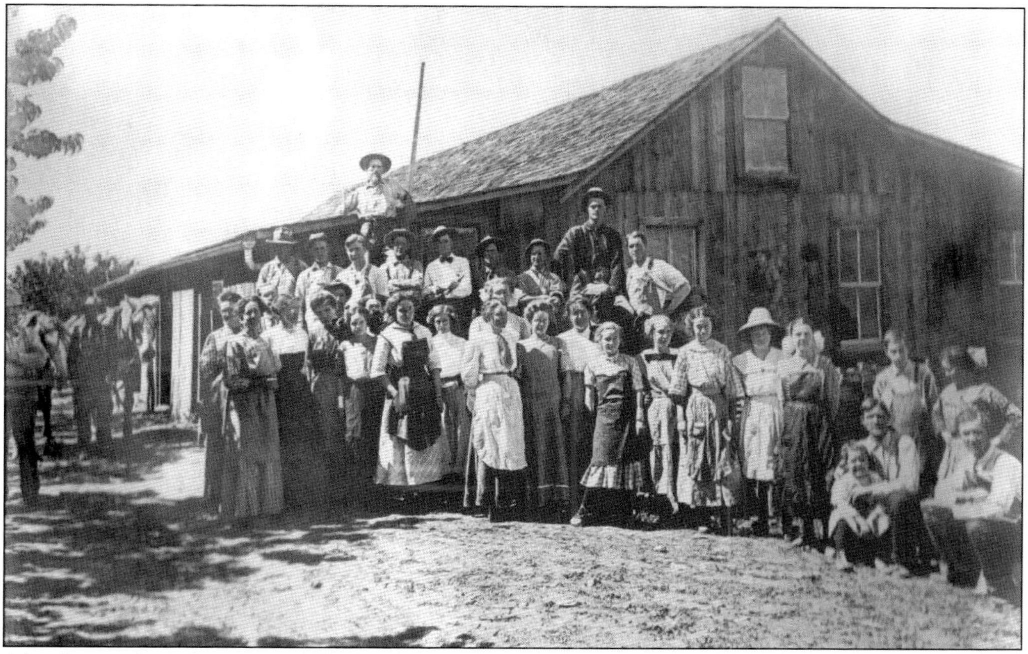

Also featured on the cover of this book, a peach-packing crew poses at the Paonia Excelsior Ranch, about 1912 or 1913. Donna Miller, with a bow in her hair, stands on the far right. (Photograph courtesy of the Delta County Historical Society, donated by Mr. and Mrs. Lloyd Miller.)

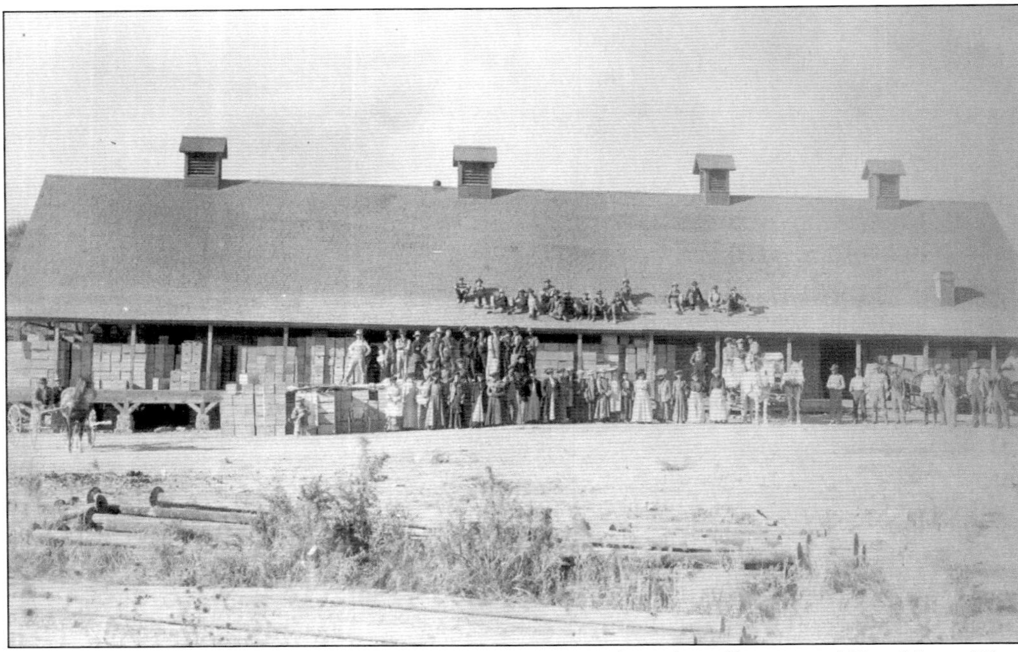

Hotchkiss Fruit Packing House was located in the North Fork Valley city of Hotchkiss. They packed a variety of locally grown fruit, including pears, peaches, apples, and possibly cherries. Notice the vast amount of wooden crates stacked along the front porch. These crates were taken to the fields and filled up by the fruit pickers. The crates were then transported by wagon to the packinghouse.

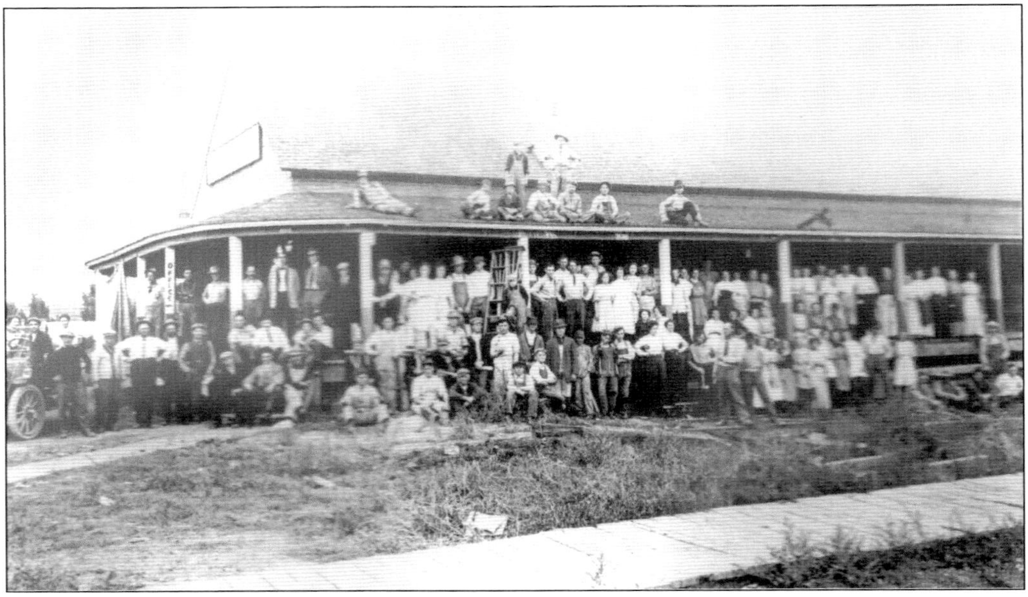

The North Fork Fruit Growers Association was mostly made up of members from Paonia, Hotchkiss, Crawford, and Cedaredge. Shown here around 1900 are over 100 of the organization's members. The association sought to promote the fruit industry and assist with growers' needs, such as market pricing, labor, and seasonal housing.

Four

Pride, Prizes, and Celebrations

The social fabric of the agricultural community in the Uncompahgre Valley was woven together by pride. At the 1893 World's Fair in Chicago, the Delta County fruit crop was honored with gold medals. In 1890 and 1902, the Delta County fruit crops took first place at every state fair (but one) in which they were entered. The valley farmers, ranchers, and residents took much pride in their industry and land, and the community that supported them. Uncompahgre Valley's businesses, farms, and families worked together and celebrated together with a variety of festivals, carnivals, or sprees—as they were called at the time.

In 1909, the Farmers Spree was born in Delta. In 1919, a Farmers/Ranchers Luncheon was added, and it is still held today. From its conception through the 1930s, this honored meal was a formal sit-down, black-tie affair, usually with more than 400 attendees. In 1935, Deltarado Days was born, a great celebration of the community's roots and agricultural industry, complete with a rodeo, donkey races, and a parade.

Around 1946, the community of Paonia began to celebrate the harvest of their most prominent crop—cherries. Cedaredge added an apple festival, as well as the Cedaredge Little Britches Rodeo—the oldest continuing youth rodeo in the nation. In 1978, the small community of Crawford held its first Pioneer Days.

Community and school sports were included in the festivities, along with prizes, ribbons, and other awards. From their inceptions, the communities used these social events as a way to visit with friends and family and simultaneously honor their shared Uncompahgre Valley lifestyles and heritage.

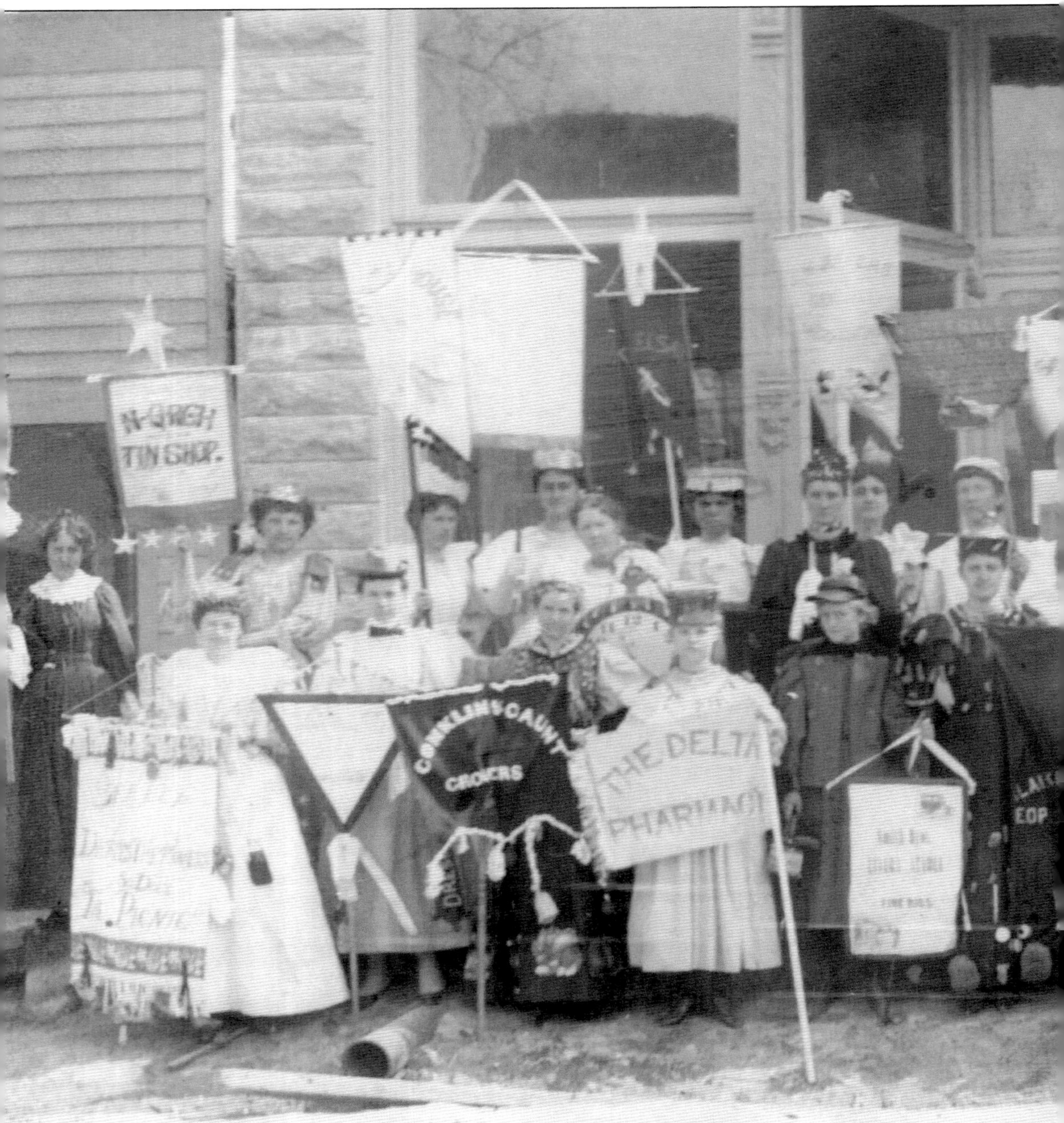

The 1897 Merchants Carnival was held at the Delta Opera House on March 31 under the auspices of the Young Women's Christian Temperance Union. The *Delta County Independent* explained that the event would feature a dress pageant in which participating area businesses would sponsor "one of Delta's good-looking girls in a costume appropriate to the firm's business." Here, in no particular order, are the pageant's 32 contestants and the businesses they represented: Edith Goodwin, Sanders Mercantile Company; Minnie Jackson, WCTU; Emma Finney, Dr. Kelsay; Arie Lewis, Delta Flour Mill; Maggie Turner, Bishop's Photo; Etta Jordan, McGrew's Meat Market; Lillie Lewis, Dr. Hunter; Sarah Lewis, People's Pharmacy; Nettie Sloan, Mabry and Kistler; Mrs. Edd

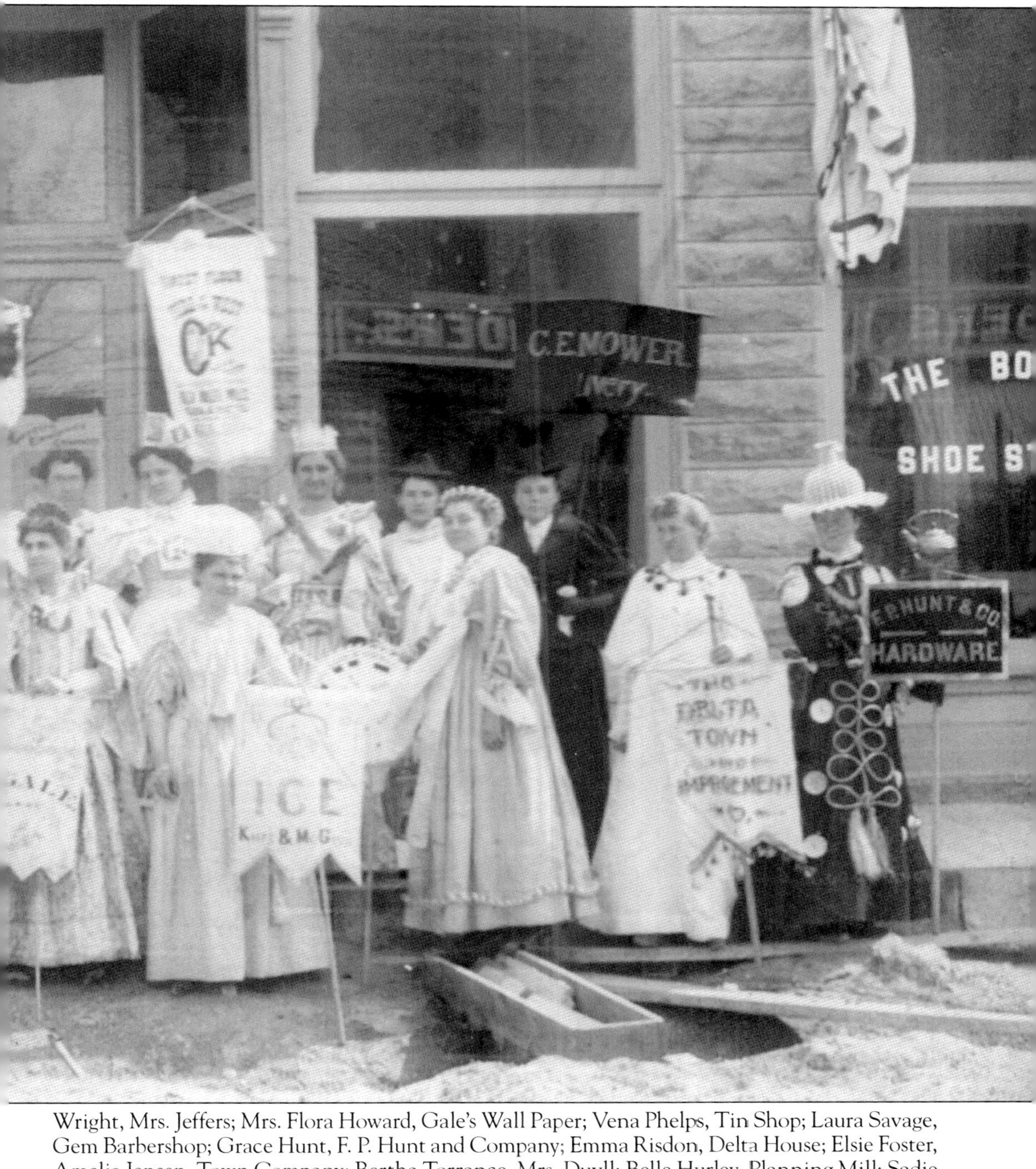

Wright, Mrs. Jeffers; Mrs. Flora Howard, Gale's Wall Paper; Vena Phelps, Tin Shop; Laura Savage, Gem Barbershop; Grace Hunt, F. P. Hunt and Company; Emma Risdon, Delta House; Elsie Foster, Amelia Jensen, Town Company; Bertha Torrance, Mrs. Duvll; Belle Hurley, Planning Mill; Sadie Jackson, McGrew's Ice House; Mabel Blair, *Delta County Independent*; Mrs. B. S. Dennison, S and H Jewelry; Viva Hawkey, Mrs. Stockham's Millinery; Dolly Ward, Conklin and Gaunt; Florance Cockrell, Mathers Dry Goods; Mabel North, Layers and Courthouse; Anna Nutter, Bowers Picnic; Stella Nutter, Nutter's Sheep Ranch; Kate Turner, R. F. Williams; Stella Graham, Mower's Livery; Amal Smith, Smith Brothers Livery; and Fern Braisted, Delta Pharmacy.

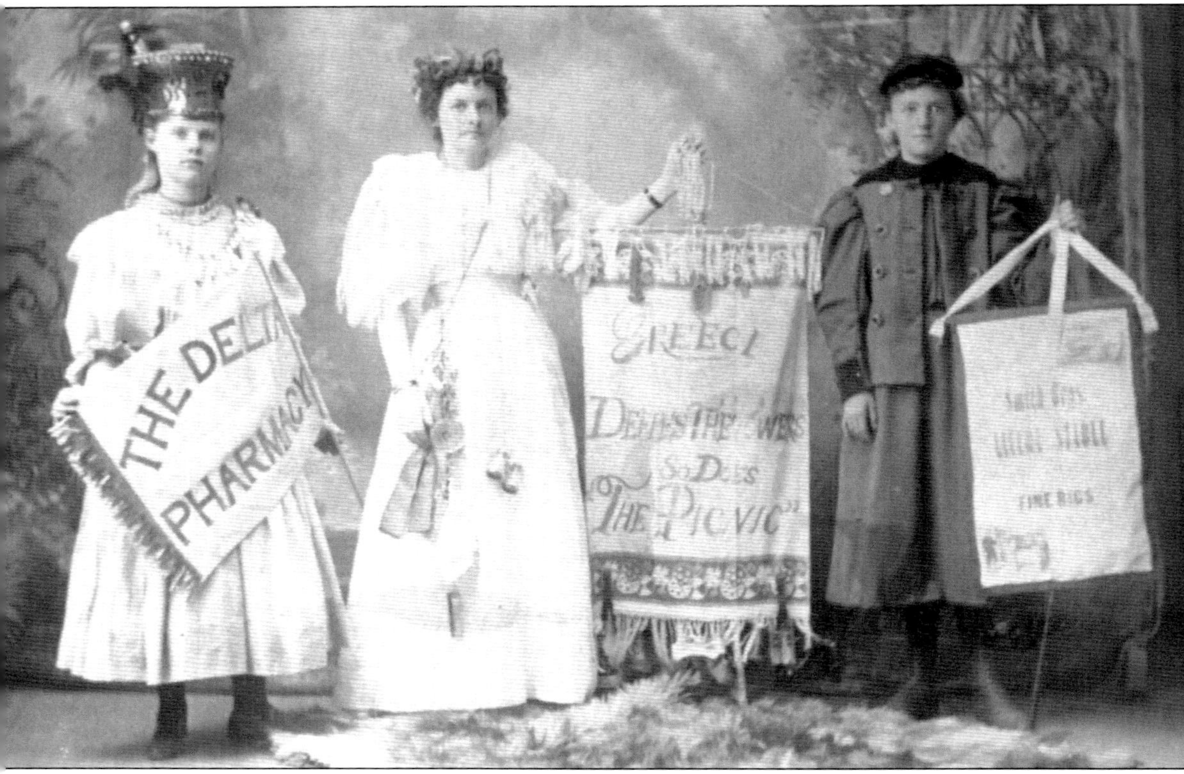

Three of the Merchants Carnival Contestants are pictured here. From left to right, they are Fern Braisted (Delta Pharmacy), Anna Nutter (Bowers Picnic), and Alma Smith (Smith Brothers Livery). After the procession of costumed "good-looking girls," a short pro-Temperance play was given to the packed house, titled "Rum or the First Glass." Three of the Merchant's Carnival Contestants—Elsie Foster, Dolly Ward, and Kate Turner—had parts in the play. The pageant's prize winners were announced the following week.

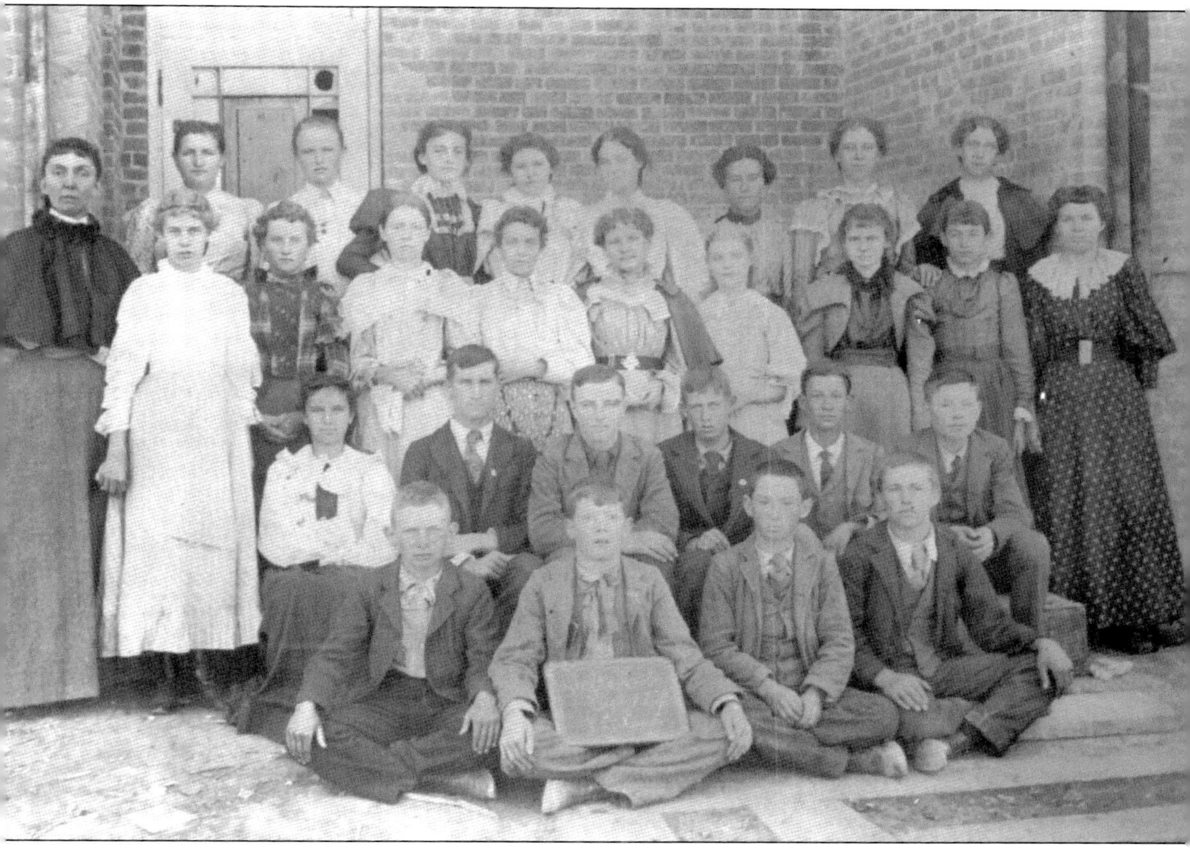

This is a photograph of a typical Delta eighth-grade class, taken on September 17, 1881. Notice that the number of girls is roughly double that of the boys; many of the young men were needed to work on the area's farms and ranches, and attending school was considered a luxury many families were unable, or unwilling, to afford. The students and faculty shown here are, from left to right, (first row) Walter Tucker, Paul Dorsey, Victor McCoy, Will Evans; (second row) Grace Holcroft, John Kelly, Bradford Skinner, Russell Hauser, Ermor Bailey, Ernest Grey; (third row) teacher Emma Meyers, Ora Gates, Lulu Geyer, Nola Goodwin, Sadie Geyer, "Vangie" Huntley, Fern Brasted, Blanche Brandt, Alice Heckman, Clara Hawkins; (fourth row) Mabel Bagley, Rose Walker, Susie Winton, May Stephens, Maymie Johnson, Mala Brown, Grace Sproule, and Florence Bigelow.

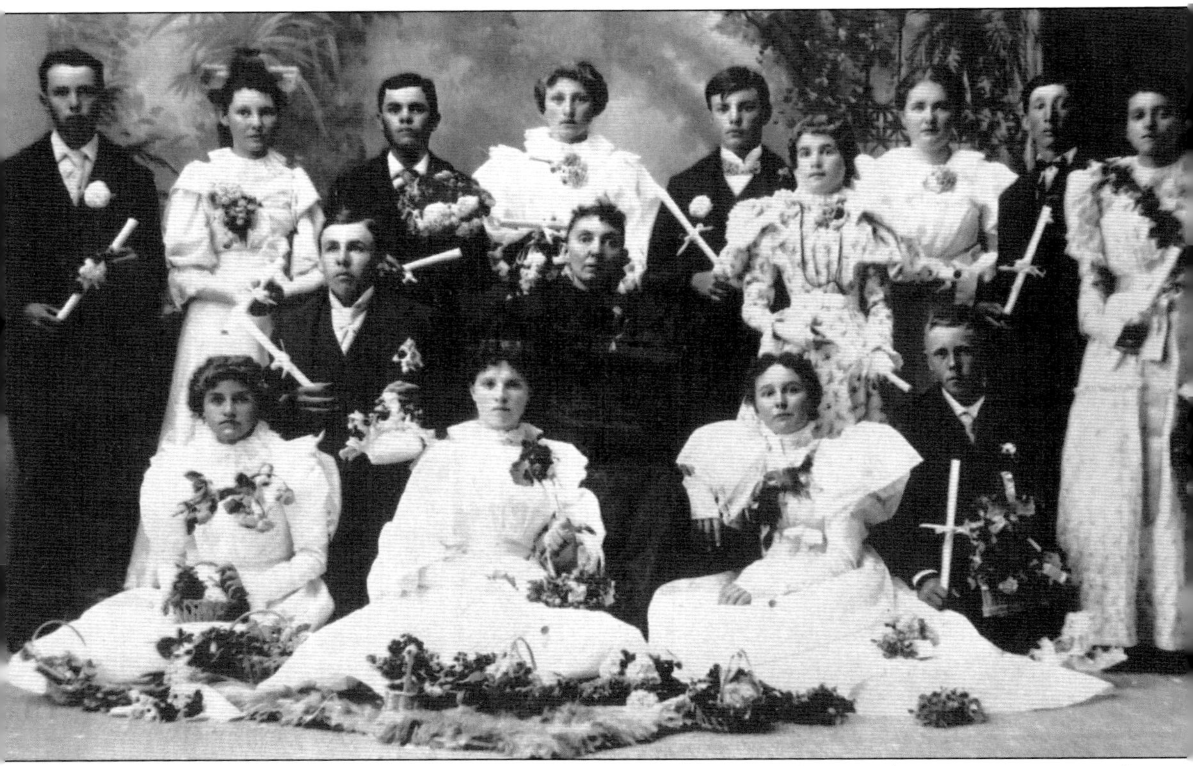

In this eighth-grade graduating class photograph from around 1895, the young women and gentlemen are dressed in their finest apparel. Their pride in their accomplishments is purely evident. The lovely gowns of the young women are adorned with fresh flowers. The handsome young men look sharp in their black suits and boutonnieres. Pictured here are (first row) Evaline Nutter, an unidentified student, Mary Dingman, Ben Laycock; (second row) Walter Smith, Emma G. Myers, Zetta Friend; (third row) an unidentified student, Mayme Johnson, five unidentified students, and Nettie Dingman.

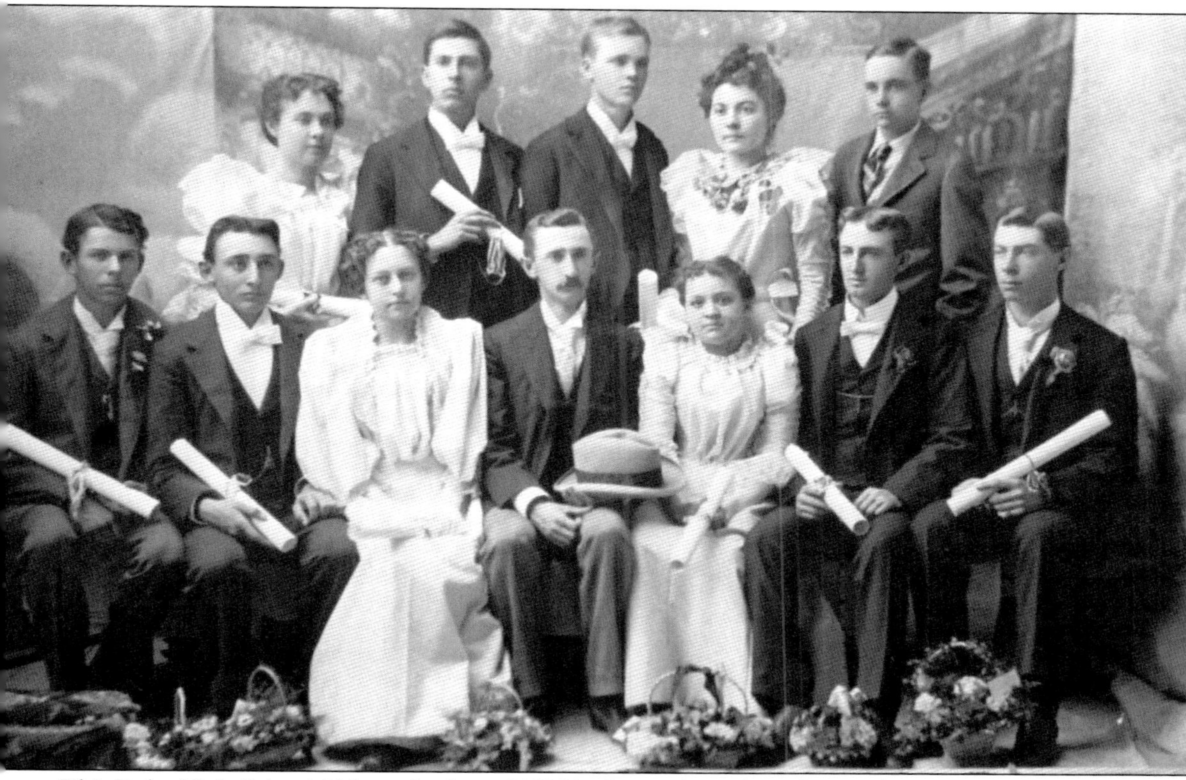

This Delta High School 11th grade class of 1898 had a total number of 12 students: four girls and eight boys, shown here with their diplomas. At their feet are basket of flowers; each gentlemen is wearing a boutonniere. From left to right are (first row) Earnest Bailey, Orion Kohnley, May R. Jones, professor W. G. Harris, Minnie Blair, J. Ernest Logan, J. Welland Jeffers; (second row) Stella Graham, Gilbert States, Harry Savage, Isabel Hurley (who later married Dr. Hunter), and Harry Stockham.

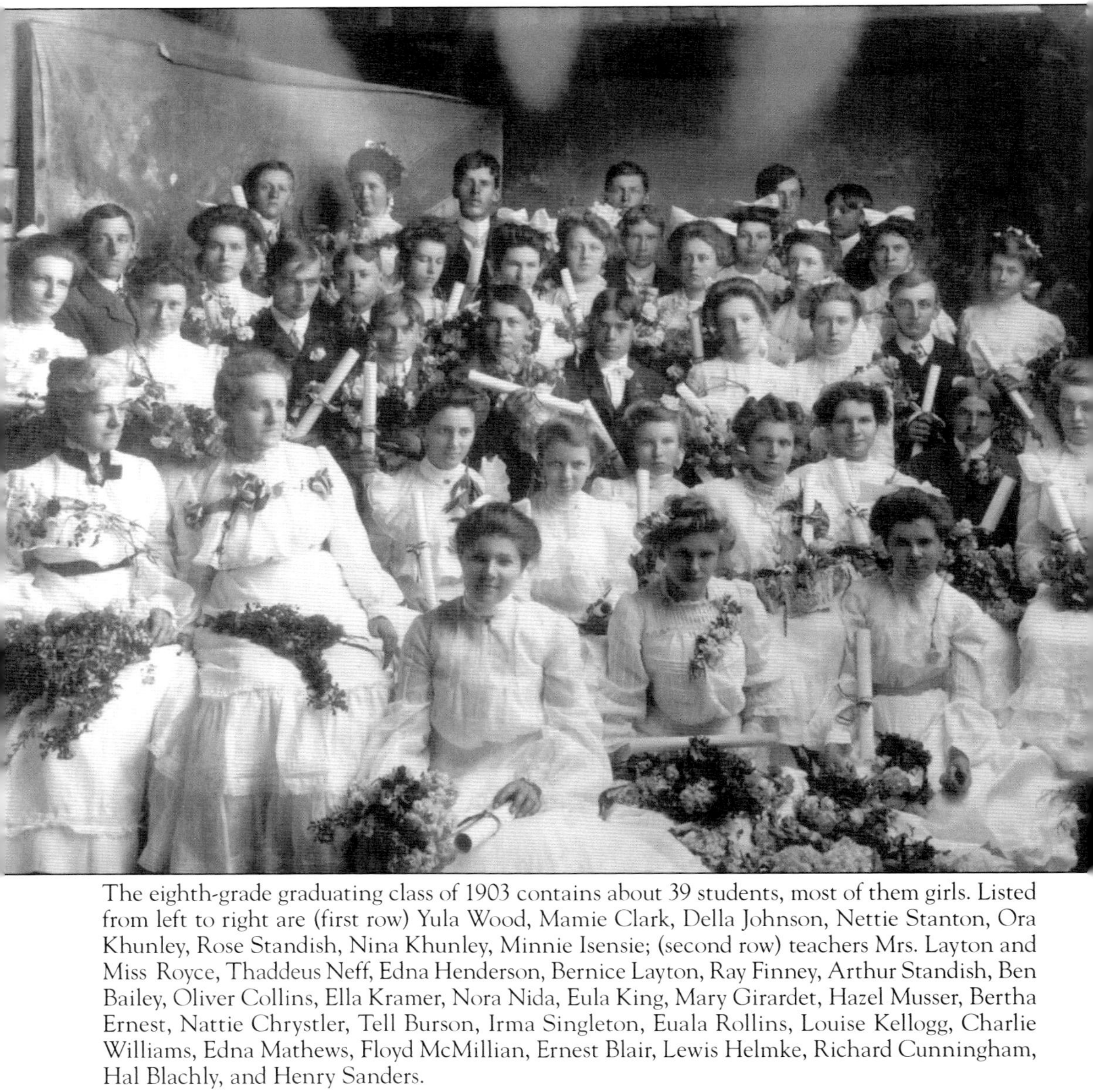

The eighth-grade graduating class of 1903 contains about 39 students, most of them girls. Listed from left to right are (first row) Yula Wood, Mamie Clark, Della Johnson, Nettie Stanton, Ora Khunley, Rose Standish, Nina Khunley, Minnie Isensie; (second row) teachers Mrs. Layton and Miss Royce, Thaddeus Neff, Edna Henderson, Bernice Layton, Ray Finney, Arthur Standish, Ben Bailey, Oliver Collins, Ella Kramer, Nora Nida, Eula King, Mary Girardet, Hazel Musser, Bertha Ernest, Nattie Chrystler, Tell Burson, Irma Singleton, Euala Rollins, Louise Kellogg, Charlie Williams, Edna Mathews, Floyd McMillian, Ernest Blair, Lewis Helmke, Richard Cunningham, Hal Blachly, and Henry Sanders.

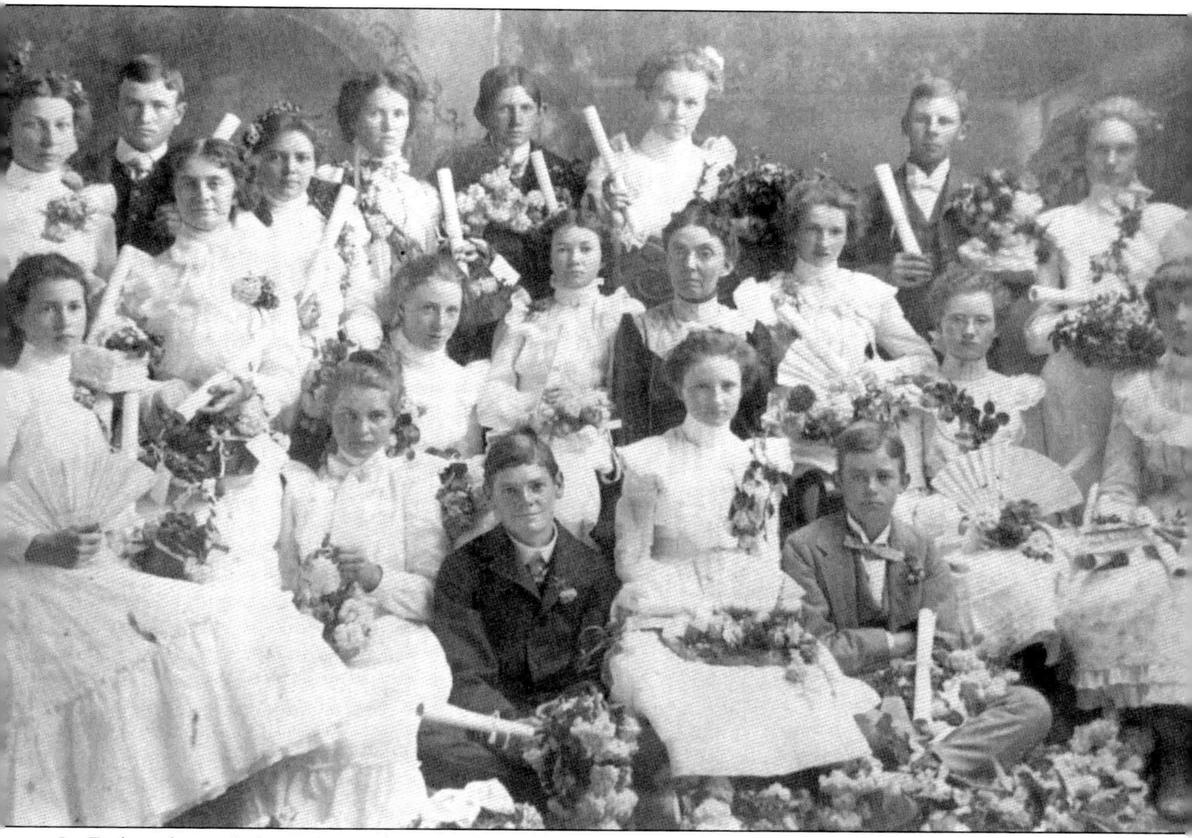

In Delta, the eighth-grade graduating class of 1901 totaled 20 students: 15 girls and only 5 boys. Note the flowers in most of the girls' hands, along with their diploma and a fan. Listed here from left to right are (first row) an unidentified student, John Johnson, two more unidentified students; (second row) an unidentified student, Nora Kellogg, Ethel Heckman, Emma G. Meyers (teacher), Hazel Musser, Pearl Haley, an unidentified student; (third row) an unidentified student, Elmer Skinner, three unidentified students, Bill Joe Stephens, Winifred Wonders, Will Lomax, and one last unidentified student.

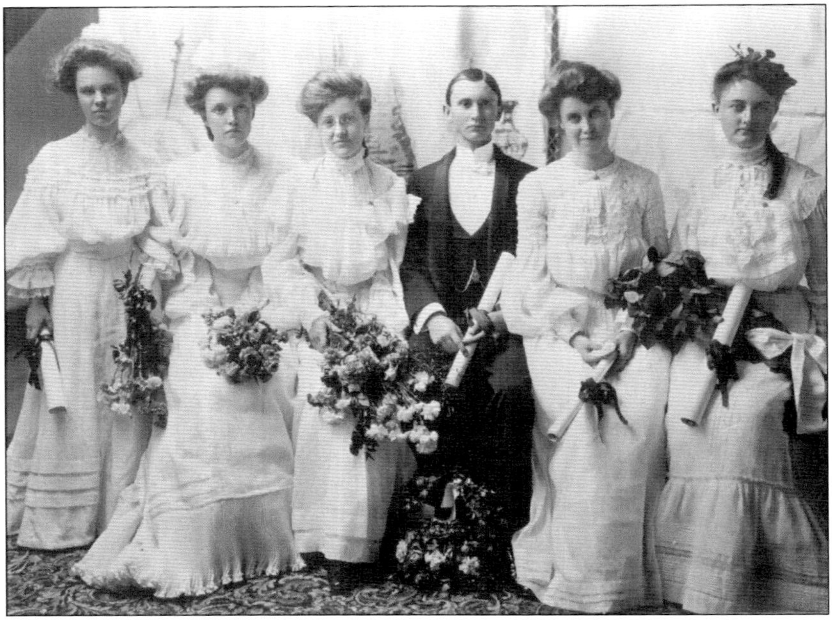

Delta High's graduating class of May 27, 1904, was made up of six students, only one of which was a boy. Each student has a bouquet of flowers along with their diploma. From left to right are Mina Merrill, Edna Ingersol, Alta Stewart, Earl Gheen, Gertrude Ashe, and Ethel Bear.

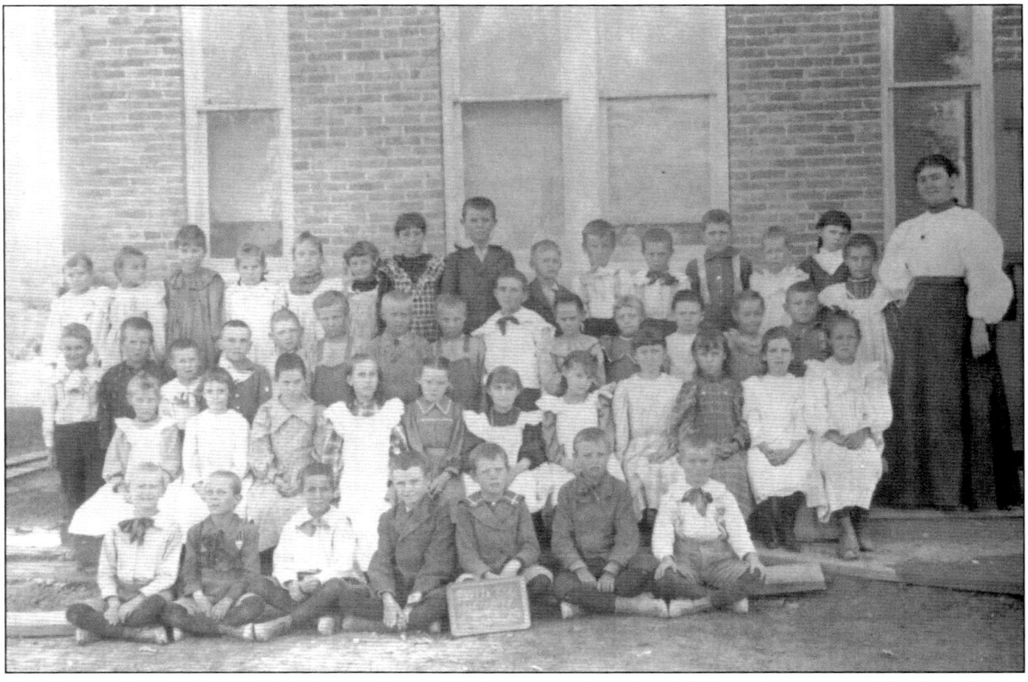

On September 15, 1897, this large class of Delta second-grade children is seen outside their brick school building with their smiling schoolteacher. In the first row, the first three students from left to right are Murray McGrew, Butler McGranahan, and Danny Thomas. In the second row, sixth from left is Nellie Stockham; and to her right is Trudie Amsbary. In the fourth row, sixth from left is Bertha Nutter.

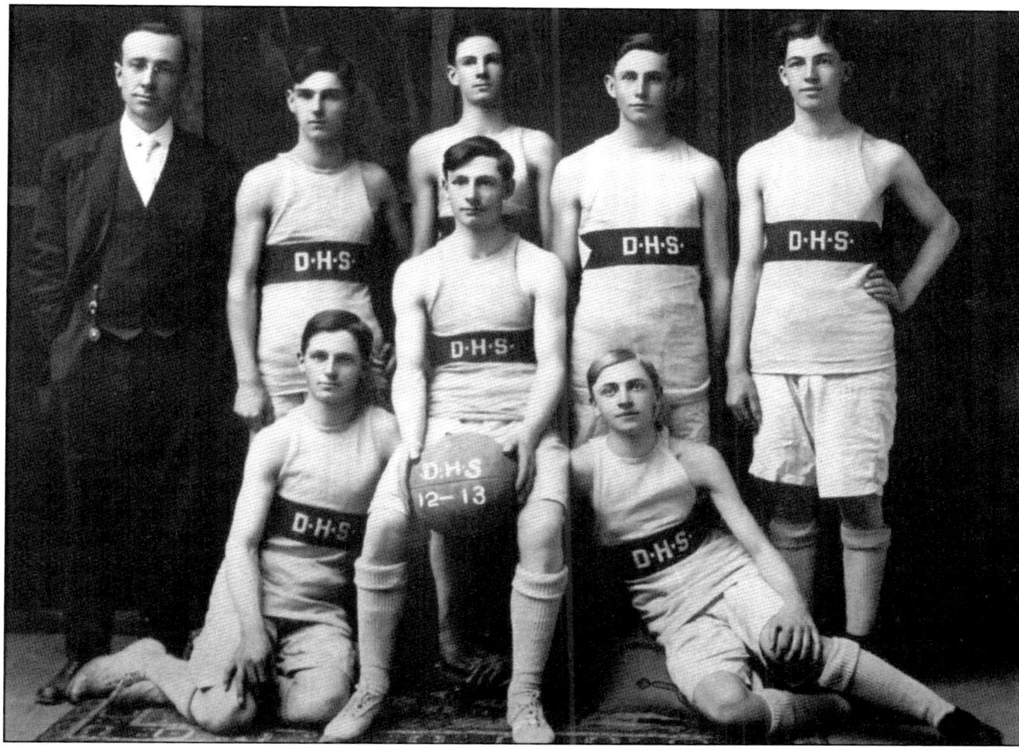

Delta's 1912–1913 high school basketball team had a total of seven players, with only one coach. From left to right, they are (first row) Rodger Nelson, Luke Meyer; (second row) Lloyd Nix, captain; (third row) Coach Seicrest, Phil Harding, Harry White, Robert Plum, and John Arthur.

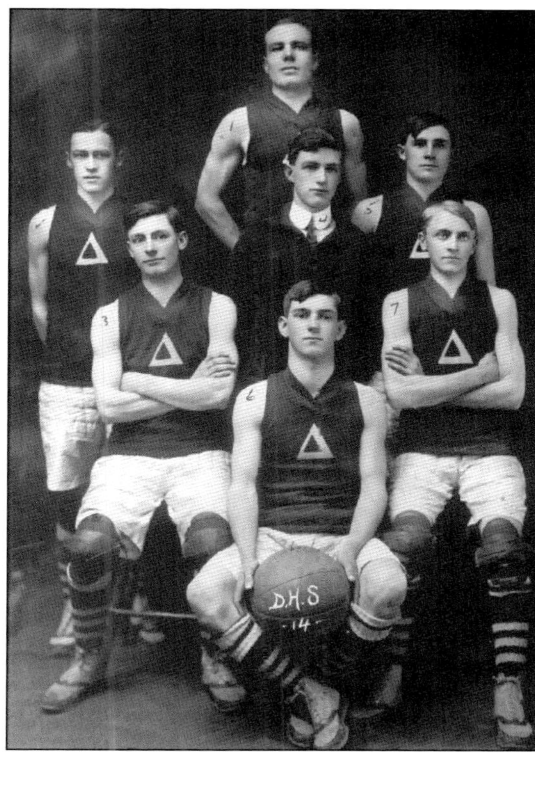

The Delta High basketball team from 1914 featured just six players and one coach. The boys are wearing high socks and two of the boys in the first row have knee guards on. From left to right, they are (first row) Phil Harding; (second row) Lloyd Nix, Luke Meyer; (third row) an unidentified player, Coach Hollingshead, Fred Stell; (fourth row) and Earl Vickery.

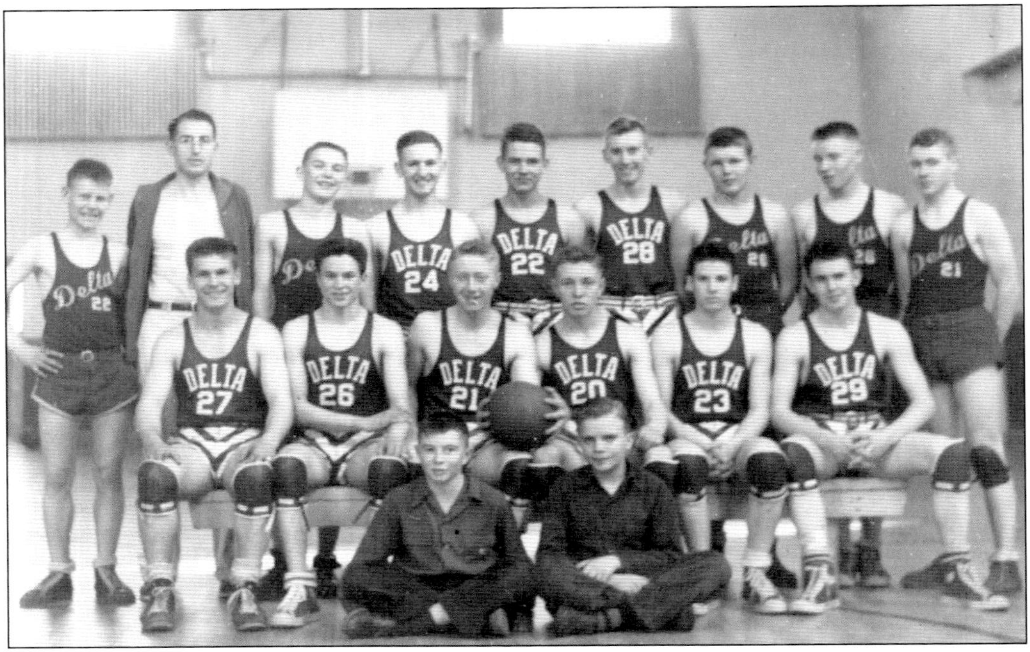

Delta High School Basketball team of 1940 was made up of 14 players, one coach and two helpers. From left to right, they are (first row) team assistants Leroy Scott and Dale Campbell; (second row) A. Farhney, Gene Bond, Whitey Huff, J. R. Ensley, Al Leonard, Ray Moore; (third row) George Barrows, Coach McCoy, Harold Blakely, Keith Crawley, Larry Sweitzer, Jack Linkletter, Dean Baldwin, and Kenny Huff. One player on the third row is unidentified.

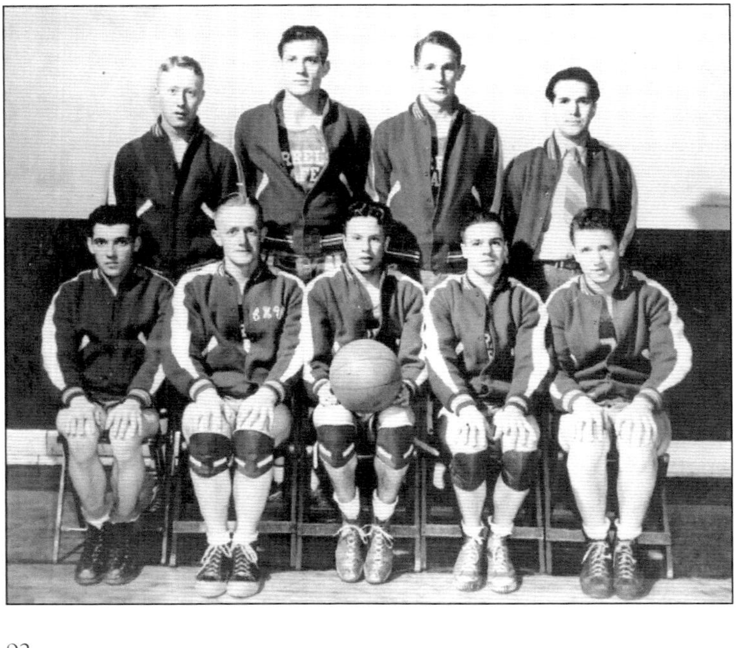

Terrell's Café Team only had about 10 players from 1940 to 1945. All of the boys here are dressed in their basketball uniforms along with their letter jackets. A few boys in the first row have their knee guards on. From left to right they are (first row) Bobby Bruttis (builder of the town's first bowling alley), Chub Lowe, Gene Bond, Gene Bussey (his father was a blacksmith), and Bruiser Gay; (second row) Jim Core, Fred Calhoun, and Al Freitas.

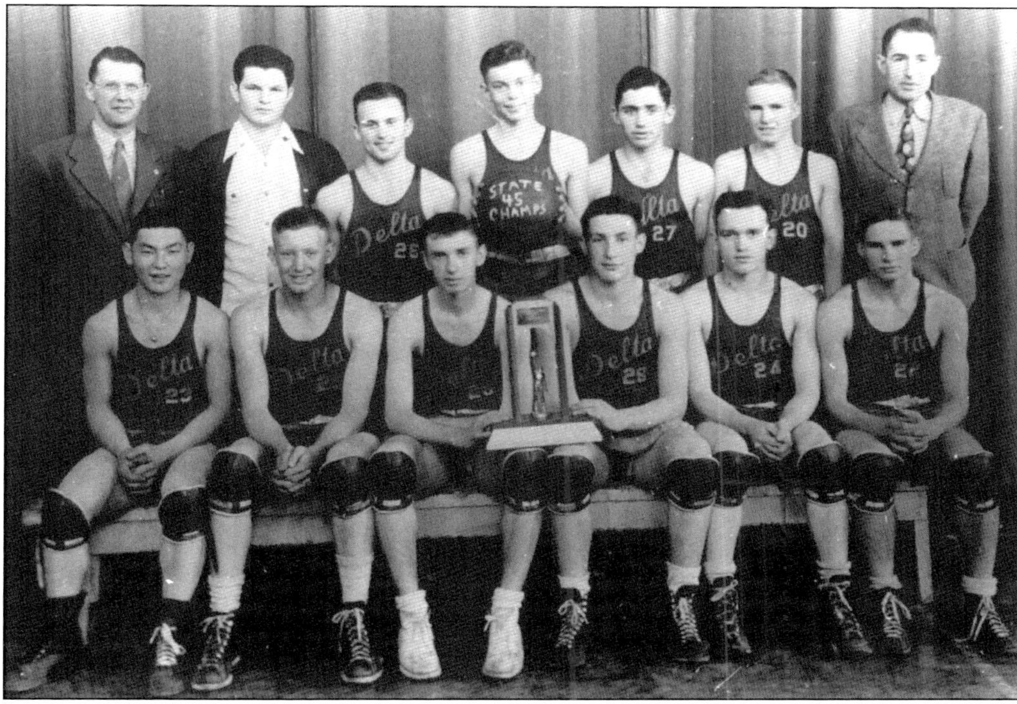

The Delta High School basketball team of 1945 were Colorado State Champions. From left to right are (first row) Bob Nakoska, Gene Pittsinger, Weldon Curry, Jim Coan, Don Ray, Sain Colbaugh; coach Carl Porath, Jerry Wethington, T. J. Harshman, Orin Duncan, Dean Cockroft, Jack Shea, and coach George Barrows.

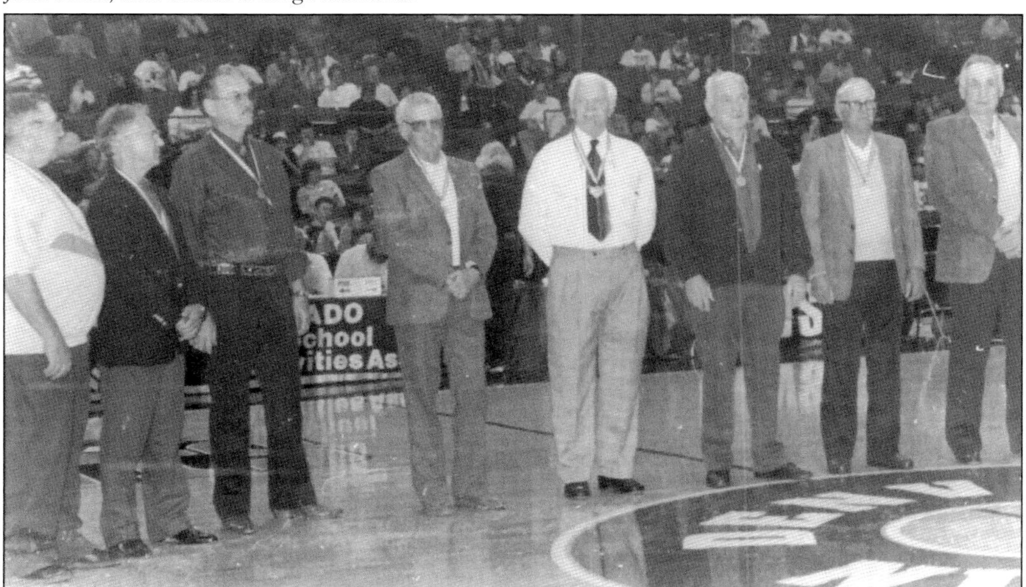

Here is a 1995 shot from the 50th anniversary ceremony for the state champion 1945 Delta High School basketball team. Pictured from left to right are Dean Cockroft, T. J. Harshman, Orin Duncan, Jack Shea, Jerry Wethington, Don Ray, Sain Colbaugh, and Jim Coan.

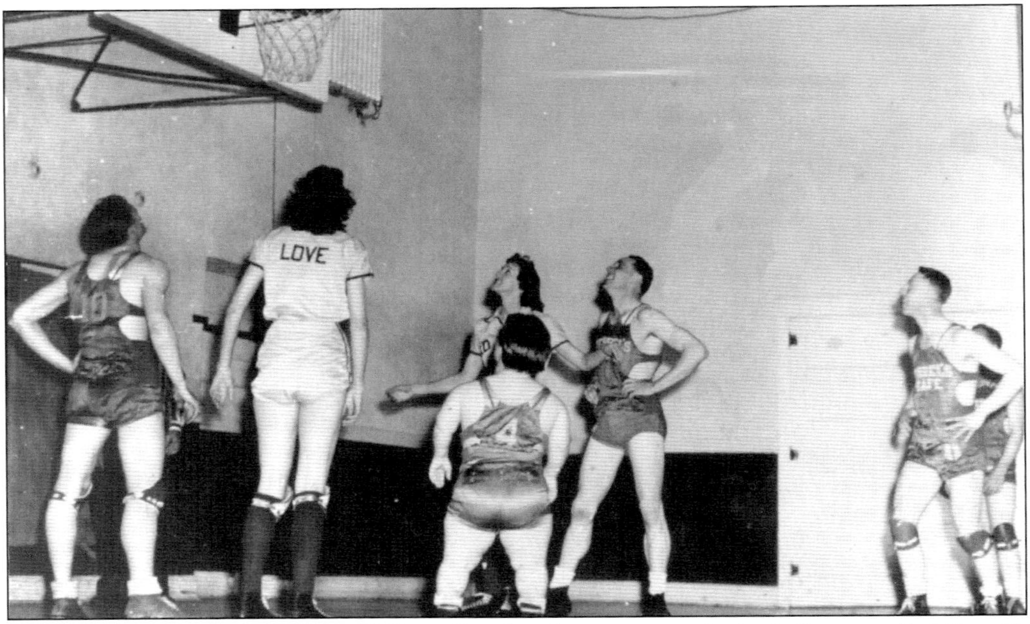

Around 1945, Royal C. Huff Sr.—"Whitey"—played on a semipro basketball team called Terrell's Café Basketball Team. Here they played a women's All-American team called the Redhead Women's Team. Left, No. 10, is Jim Core of Western State College. To his right is Love, a 6-foot-5 woman player. Stubby Hocker, whose family owned the grocery store on Ninth and Main Streets, is No. 4. Right of Hocker is Fred Calhoun, who became a judge. To the right of him is this book's coauthor, Whitey Huff.

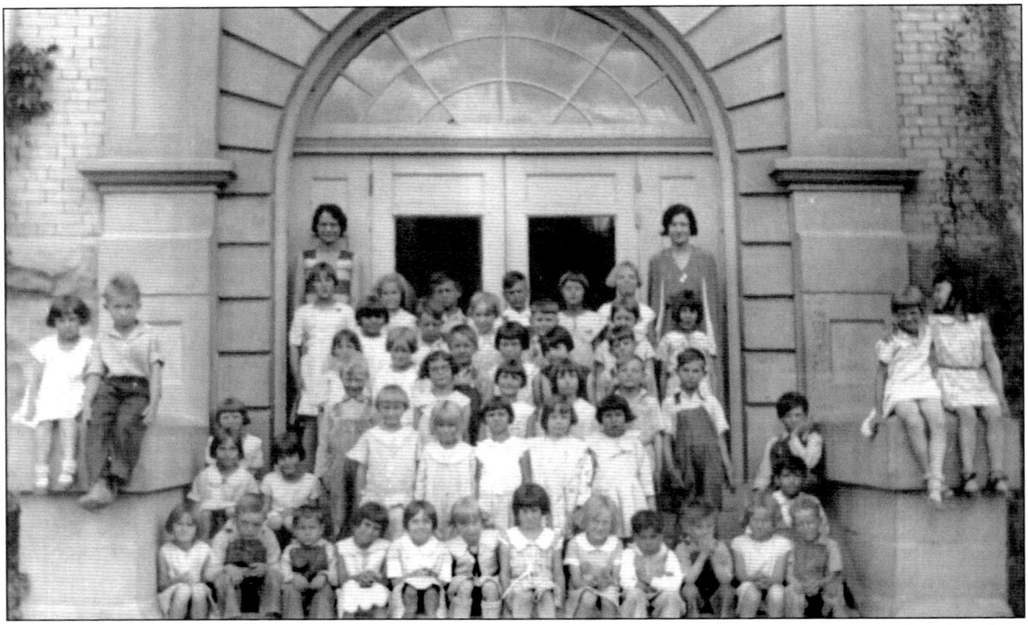

In this photograph is Whitey Huff's second-grade class, posing in front of Delta High School in 1932. There are 50 students in this class, along with two teachers. Notice how nearly all the boys are wearing coveralls, and all of the young women are wearing dresses.

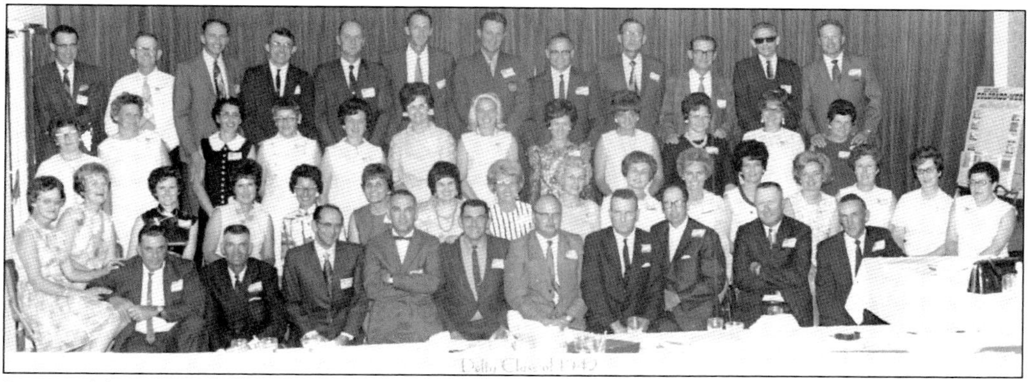

Pictured here in 1962 are attendees of the 20-year class reunion for the Delta High School graduating class of 1942. Fifty of the original class attended the reunion. In the photograph, everyone has big smiles and some are even laughing. A few couples that had met in high school were still together at the reunion.

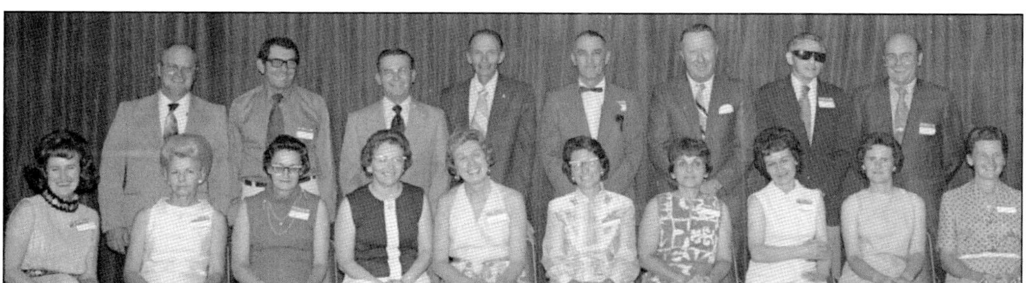

At the 30-year reunion of the Delta High School class of 1942 in 1972, 18 out of the original 50 students (from the second grade) attended the reunion. All the women still wore dresses, but now the men attended wearing suits and ties.

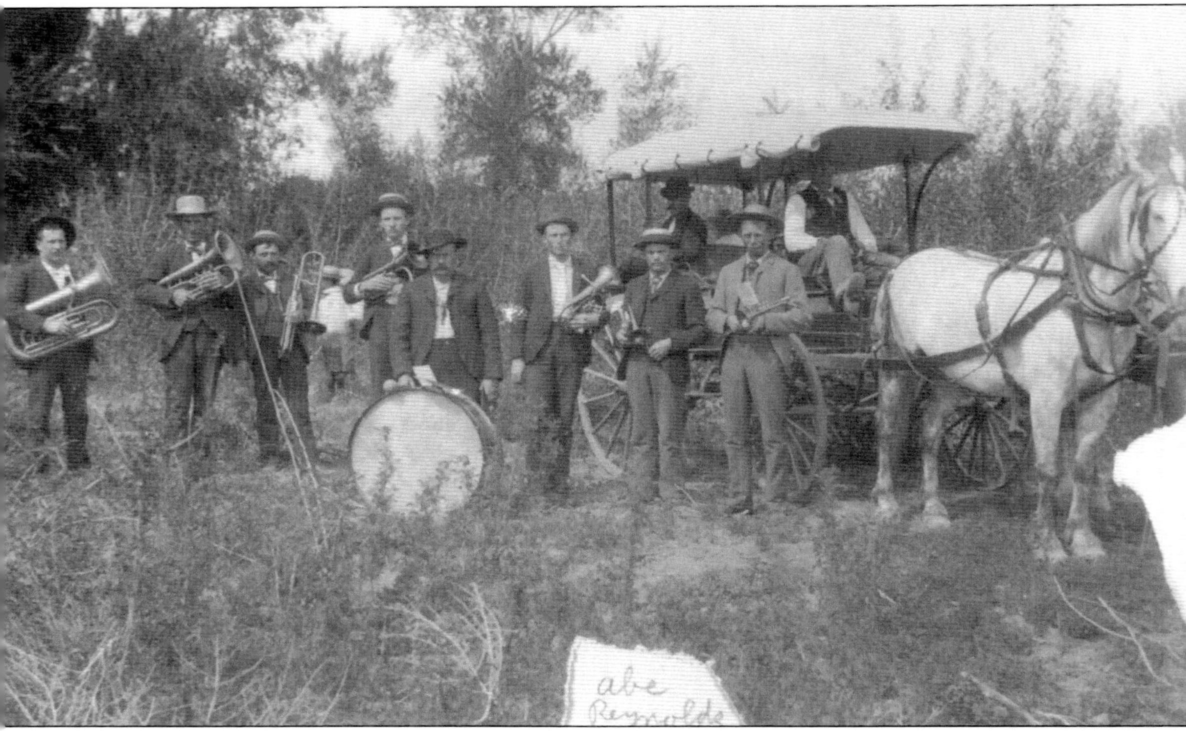

In February 1891, the young men of Delta decided to organize a brass band. Their idea was to play immediately. Instruments were ordered. The band leader was Professor F. Jackson. The band gave free concerts on the street every Saturday afternoon. Soon the band became one of the leading bands in Colorado and a source of pride to the town. Members shown here, in no specific order, are F. Jackson (E-flat cornet), L. Croster (first B-flat cornet), A. Maxwell (second B-flat cornet), E. Clack (solo alto), S. Findley (second alto), C. M. Snider (second tenor), H. Wilson (trombone), H. Price (baritone), C. Downing (tuba), M. Graham (side drum), and W. R. Gale (bass drum).

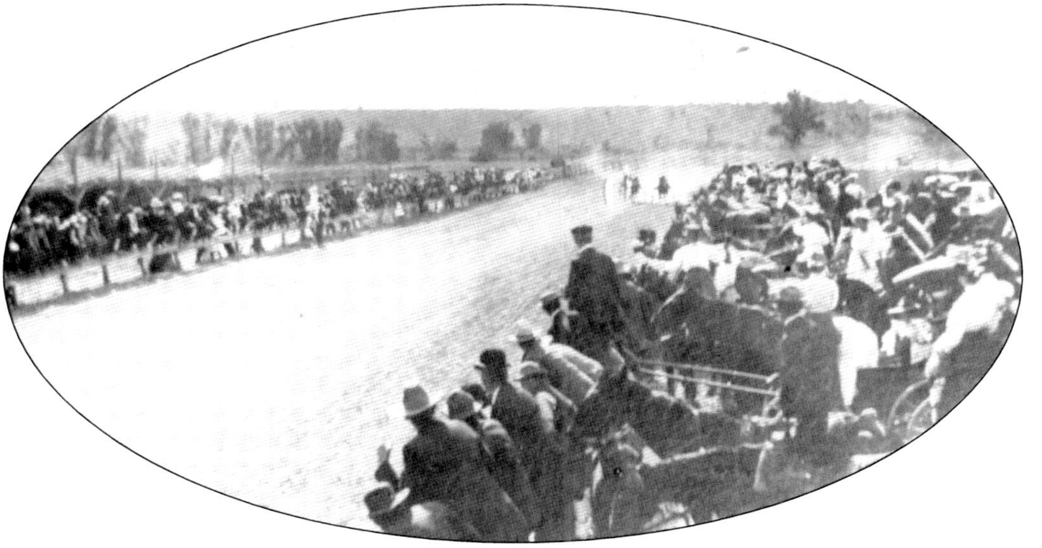

The Delta County Fair Association formed about 1897. They built a race track complex, which consisted of new stables, a grandstand, and a half-mile dirt track lined with post and rails. In the race pictured here, spectators fill the grandstand and line the rails. On the right side of the photograph, some spectators have pulled their horse and buggies right to the rail line and used them for seating.

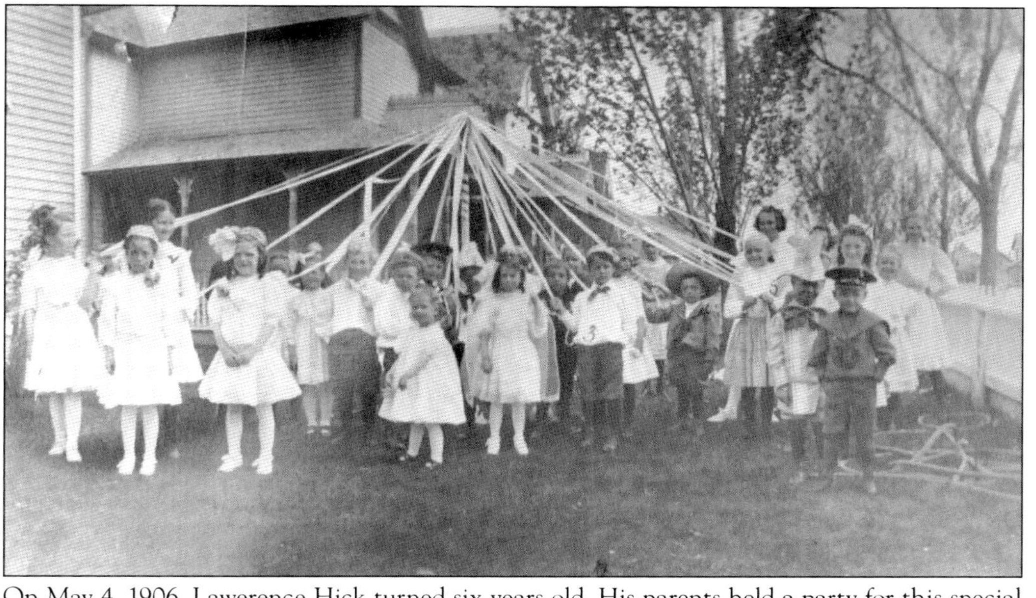

On May 4, 1906, Lawerence Hick turned six years old. His parents held a party for this special occasion. The Maypole Dance was very popular with children during this time; the little ones pictured here taking part in the dance include Doris Singleton (Pittser), Vera McCartney, Lawrence Hick, Chester Castle, Edith Castle Parker, Elsie Ault, and Eleanor Kurz Adams.

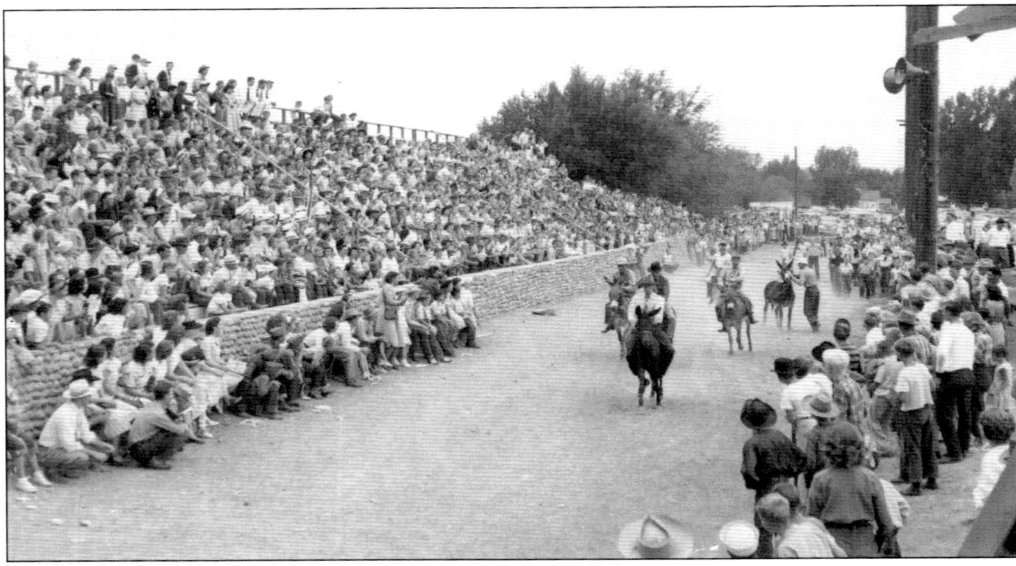

The early settlers of the Uncompahgre Valley enjoyed a good time, fellowship, and an occasional friendly competition. Here the Delta Jaycees sponsor burro races at the Hotchkiss Fairgrounds. The crowds have filled the stands, and much to their enjoyment, some of the riders are having a hard time with their mounts.

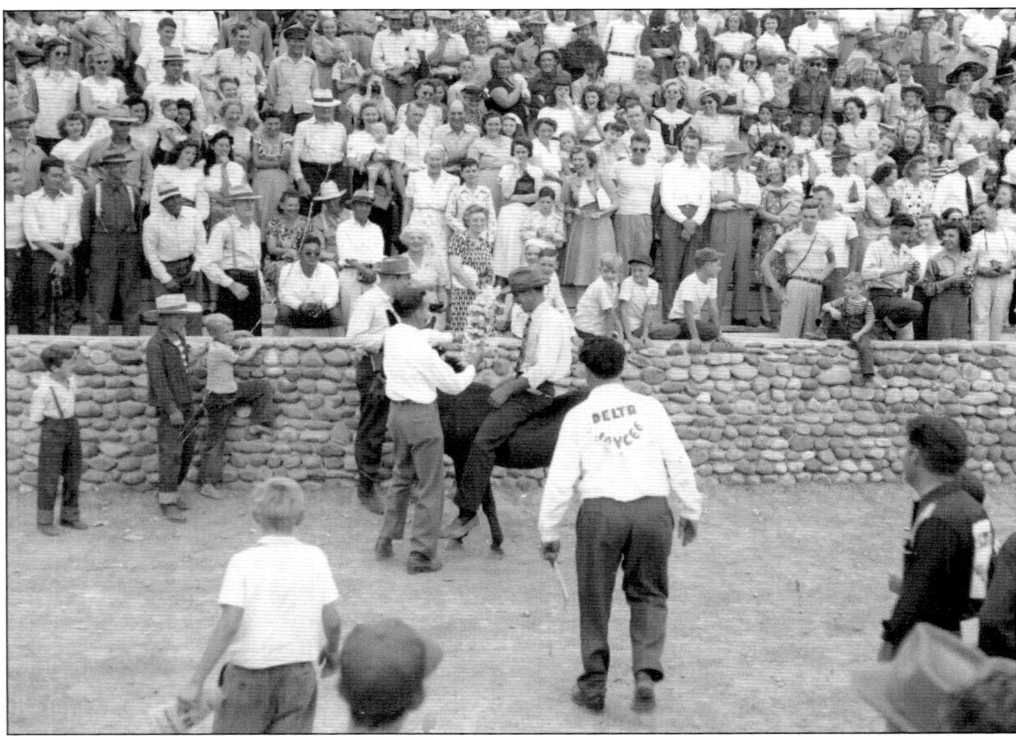

As the crowd looks on in 1909 at the winner of the Jaycees burro race, the winner is given a ring of flowers. As seen here, the riders rode the animals bareback. Roy E. Dickson is the hat-wearing boy on the track to the left of the burro.

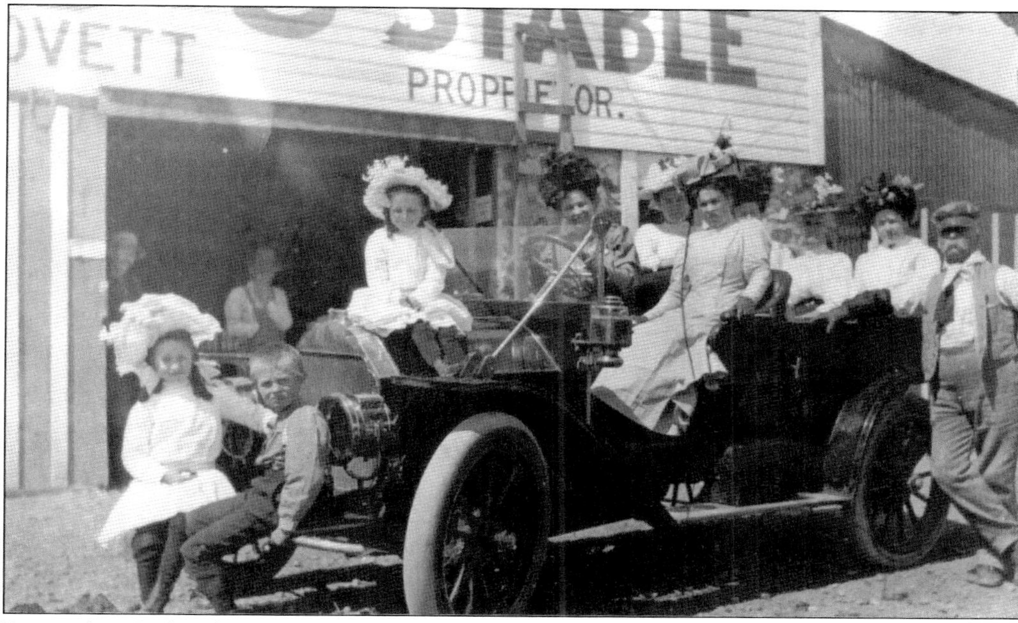

Pictured in Cedaredge in front of Sam Lovett's Livery Stable with their shiny new iron horse in 1910 is a group of well-dressed local women and children. From left to right are Lucille Bolton, Lester Holland, Edna Bolton, Mrs. L. C. Bolton, Ruby Hart (McMillian), Mrs. John Conner, Edith Van Aken, Edna Seay, and livery owner Sam Lovett.

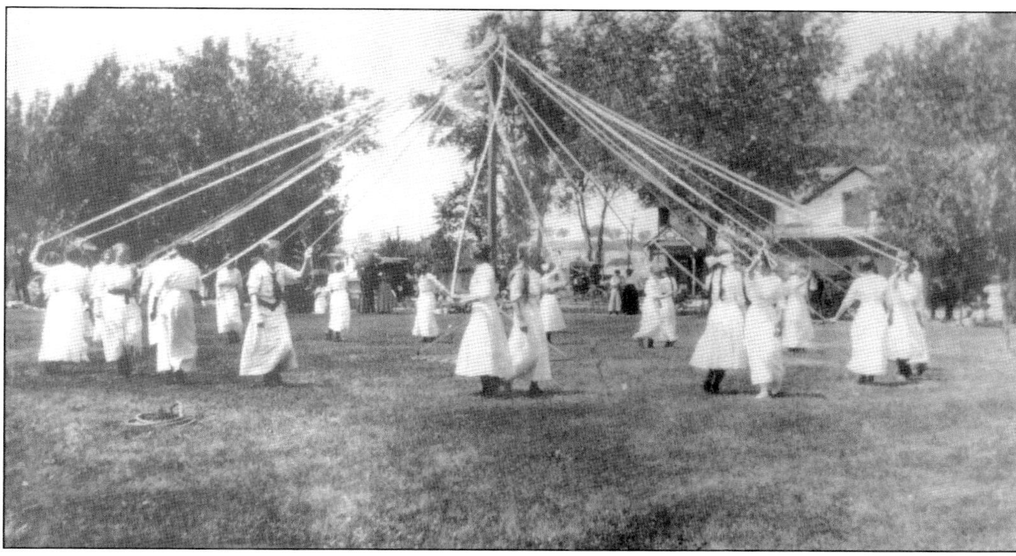

Each year, the high school girls participated in a number of dances, including the Highland Fling and the Maypole Dance. In this 1916 image, physical education teacher Grace Cummings directs the girls in a dance on the courthouse lawn. Note that some of the women in the audience are using parasols to shield them against the sun. The Frank Sanders home stands in the background.

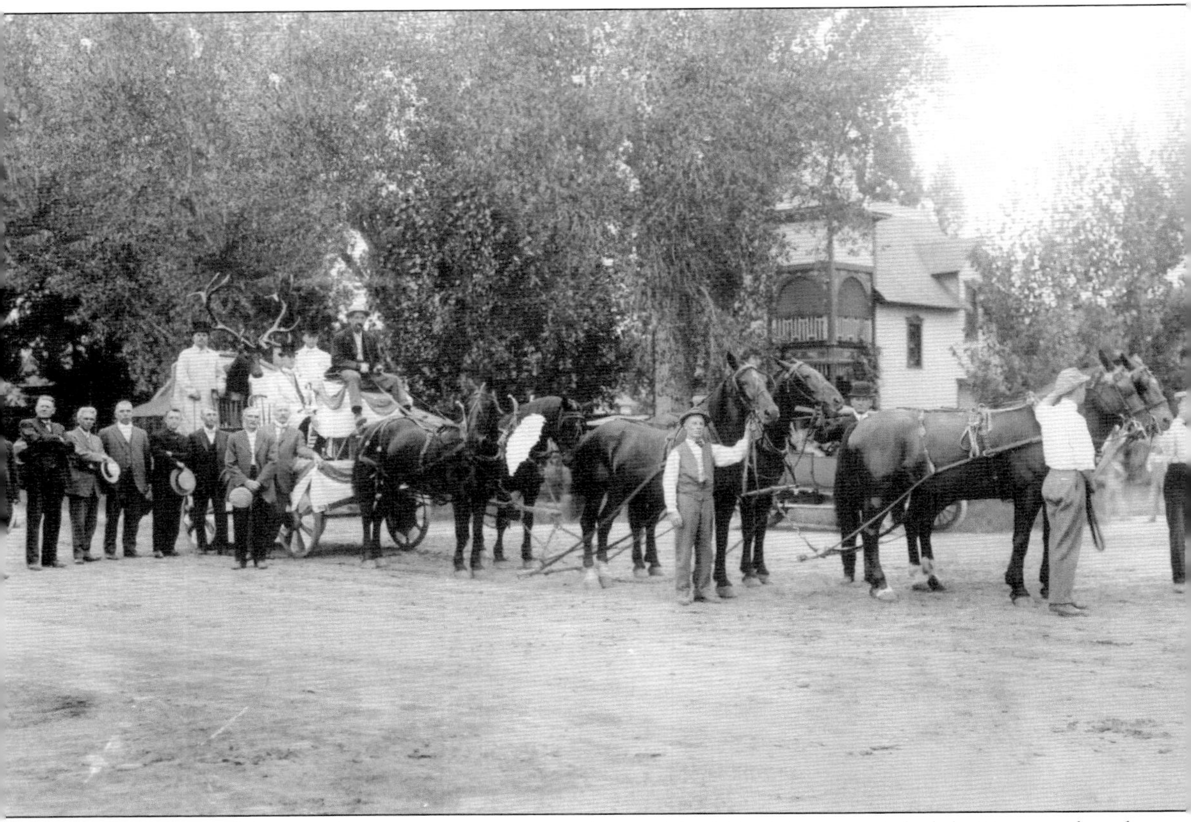

Delta's local Benevolent and Protective Order of Elks (BPOE) is a social club. Deceased and otherwise absent lodge members are recalled each evening at 11:00 p.m. when the lodge esquire intones, "It is the Hour of Recollection." The exalted ruler or a member designated by him gives the 11:00 p.m. toast. The Delta Lodge No. 1235 is shown here in 1914 with a carriage adorned by their prize elkhead, reportedly won by the lodge for the best story. Lodge members accompany their float, which is pulled by two teams of horses. The first team on the right is held by John Vanderpool; Mike Ween holds the second team.

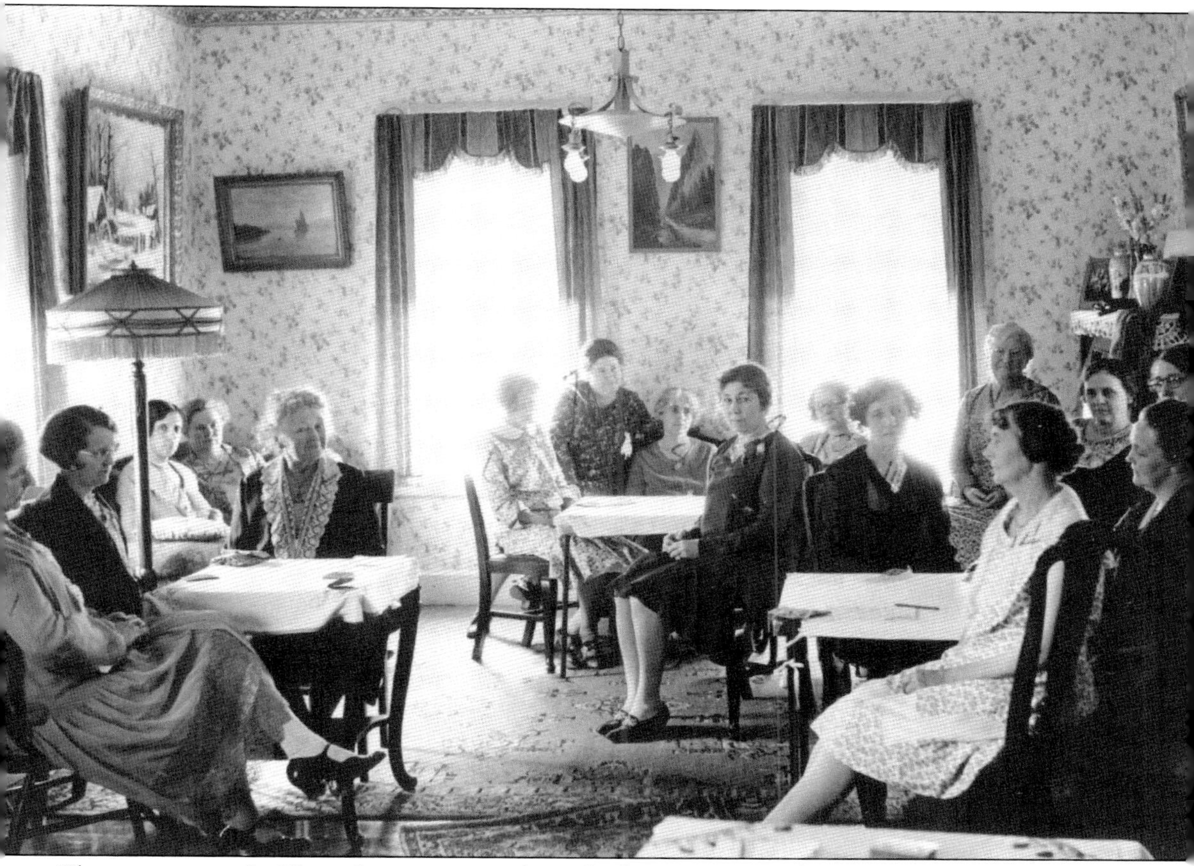

These women at the Himes home are attending a bridge party, a popular social gathering among friends in the early 20th century. Pictured from left to right are Mrs. Ernest Englehardt, Mrs. Lee Bast, Mrs. Will Marshall, Mrs. Avon Remington, Mrs. Robert S. Kelso, Mrs. Travis, Mrs. Snyder, Mrs. W. A. Day, Mrs. C. R. Hollems, Mrs. K. C. O'Dell, Winnie Darling (sister of R. S. Himes), Mrs. R. B. Wilson, an unidentified woman, Mrs. W. D. Himes, Mrs. O. B. Whipple, and Mrs. R. E. Piner.

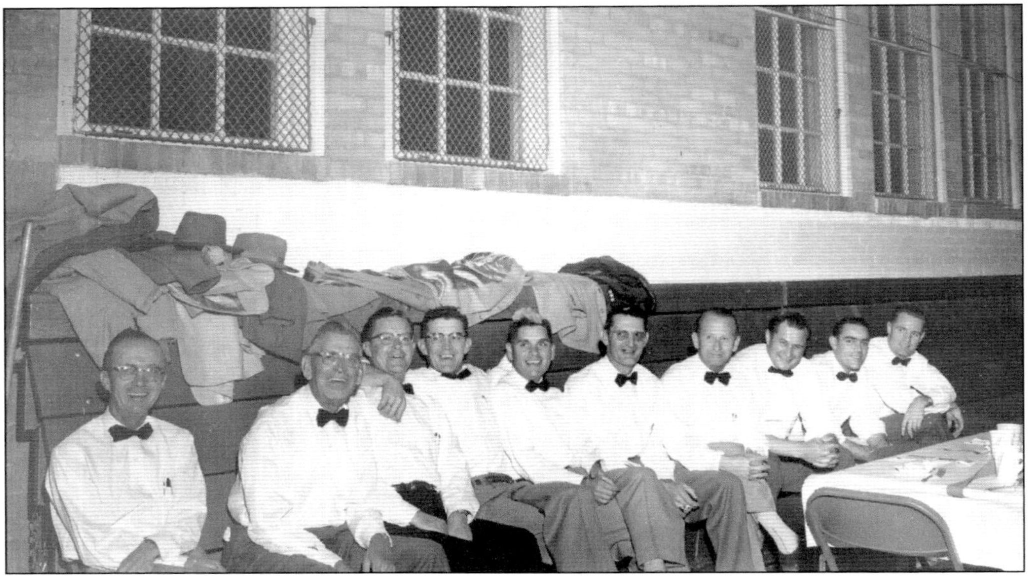

Here on November 17, 1954, the Paonia 4-H Dinner is held with several Delta County Community leaders present. Pictured from left to right are Mr. Hebrew, Mr. Hamman, Mr. Averette, Mr. Peterson, Mr. McKnight, Mr. Renfrow, Mr. McKnight, Mr. Roberts, Mr. Willie, and Mr. Peters. Many of these men were very active in Delta County communities and are counted among the founding fathers of the county's cities and towns. In the present day, you can still find their descendants active in leadership positions all over Delta County.

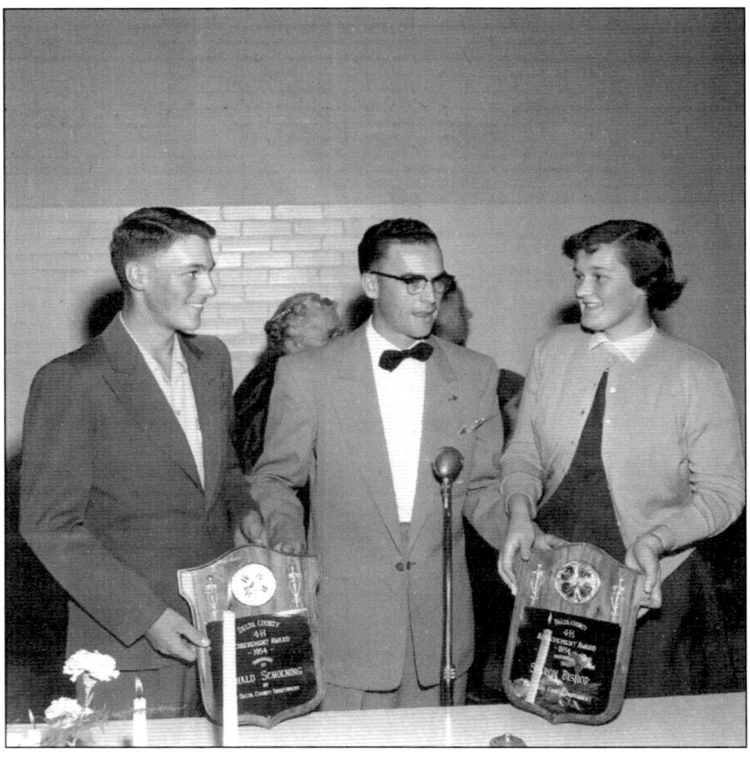

Agricultural roots and pride have carried down through the succeeding generations of the Uncompahgre Valley. In 1954, the *Delta County Independent* newspaper presented 4-H awards to young Mr. Schoening and Miss Bishop, budding agriculturalists, at a local event.

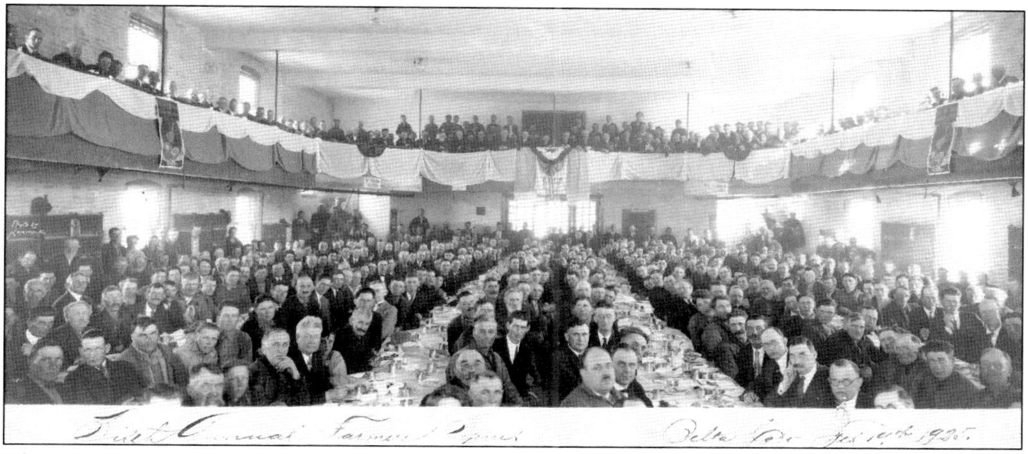

The sixth-annual celebration of the Farmers Spree was held on February 19, 1925. This celebration was held in the Delta Armory Building on Grand Avenue. This was a formal sit-down dinner, complete with a dinner jacket, for several hundred farmers. They used metal silver-plated cups and silverware. Note that no women are present in this photograph.

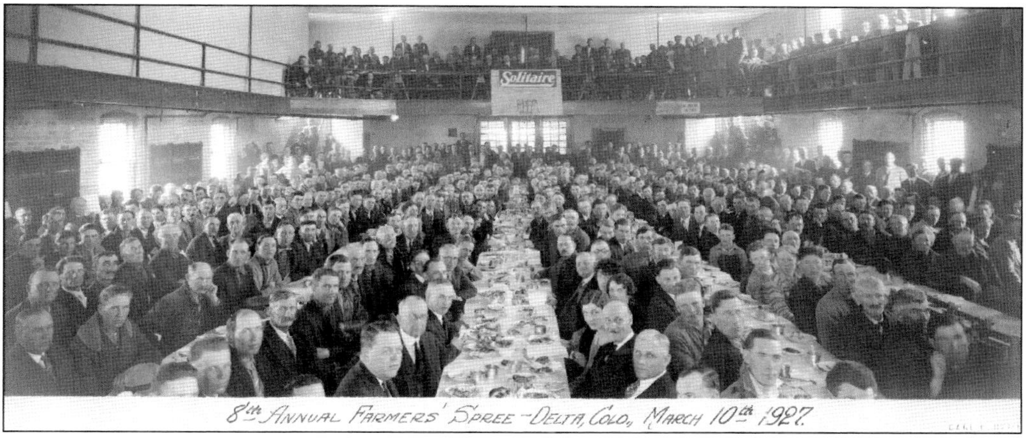

On March 10, 1927, at the eighth-annual Farmers Spree, it was business or celebration as usual, complete with a written program. The meal included a main course complete with rolls and butter, topped of with some of the valley's famous fruit served in a pie. At this celebration, there are three women pictured in the middle row toward the front.

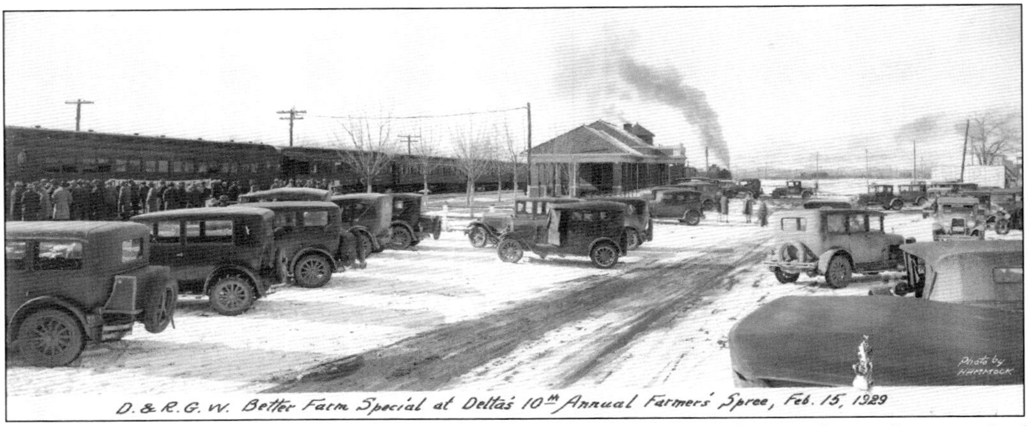

This wintry scene at the Delta Station for the Rio Grande Railroad West shows the arrival of some of the participants in Delta's 10th-annual Farmers Spree held on February 15, 1929. The celebration drew a big crowd of local farmers and ranchers together to share their stories and talk about plans for the coming year. The event would later be known as the Farmer and Ranchers Luncheon, and is still celebrated annually during Deltarado Days in the summer.

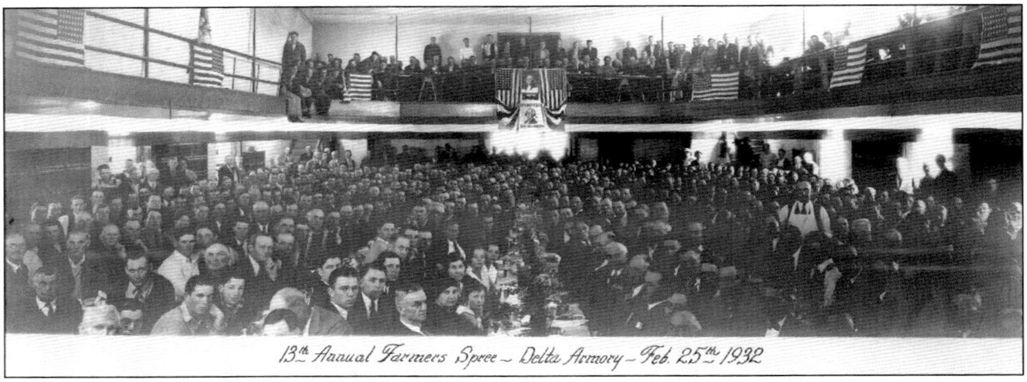

The 13th-annual celebration of the Farmers Spree was held on February 25, 1932. This celebration continued the tradition of being held in the Delta Armory Building on Grand Avenue. This year was noted as the 200-year celebration of George Washington's birth; Washington was, of course, a fellow planter. This photograph reveals that at the 1932 spree, a few women and girls were present.

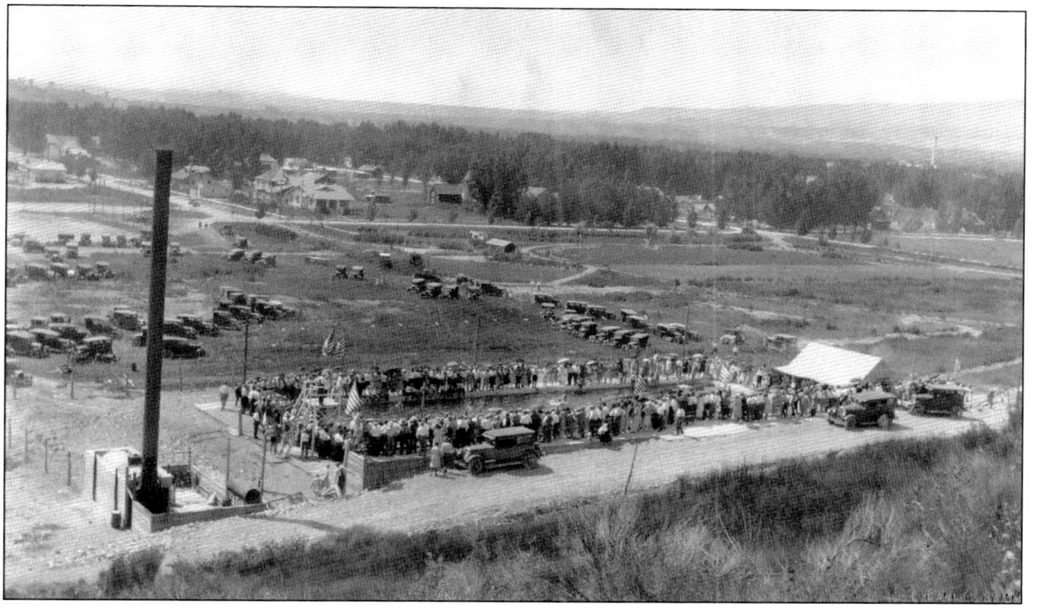

In 1927, Delta enjoyed the fruits of its labors with the opening of a public swimming pool and bathhouses. In his dedication speech, Dr. W. Cleland said, "You have talked of this pool for five years. Here it is. Hop in." The above photograph looks down from Ninth Street Hill. In the background stands the distant white stack of the sugar beet factory. A collection of Model A and Model T Fords dot the landscape. The stack for the furnace that heats the pool is visible in the left foreground. The old high school and middle school buildings have not yet been built, and Cleland Park is only an empty field. In the image below, several of the valley residents who came to the dedication ceremonies as spectators have quickly converted into swimmers. (Photograph by Earl G. Hammock.)

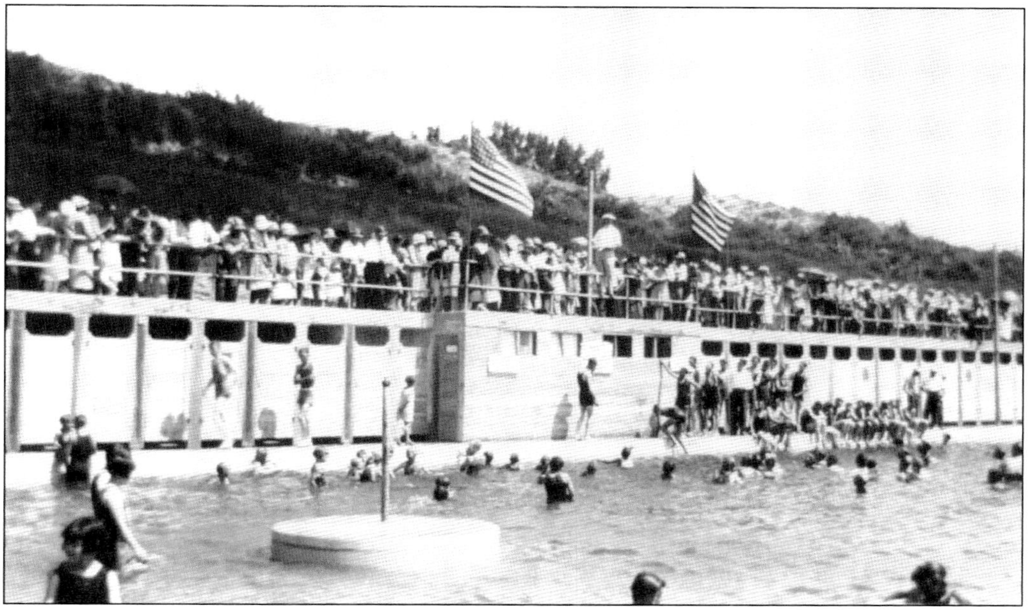

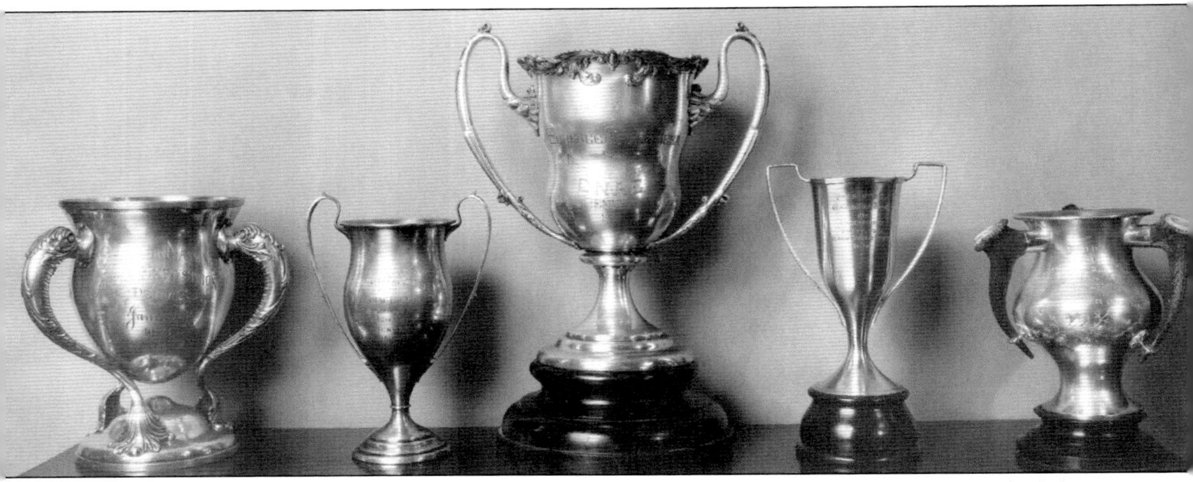

This photograph shows a number of silver cups won in 1910 by valley businesses. At far left is an award from the 1910 Colorado National Apple Exposition (CNAE) in Denver; to its immediate right is a cup presented to Justin E. Miller by the Merrimac Chemical Company, Manufacturers of Lead; third from left is a large cup won by Surface Creek Mesa at the 1910 CNAE; second from right is a cup presented by Olathe State Bank for Sweepstakes Bushel Corn at the Olathe Corn and Potato Show; and at far right is a trophy from the Denver Apple Show.

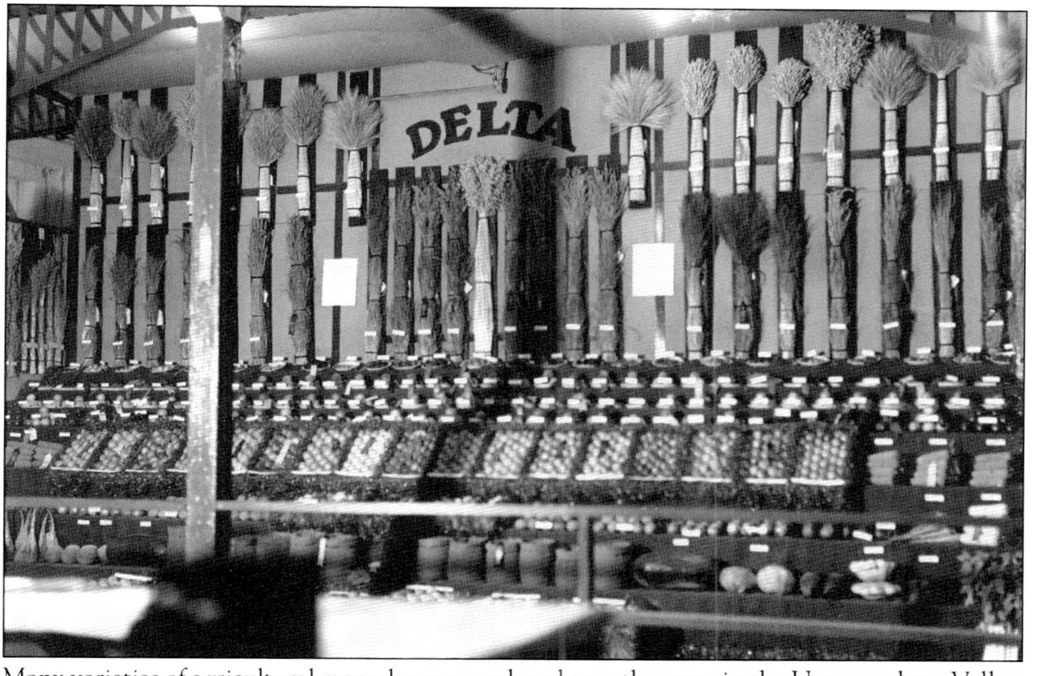

Many varieties of agricultural marvels were produced over the years in the Uncompahgre Valley. Here is an extensive display at the 1935 Colorado State Fair including approximately 48 varieties of grains with the other agricultural crops. Delta's booth design remained the same; their constant theme was the wide variety and bountiful crop yields in Delta.

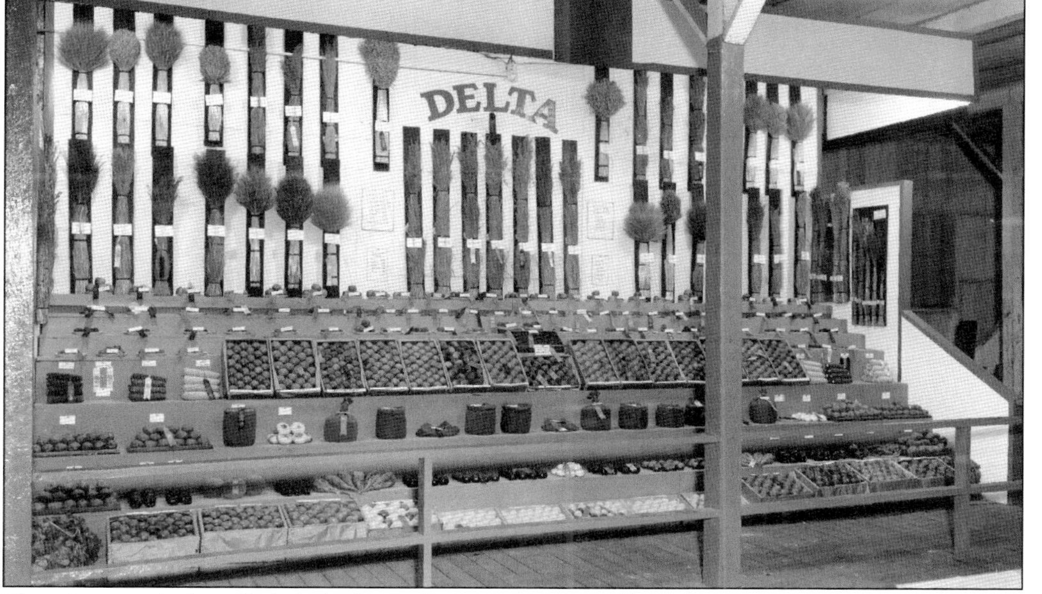

This photograph shows Delta's display at the State Fair in Pueblo, Colorado, held August 24–29, 1936. A beautifully arranged booth brimming with locally grown fruits, vegetables, and several varieties of grains was the star of the show. In 1936, Delta took top honors for its artfully arranged bounty, bringing home over 149 ribbons and placing or winning in almost every category entered.

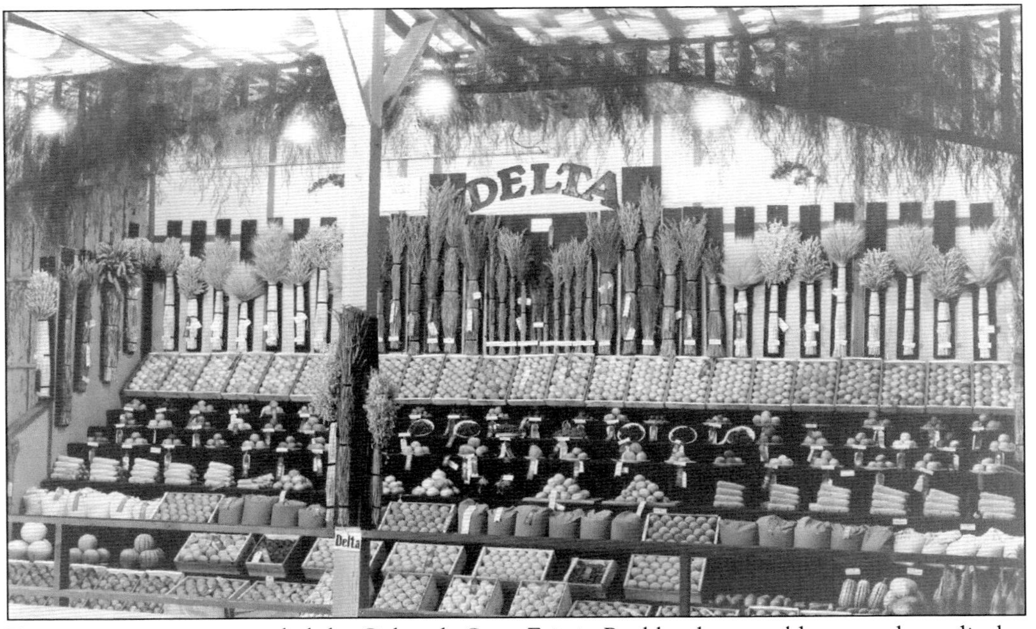

Every year counties attended the Colorado State Fair in Pueblo, they would set up a huge display of all the agriculture grown in Delta that had entered. Year after year, Delta took a large portion of the ribbons for their crops. There are about 79 ribbons displayed the various grains, fruits, and vegetables in this display.

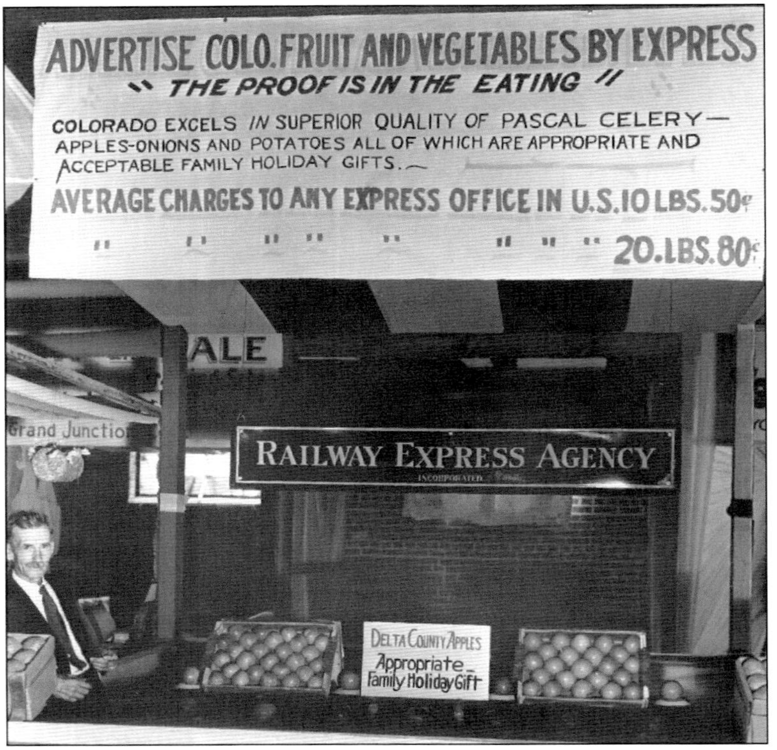

Even local businesses such as the Railway Express Agency got into the market of promoting the valley's highly desirable fruits and vegetables to the rest of the United States. Seen here is a booth promoting local produce as holiday gifts with an average shipping cost of 10 pounds for 50¢.

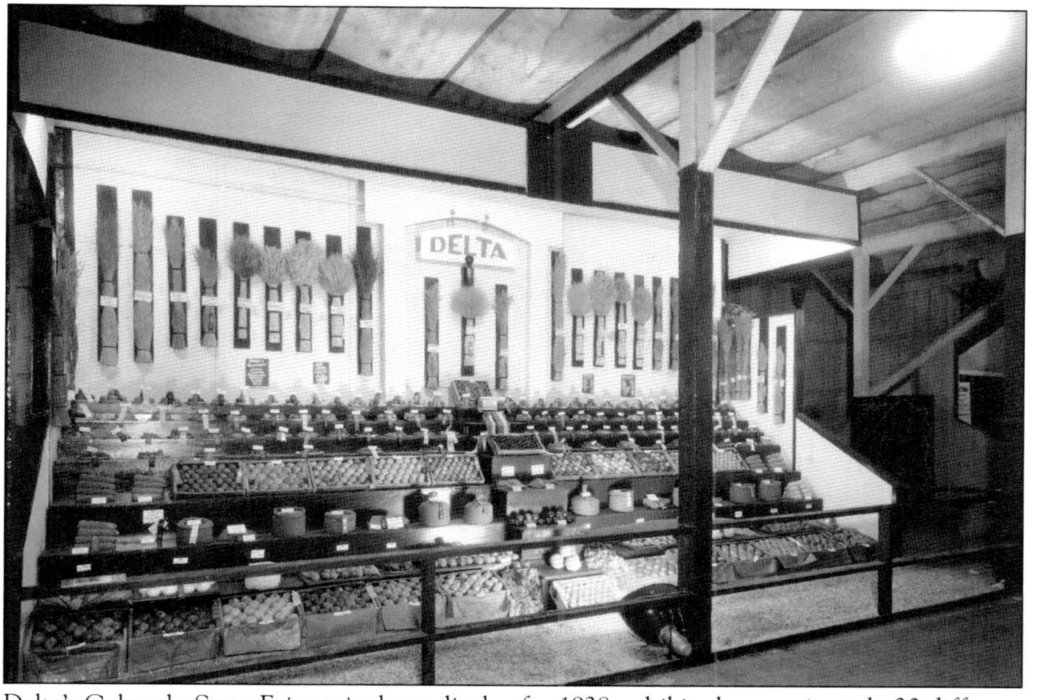

Delta's Colorado State Fair agriculture display for 1938 exhibited approximately 30 different grains and 175 varieties of fruits and vegetables. The coloring, size, and juiciness of Delta County's produce were not matched by that of any other county in the state.

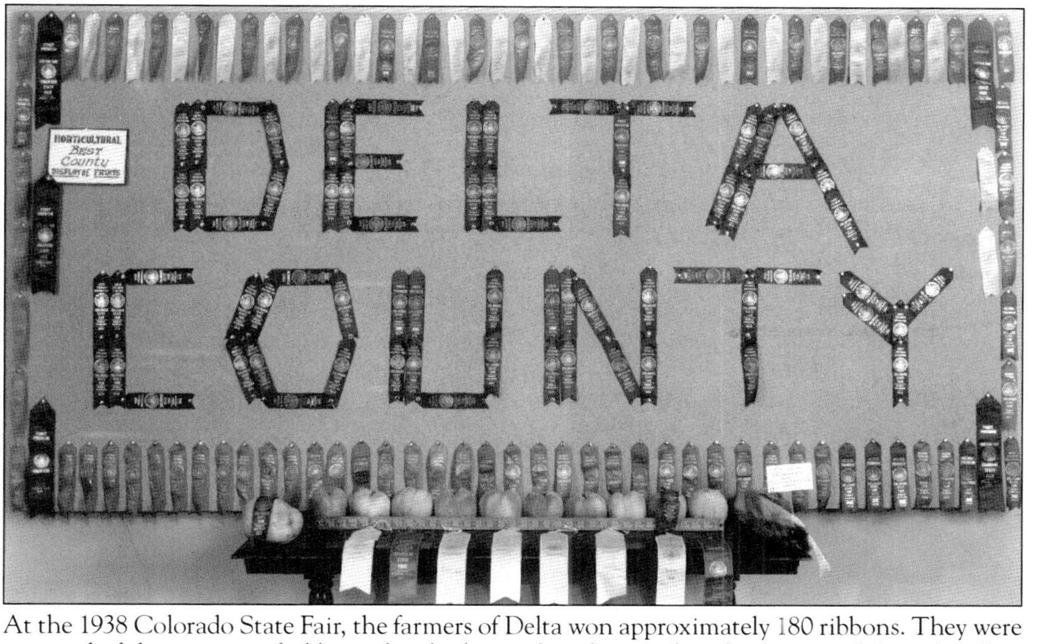

At the 1938 Colorado State Fair, the farmers of Delta won approximately 180 ribbons. They were so proud of the amount of ribbons they had won that they made a display out of them for all to see. Champion produce displayed here included prize fruit, a potato, and an ear of corn. The tiny sign on the corn at lower right reads, "Grown by Ira Markley with sulfur fertilizer N. Delta."

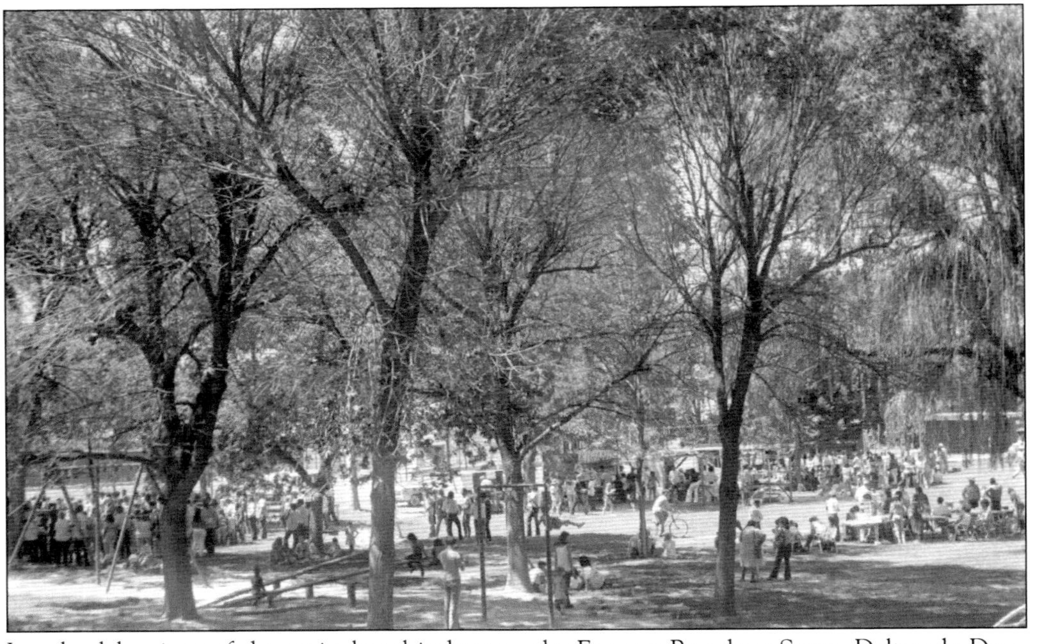

Local celebrations of the agricultural industry—the Farmers Ranchers Spree, Deltarado Days, Cherry Days, the Apples Festival—have remained popular in the valley. Communities come together to celebrate their heritage and socialize.

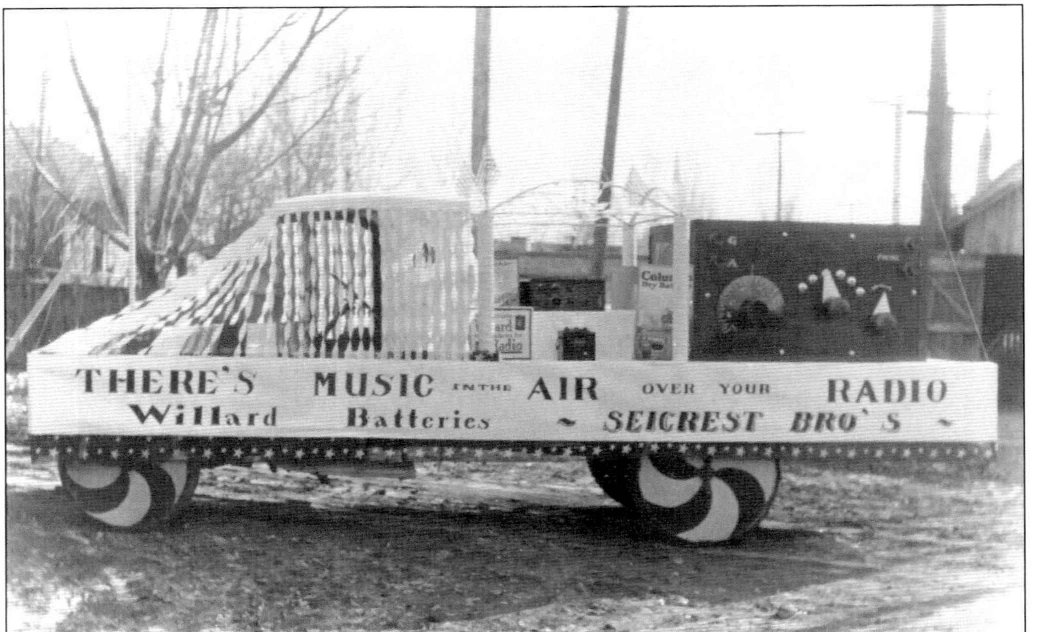

In the 1920s, radio was new to the valley. The Seicrest brothers built a float advertising Willard batteries and promoting the novel medium with a mock, oversized receiver (with dials) on a flatbed truck decorated with streamers. Floyd Hinton sat inside the "radio" playing phonograph music. The float won first prize in the parade.

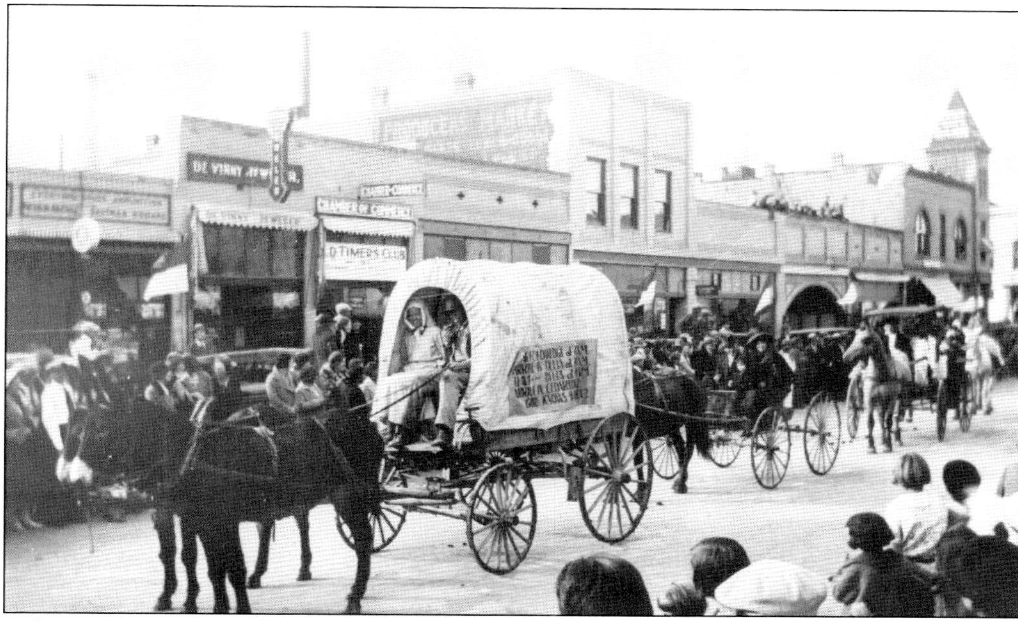

Delta was formed on February 11, 1883. In 1933, the community had its 50-year celebration. There were several parade floats for the commemorative occasion. Several were horse-drawn wagons and carriages. This covered wagon pulled by mules has a banner on the side that reads: "LEAVE Cedaredge at 2 AM; ARRIVE IN DELTA at 11 AM; LEAVE . . . DELTA at 4 PM; ARRIVE Cedaredge: GOD KNOWS WHEN?"

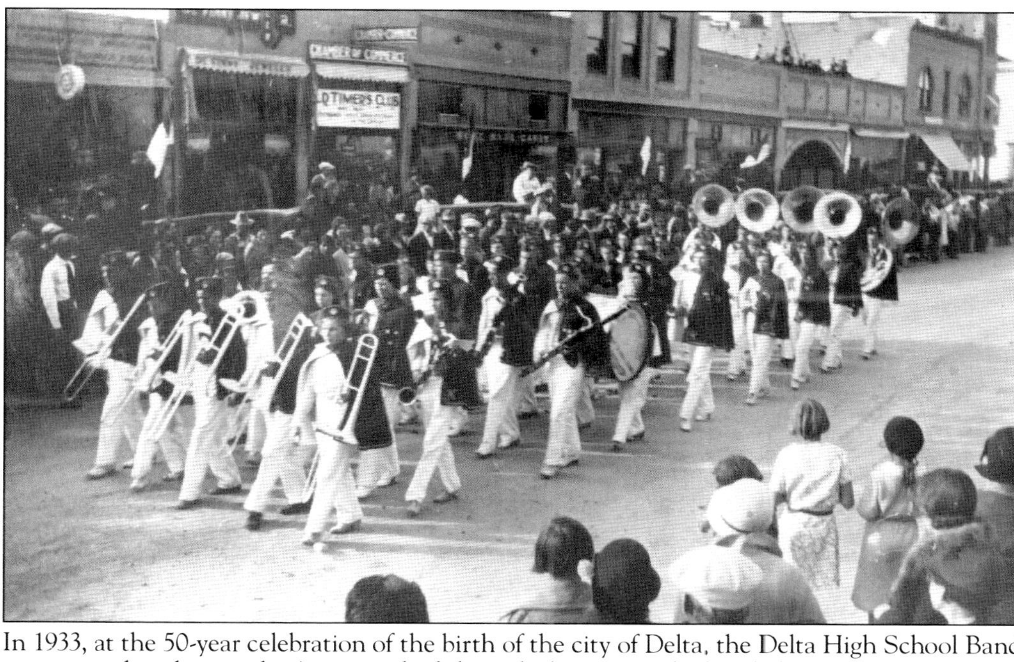

In 1933, at the 50-year celebration of the birth of the city of Delta, the Delta High School Band participated in the parade. As it marched through the streets, the band played a variety of tunes for onlookers.

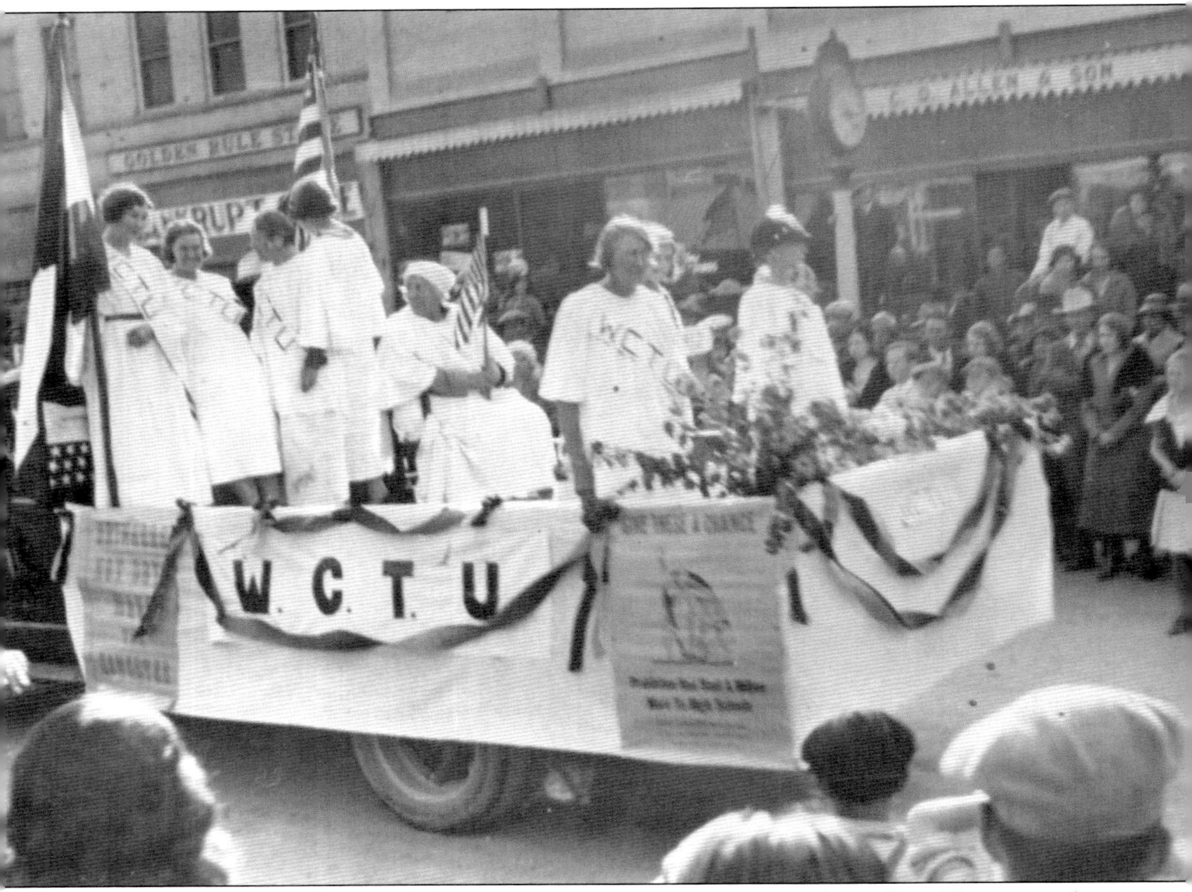

The Women's Christian Temperance Union was ever active in the valley. They were always participating in the various festivals and events, and are shown here in the 1933 50-year celebration parade. The group spearheaded the crusade for Prohibition and were very interested in a number of social reform issues including suffrage, labor, prostitution, public health, sanitation, and international peace. The purpose of the WCTU was to combat the influence of alcohol on families and society. They were inspired by the Greek writer Xenophon, who defined temperance as "moderation in all things healthful; total abstinence from all things harmful."

The 50-year celebration was a time for all the settler families and friends to participate in the celebration in any fashion they saw fit. Local gentlemen dressed in their best suits complete with top hats and walking canes and joined in the parade. Pictured here are, from left to right, A. C. Remington, Albert Newton, and Charles Holtgreen. The men have stopped to pose for a photographer on Main Street, between Third and Fourth Streets.

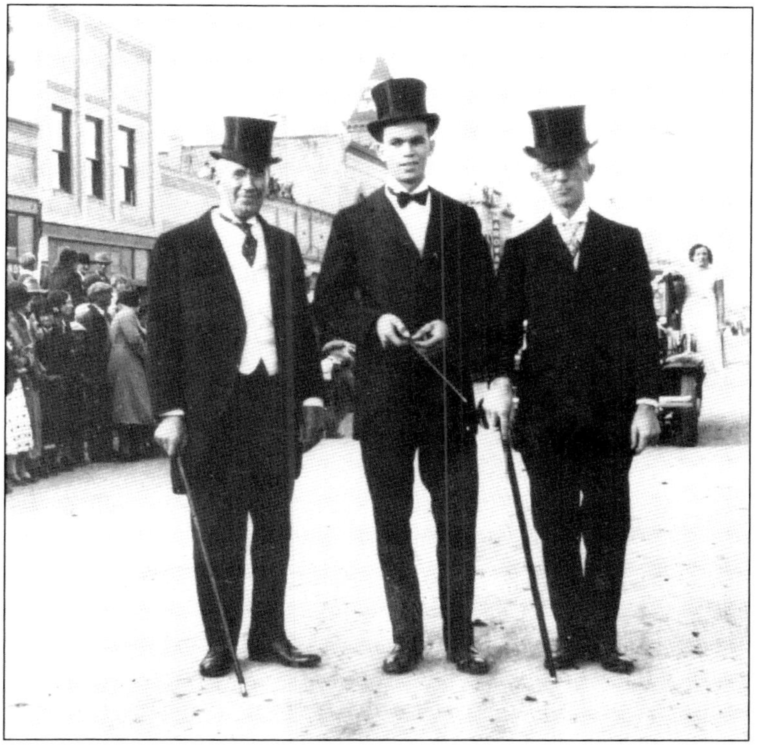

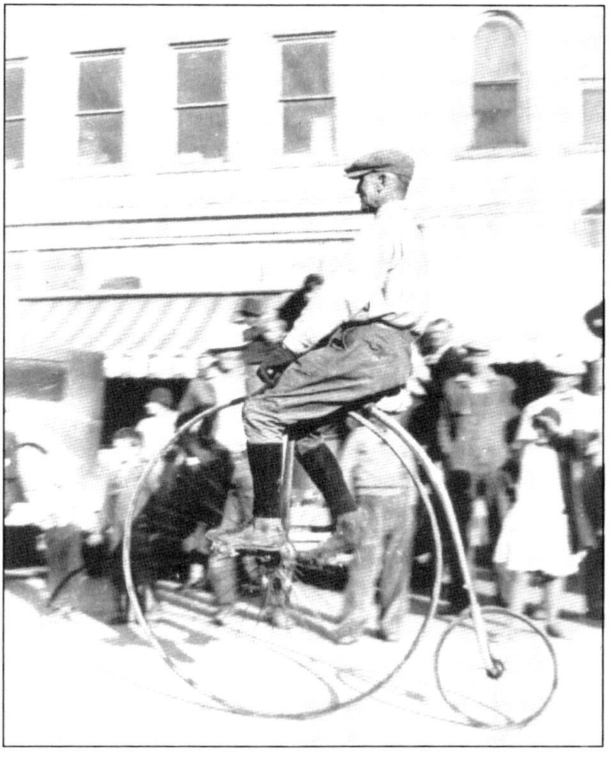

R. B. Wilson rode his "high-wheeler" bicycle during the 50-year celebration parade. The high-wheeler (or bone shaker) bicycle such as the one Wilson rides here had a front wheel from 48 to 52 inches high and a back wheel between 10 to 14 inches high. These bicycles might stand as tall as 66 inches high and were very popular in the late 1800s.

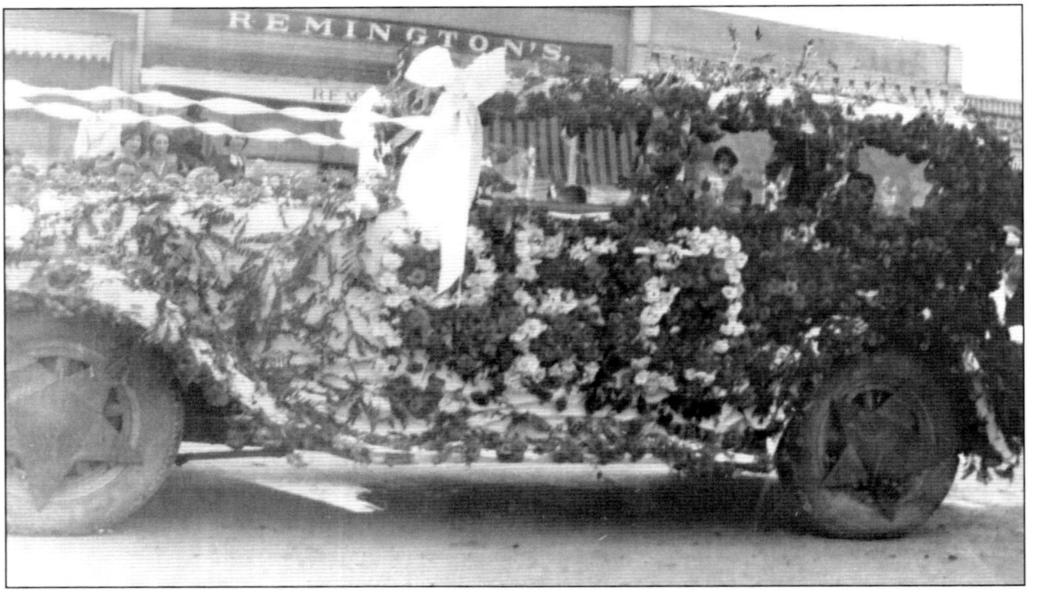

The Philanthropic Educational Organization (PEO) Sisterhood was passionate about its mission: promoting educational opportunities for women. They decorated every square inch of this car with flowers and leaves.

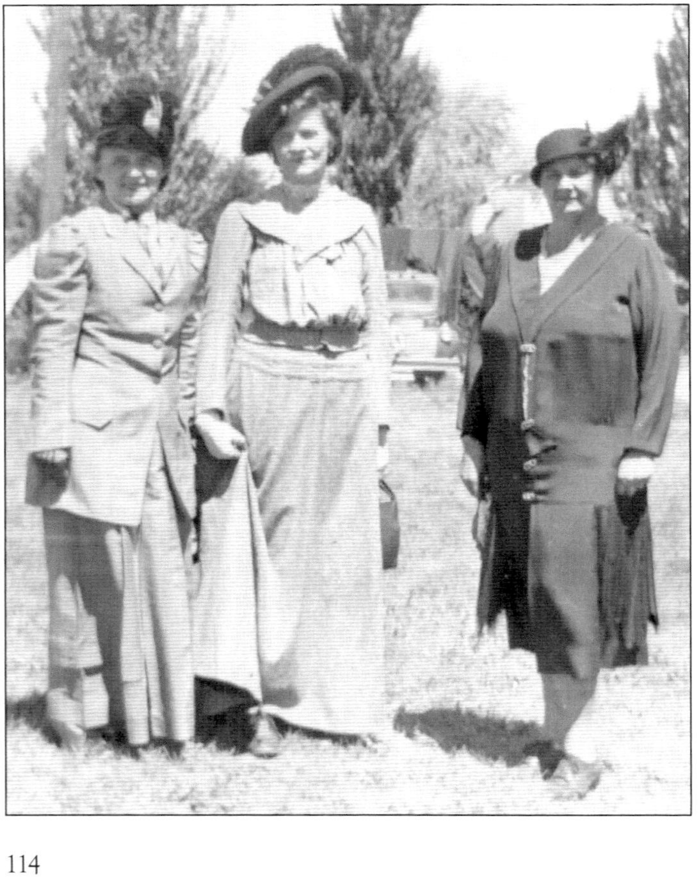

At one Deltarado Days event, Edith Parker (left) wore a period two-piece dress complete with a scarf and thigh-length jacket, complete with a hat. Grace Stewart (center) wore a full-length dress with a high-neck lace collar and a large hat. Ethel Smock (right) was dressed in more current attire; she wore a woman's drop waist banded dress, a V-neck, long sleeves, and a small hat with a dark feather plume.

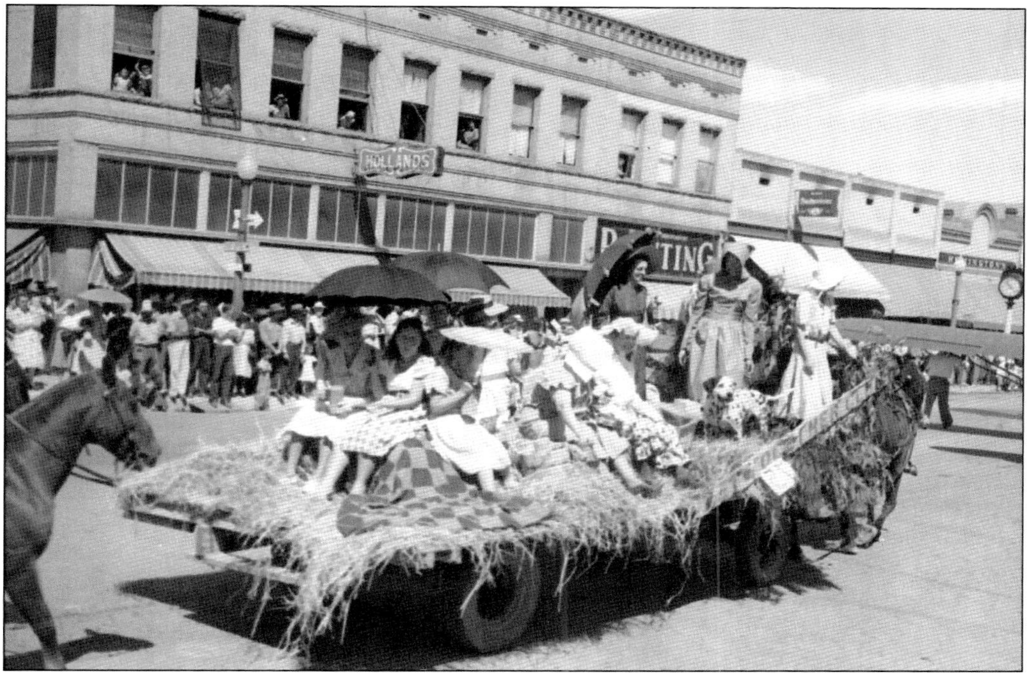

There was nearly always a parade to go along with every community celebration. Shown here on the streets of downtown Delta are women and children riding a float that they had made themselves for the 1948 Deltarado Days.

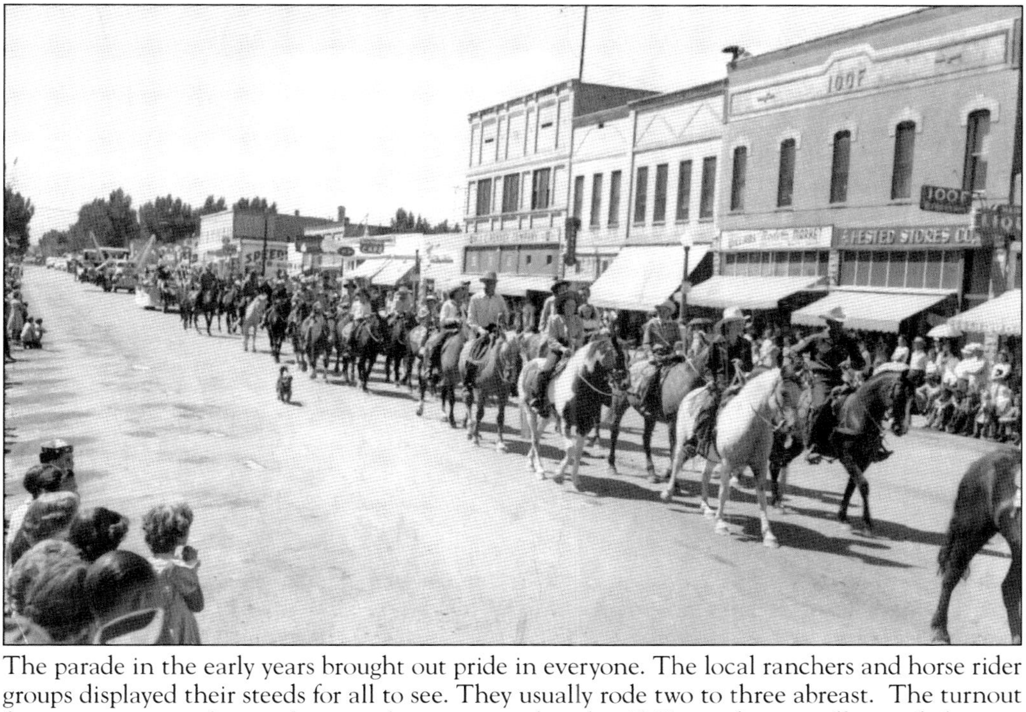

The parade in the early years brought out pride in everyone. The local ranchers and horse rider groups displayed their steeds for all to see. They usually rode two to three abreast. The turnout for spectators was also good; certainly, it appears that this 1948 parade was well attended.

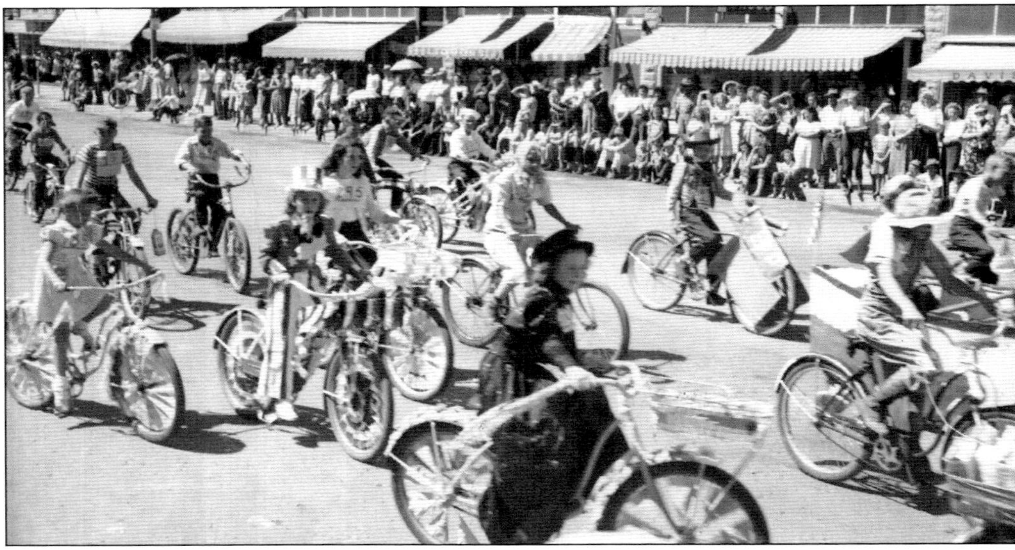

This parade in 1948 included something for everyone as a participant. Here local children entered into a bicycle decorating contest. Some of the children even wore costumes with their entry numbers pinned to their chest. Front middle is a young woman in a frontier dress with bonnet, behind her to the left is a young man dressed as Uncle Sam, and top row to the right is another young man dressed as a cowboy.

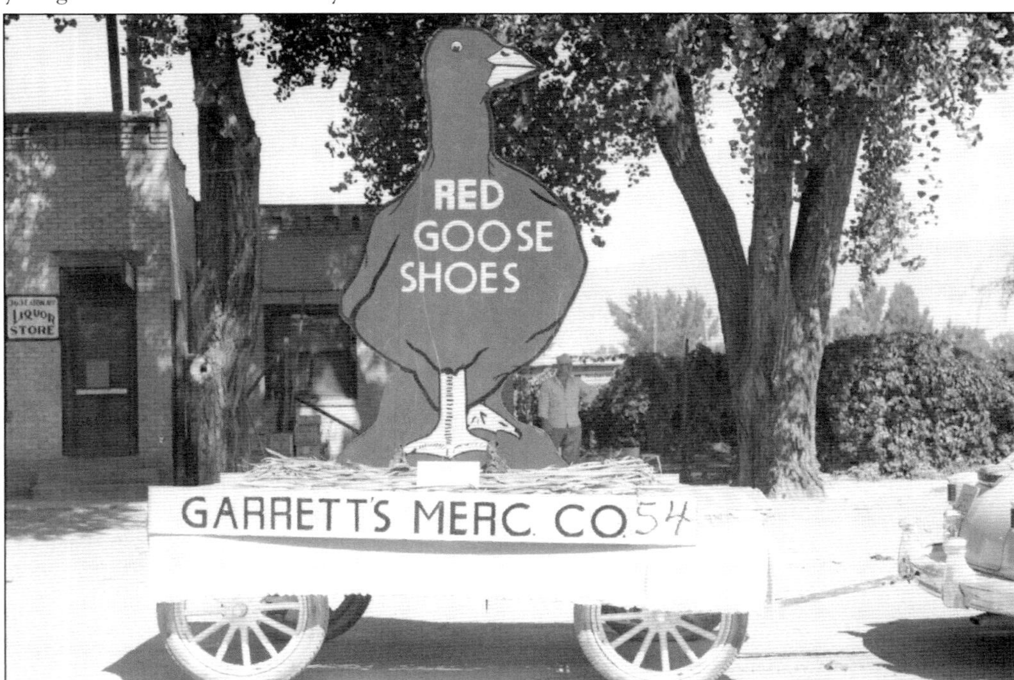

Passing the liquor store on 363 Eaton Avenue in the 1948 parade is a float built by Garrets Mercantile Company. The flatbed trailer is decorated with a large Red Goose Shoes cutout. On the floor of the trailer are stalks used as a "nest" with an old boot on the left and a new boot on the right.

In 1948, Remington's float featured a giant pair of Lee Rider jeans on a flatbed truck. They were held up on all four corners with supports wrapped in colored paper streamers and the Lee Rider promo doll holding them up. In the store window hangs a Deltarado Days poster.

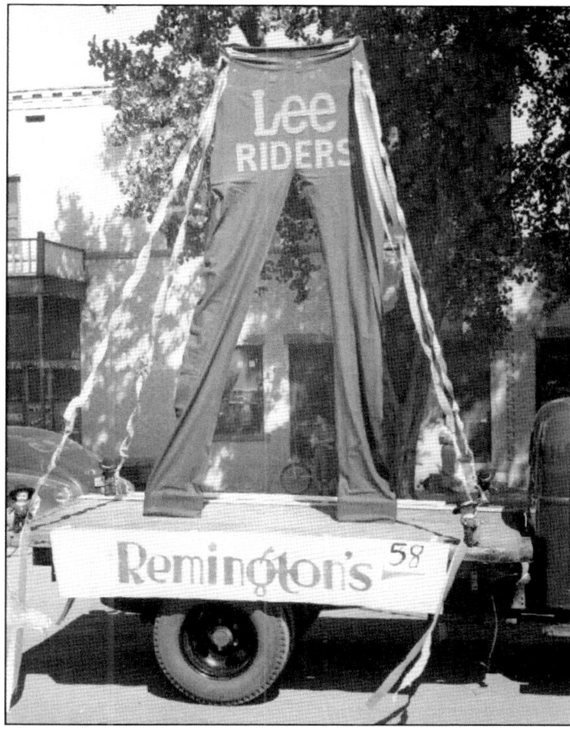

The 4-H was strong in the valley; a number of Delta's young people were members of this agriculturally minded youth organization known by its 4-H Clover symbol (standing for Head, Heart, Hands, and Heart). Here two young 4-H members on a parade float hold signs promoting Home and Church, above a club sign reading "Building Today for a Better Tomorrow."

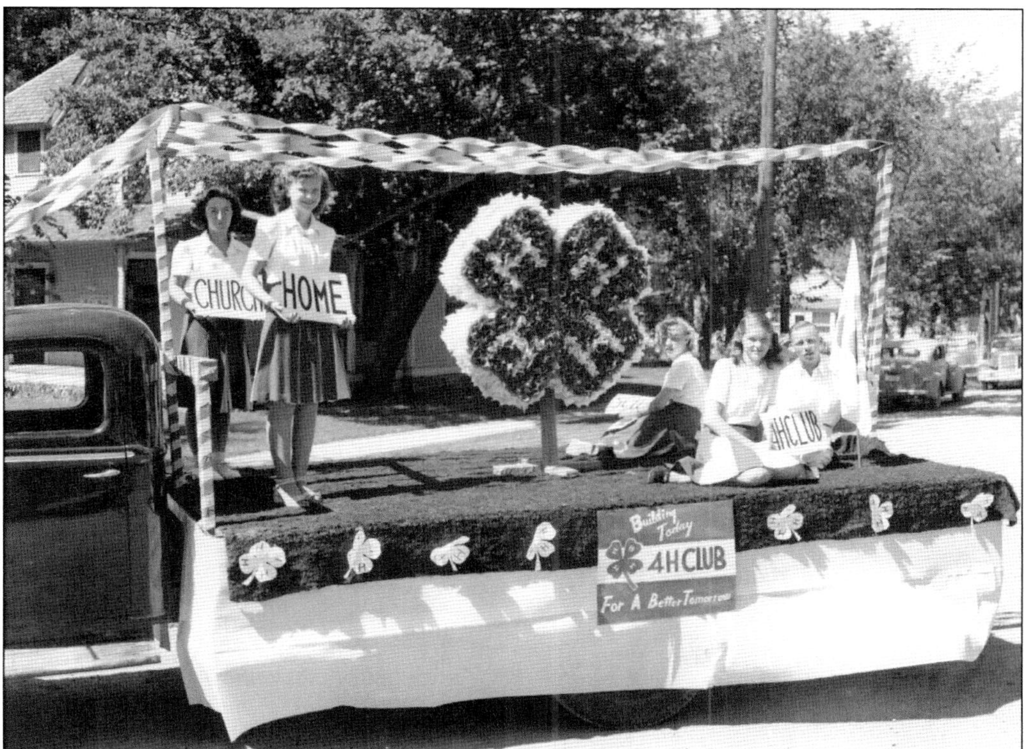

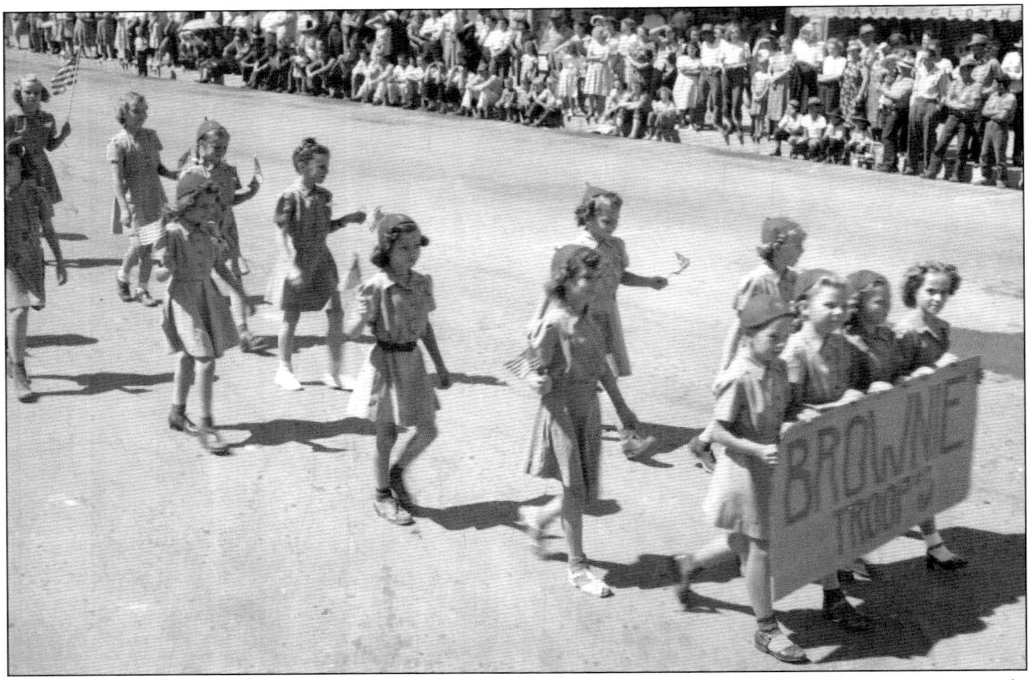

The local Brownie Troop No. 5 participated in the 1948 Deltarado Days parade. Approximately 15 to 20 girls marched the parade route carrying small American flags. Here they are passing Davis Clothing (top right) located on the corner of Main and Fourth Streets.

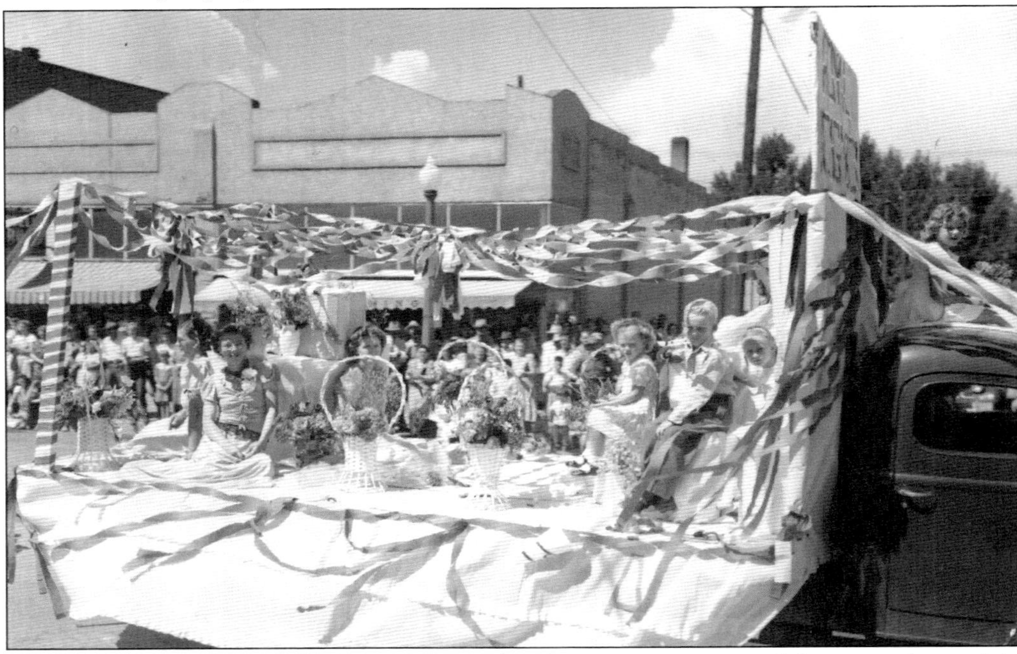

This 1948 Deltarado Days float was decorated with paper streamers and flowers in large white wicker baskets on a flatbed truck. Three women and four local children pictured here as they pass through Main and Fourth Streets.

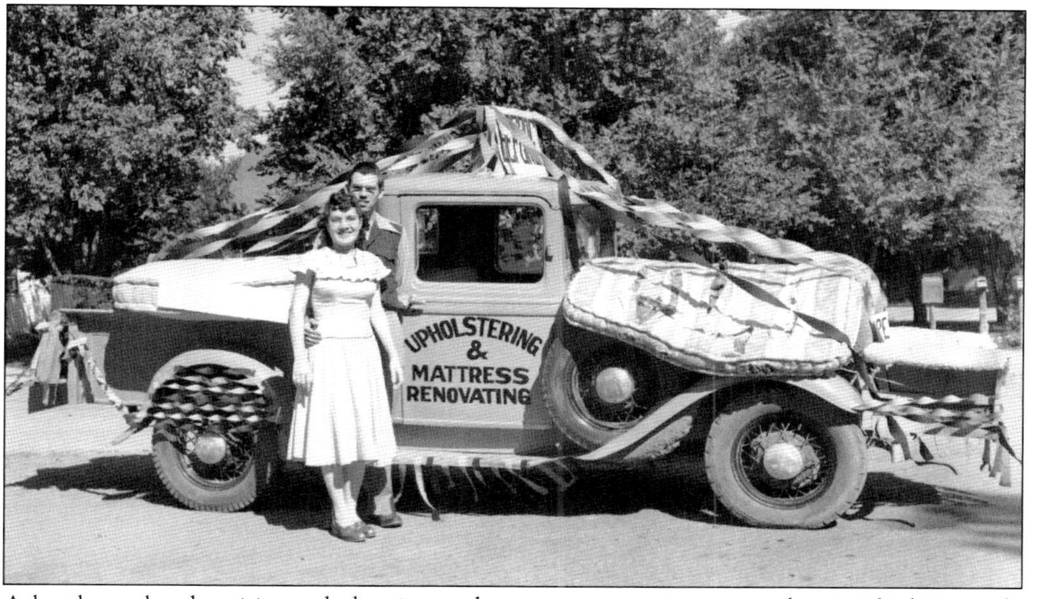

A local couple advertising upholstering and mattress renovations poses here with their truck, which is decorated with an old mattress and a chair. Paper streamers flow from front to back. Located across the bed of the pickup truck is a new innerspring mattress; by 1948 the innerspring mattress was becoming popular with postwar consumers.

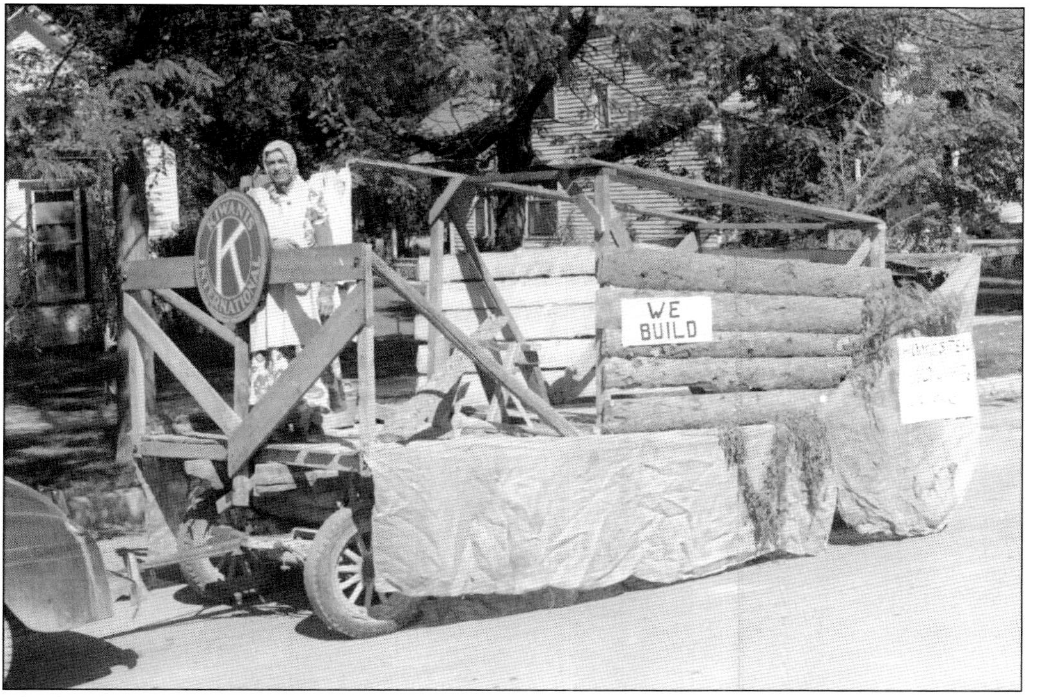

The local Kiwanis International group took part in the 1948 Deltarado Days parade. One of its male members dressed as a woman on a trailer decorated with a partially built structure and a sign reading, "We Build."

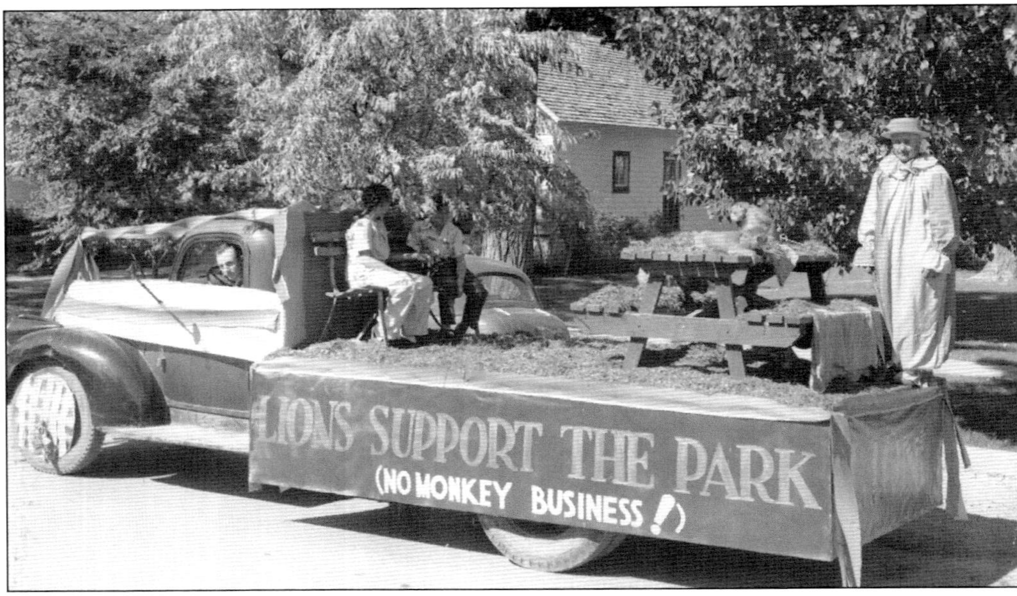

The local Lions Club built a float for the 1948 Deltarado Days parade that came complete with a monkey. As noted on their banner, they were supporters of a new local park, and their flatbed truck included a picnic bench decorated with grass, a monkey tender in a clown suit, and a boy and girl nearing courting age sitting on a park bench, above a banner reading, "No Monkey Business!"

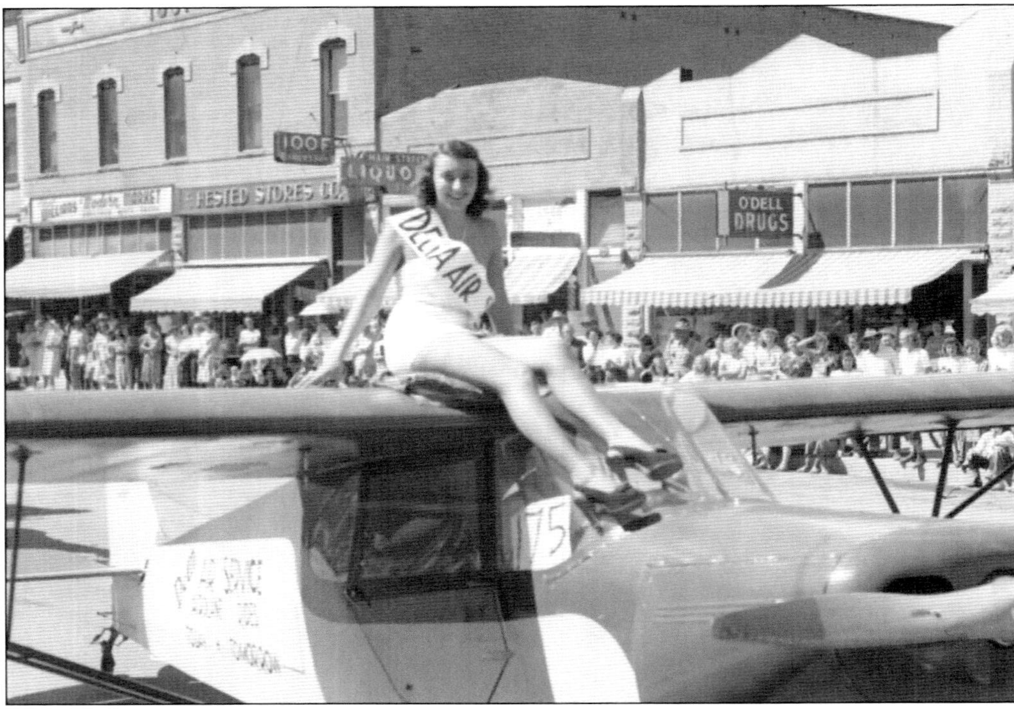

The Delta Air Service pulled one of the light weight planes as a float in the 1948 parade, adorned with a lovely local woman wearing a sash reading, "Delta Air." The sign on the plane read, "Delta's Air Service, Airplane Rides Today and Tomorrow."

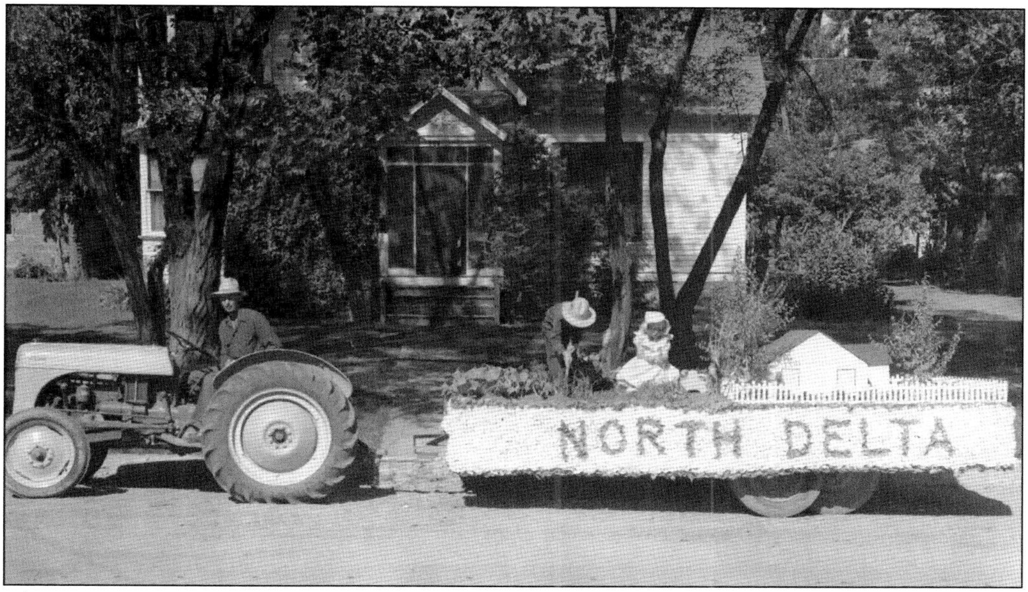

The entire county and valley participated in the 1948 Deltarado Days. A farmer from North Delta built a float pulled by his Ford tractor. Displayed is a mini-farm complete with a white picket fence, trees, and a vine ground crop. The boy is hoeing the crops and the young girl is dressed in an early pioneer costume complete with a bonnet.

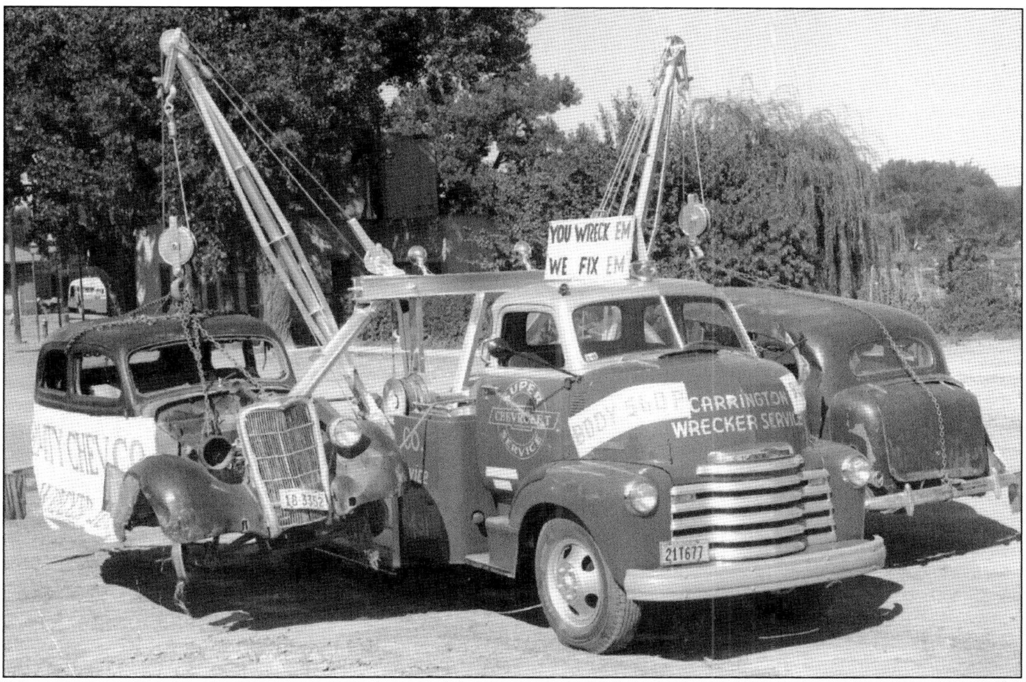

Scott Carrington owned a Chevrolet dealership on Main Street. For the 1948 parade his entry was an impressive monster tow truck. It featured two swing arm tow hitches that made the truck capable of carrying two full vehicles at a time. Carrington's slogan, "You Wreck Em We Fix Em," reflects the fact that, along with the wrecker service, he also owned a body shop.

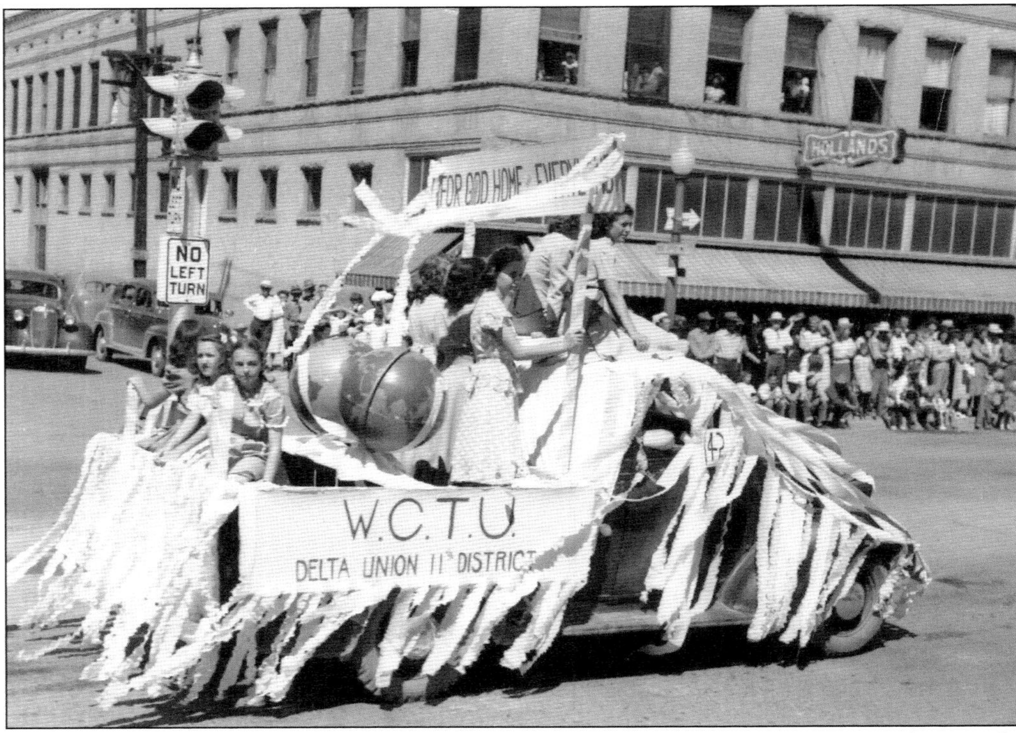

Entry 42 in the 1948 parade was entered by the WCTU Delta Union 11th District. This was the Women's Christian Temperance Union Club. Their sign reads "'For God, Home and Every Land." The white ribbons symbolize purity, the globes symbolize the group's commitment to peaceful coexistence between nations. The WCTU's watchwords were "Agitate—Educate—Legislate." WCTU members chose total abstinence from all alcohol and tobacco as their lifestyle.

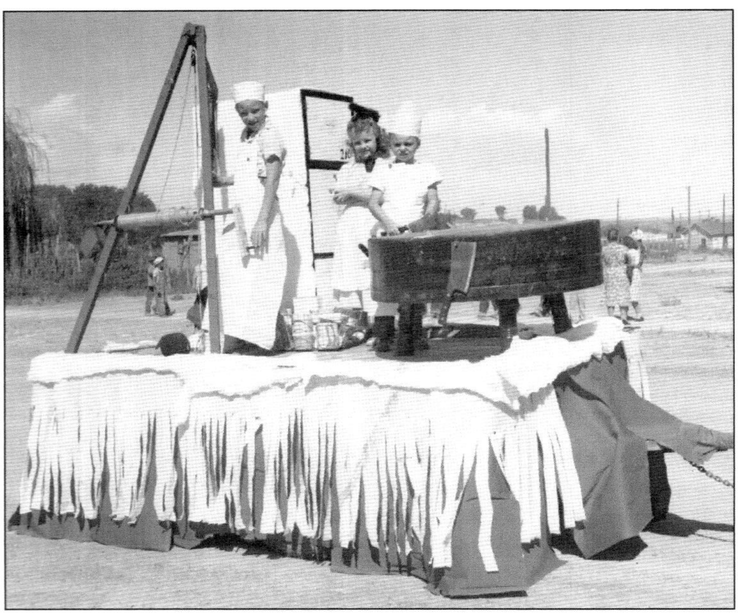

Local children man this float for a butcher's store in the 1948 parade. One young man stands behind a chopping block, holding a small (but real) meat cleaver; behind him stands another boy manning a frame wench, used for holding up large slabs of meat.

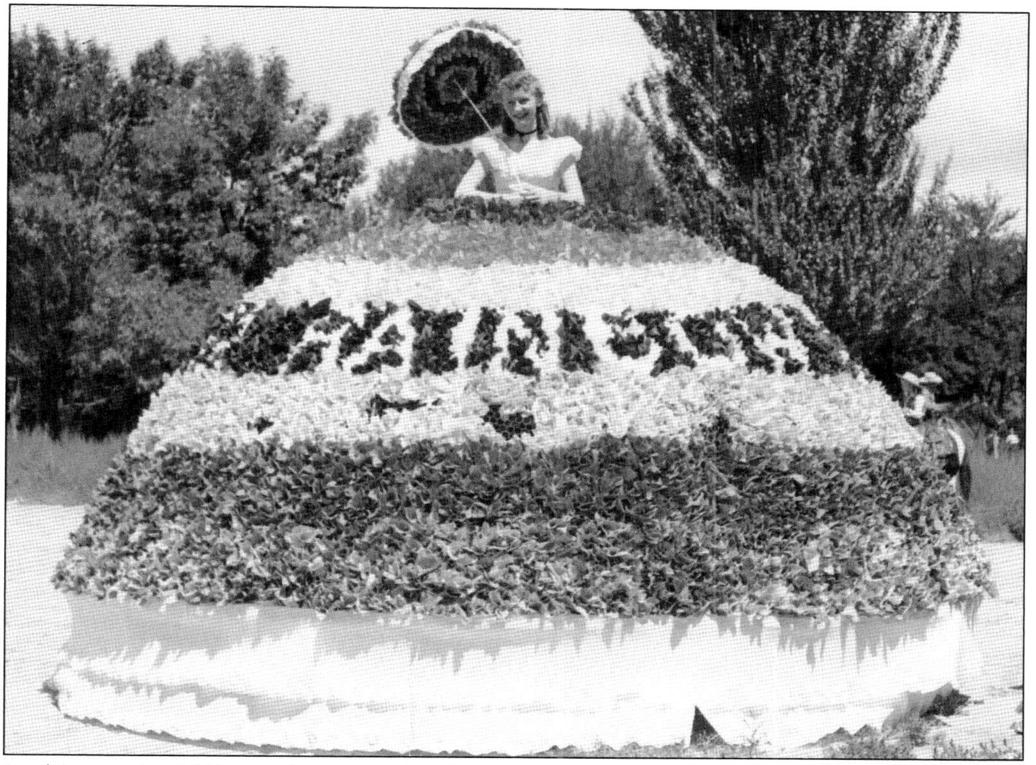

In this creative 1948 parade entry, a lovely young woman stands in the middle of her massive Annabelle dress. The dress was made of thousands of paper flowers put in place to resemble a hoop skirt. The outfit was complete with a color-coordinated matching umbrella.

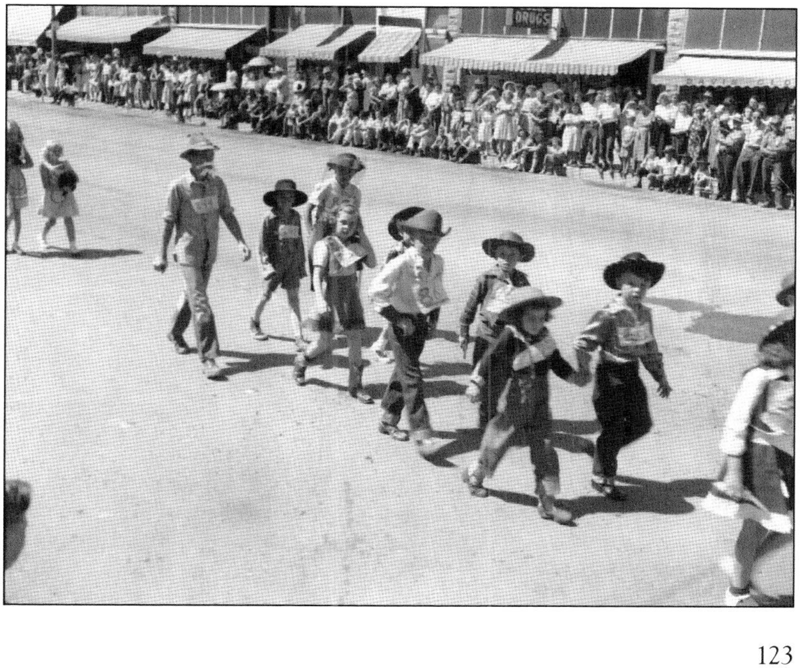

In the 1948 parade, this group of young children in cowboy and cowgirl costumes pay homage to the area's Western heritage. (Behind them are two little girls not in costume but carrying puppies.)

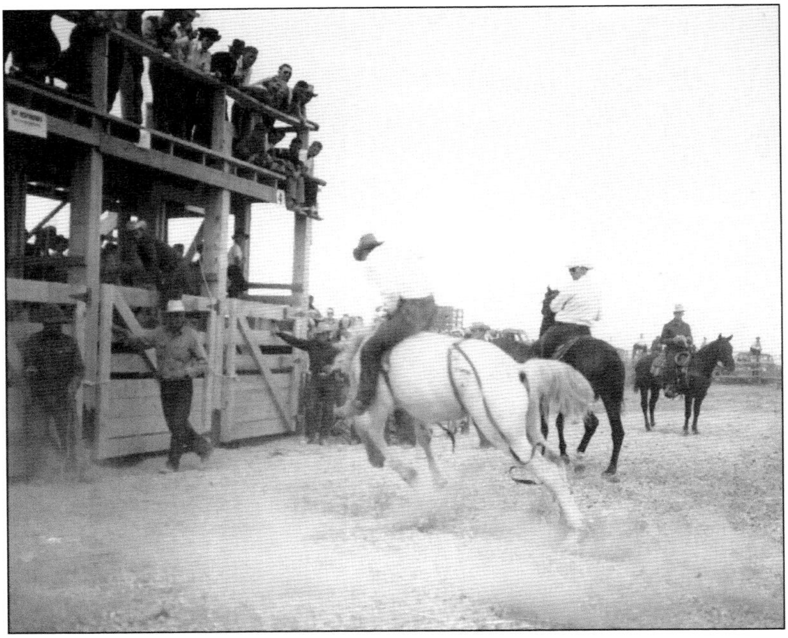

Donkeys and burros were not the only wild rides taken at the Hotchkiss Fairgrounds. Shown here during the 1948 Deltarado Days rodeo is a contestant riding a bucking bronco. Other contestants watch from the chutes and the overhead walk.

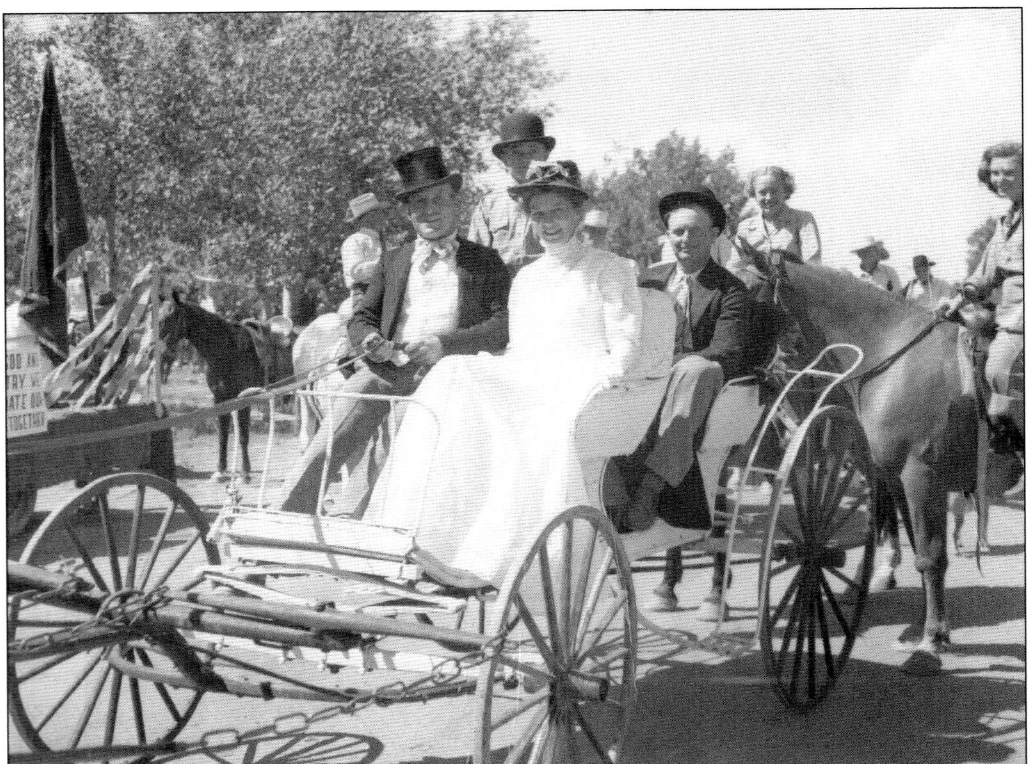

Seen here in the Deltarado Days Parade of 1948 is a horse-drawn carriage. The participants are dressed in c. 1900 clothing. In the front seat are Mr. and Mrs. Harry Lane. In the back are Gordon Lell (left) and Kenneth Brown.

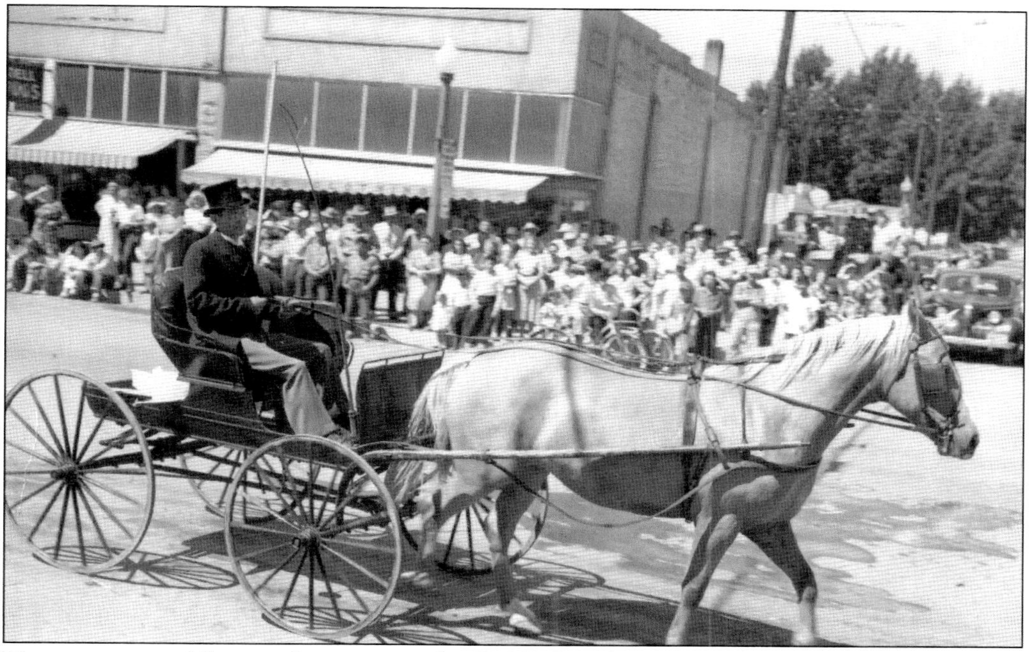

There were several floats and carriages in the 1948 Deltarado Days Parade. This turn-of-the-century two-person buggy (complete with a whip for his horse) was owned and entered by Dr. E. Phillips. The beautiful white horse prancing down the street pulling Dr. Phillips's prize buggy was named Pandora. Here they are crossing the corner of Fourth and Main Streets.

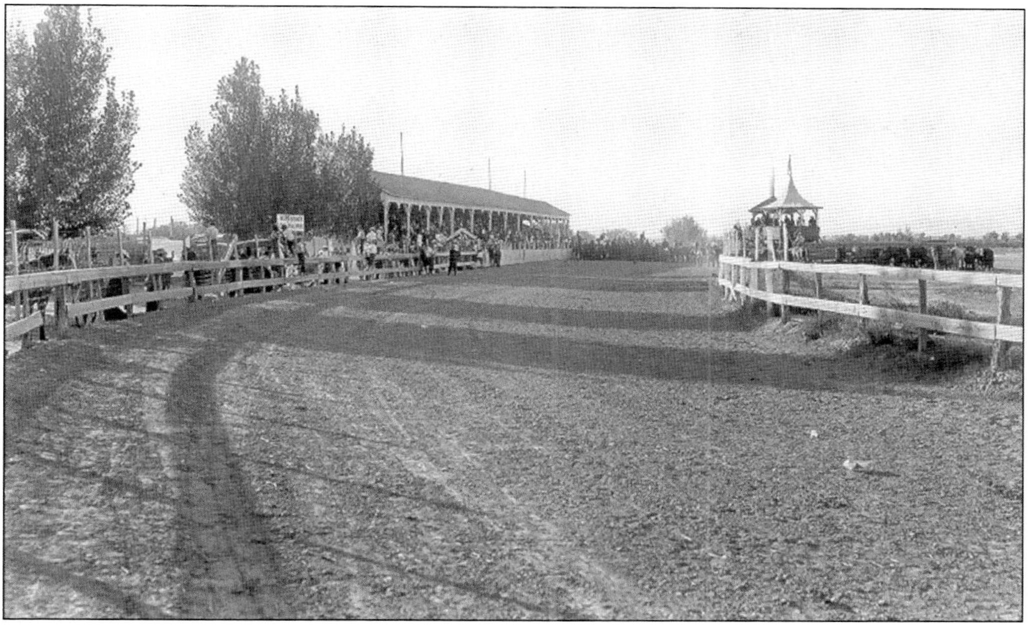

The grandstand at the Montrose Fairgrounds in September 1914 shows that a huge crowd has gathered to enjoy the day's events. Residents from all over the valley came to exhibit their fine agricultural bounty and livestock. At the moment of this photograph, the track stands ready for a race or a display of skilled horsemanship.

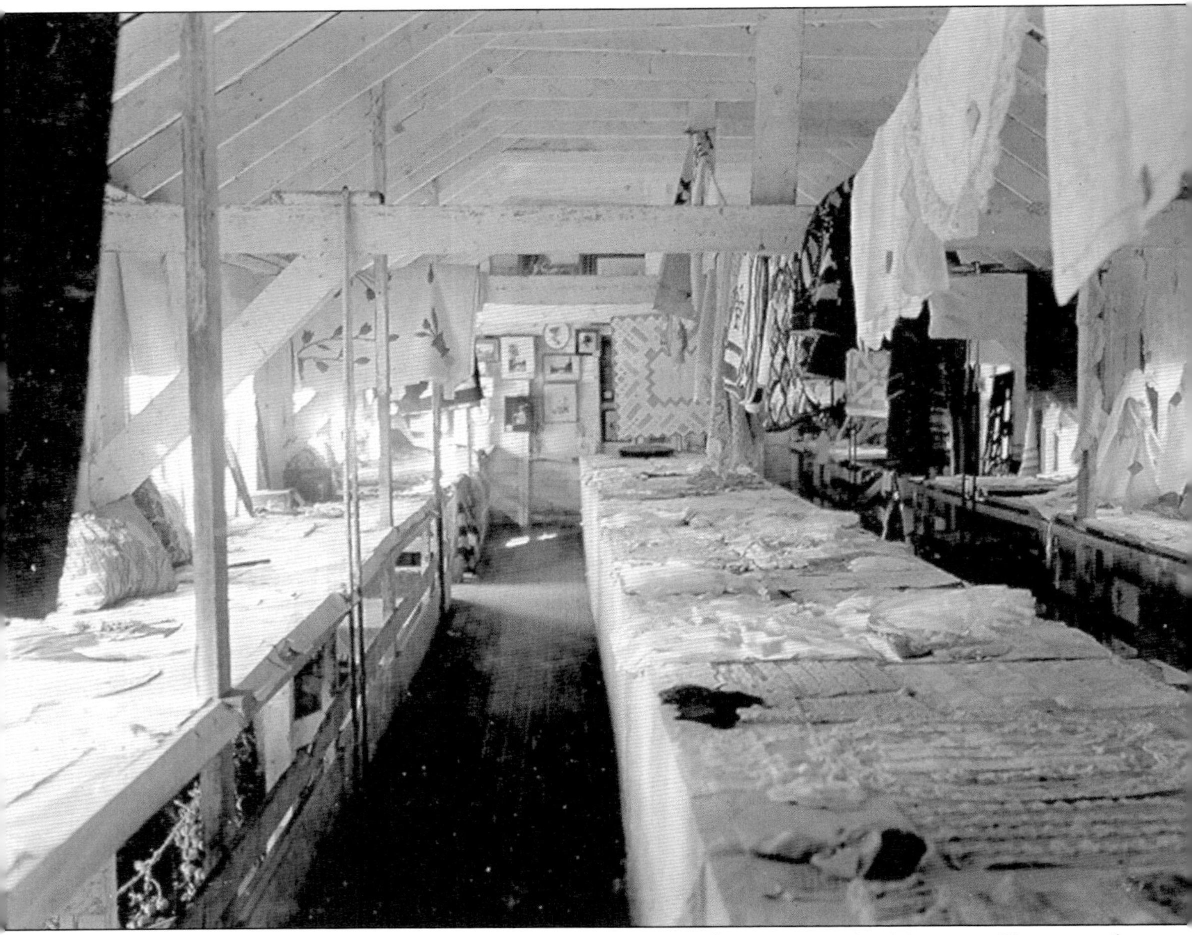

Seen here is the Fancy Work Exhibit at the Western Slope Fair at the Montrose Fairgrounds in September 1914. The different displays represent hours of tedious work and intricate detail, resulting in hundreds of useful masterpieces, works of art of heirloom quality to be shared with generations to come. Some of the different pieces represent a dying art and can be seen almost exclusively in museums today.

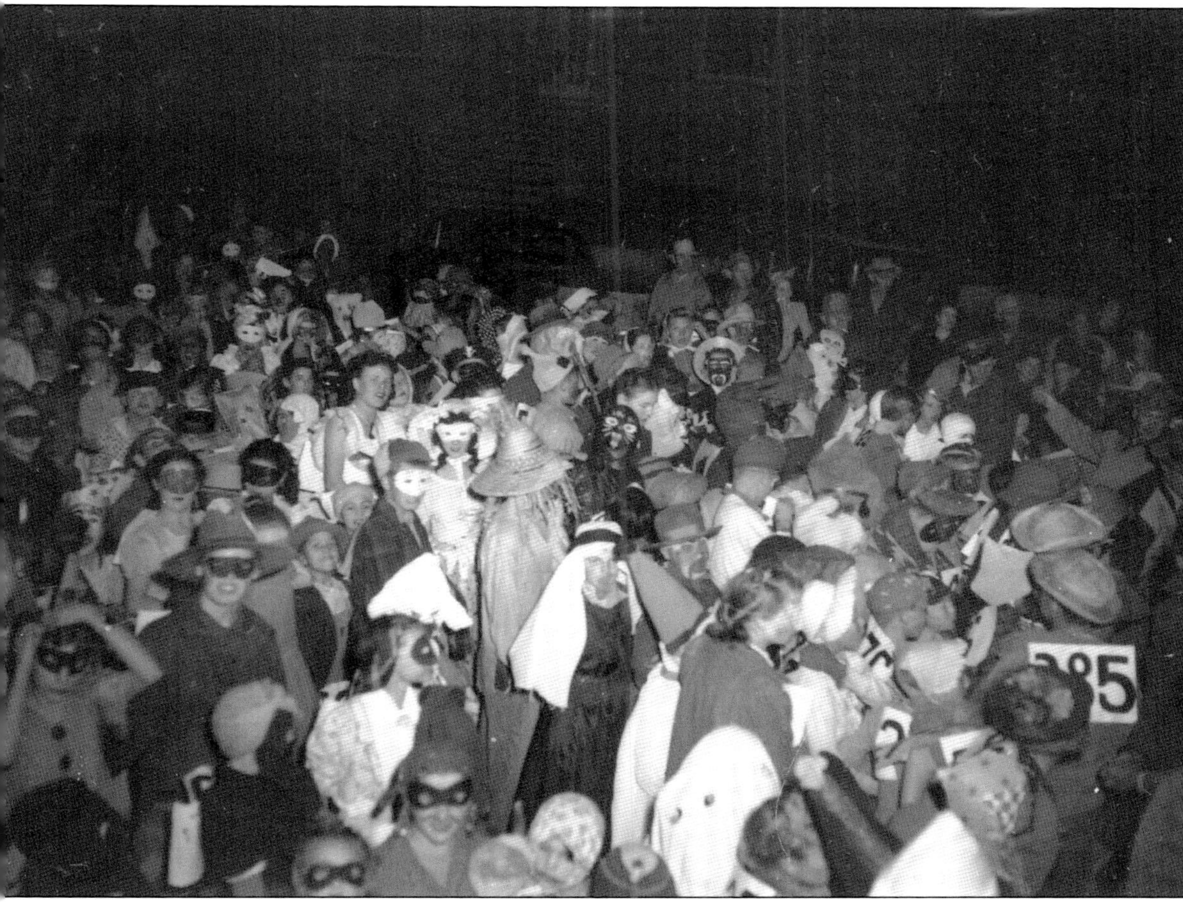

Every Friday night before Halloween, all of the businesses in Delta opened their doors for local children to come in and do some trick-or-treating. This event normally would start around four or five in the afternoon; all of the children would come dressed in their costumes. This tradition continues today.